SYRACUSE UNIVERSITY
The Tolley Years

Campus view, c. 1962

SYRACUSE UNIVERSITY

Volume Four · The Tolley Years

1942–1969

JOHN ROBERT GREENE

With Karrie A. Baron

With a Foreword by
Chancellor Kenneth A. Shaw

Syracuse University Press

First Edition 1996

96 97 98 99 00 01   6 5 4 3 2 1

This book is published with the assistance of
a grant from Syracuse University.

Illustrations courtesy of Syracuse University Archives.

The paper used in this publication meets the minimum requirements of
American National Standard for Information Sciences—Permanence of
Paper for Printed Library Materials, ANSI Z39.48–1984.

The Library of Congress has catalogued volume 3 as follows:

Galpin, William Freeman, 1890–1963
    Syracuse University.

        Vol.3 rev. and edited by Richard Wilson, from a text prepared by
W. Freeman Galpin and Oscar T. Barck, Jr.
    Includes index.
        CONTENTS: v. 1. The pioneer days.—v. 2. The growing years.—
v. 3. The critical years.
        1. Syracuse University—History. I. Wilson, Richard, 1920–   .
II. Barck, Oscar Theodore, 1902–   . III. Title
LD5233.G3   378.747   52-2118
ISBN 0-8156-8108-9 (v. 3)

V. 4. The Tolley years
ISBN 0-8156-2701-7 (cl.)

Manufactured in the United States of America

As always, for

Patty, T. J., Christopher, and Mary Rose,

and for Robert W. Tozer

TOLLE ET LEGE

JOHN ROBERT GREENE is professor of history and communication at Cazenovia College, where he has taught since 1979, and lectures at Syracuse University's University College. His previous books include *The Crusade: The Presidential Election of 1952*, *The Limits of Power: The Nixon and Ford Presidencies*, and *The Presidency of Gerald R. Ford*.

A university, as its name suggests,
should have an educational program designed
to serve the needs of everyone. Its field of study is as
wide as the universe. It is concerned with all of men's
ambitions and wants. It must be prepared to teach
whatever anyone desires to study and learn.

—William Pearson Tolley (1954)

Contents

Illustrations

MAPS

Foreword

*A great man need not be virtuous, nor his opinions right,
but he must have a firm mind, a distinctive character.*

—George Santayana, *Winds of Doctrine* 1913

I KNEW about William Pearson Tolley long before I met him. As a student of and then practitioner in higher education, I encountered his vision and his legacy in any discussion of the great postwar growth period in our field and of the creation of the handful of American institutions that could claim to be major research universities. I knew Tolley as an innovator, a risk-taker, a consummate fund-raiser, and a courageous supporter of unfettered pursuit of knowledge.

He was a force to be reckoned with and a giant in the history of Syracuse University and in national higher education. I was therefore honored to have met him in person, however briefly. Although I had only a few discussions with him, I came to know him also through his many admirers and even his detractors. I was eager for more information and looked forward to his volume in the continuing history of Syracuse University.

For those of us who are relatively new to this community, *The Tolley Years* is an opportunity to follow the life of a man who is a key to the university's past and an important shaper of its future. We learn about his extraordinary responses to the demands of a world war, the press of the postwar G.I. Bulge, the assaults on academic freedom in the 1950s, and the upheaval generated by the civil rights and antiwar movements of the 1960s. We have a chance to observe a chancellor who was not only a highly skilled administrator and a deft

XIII

persuader but was also a thoughtful advocate of the life of the mind and the centrality of the liberal arts. We meet a man who made mistakes and acknowleged them openly.

For those who knew Bill Tolley as a colleague, student, or friend, this book offers a different experience. This is a chance to relive moments, even decades, of great significance for the country and for each member of the university community. Each of these readers will bring a different perspective to the events as they unfold in this volume, and some may wish to challenge the author's impressions. Nevertheless, those who fondly claim Dr. Tolley as *their* chancellor will find much to add to their knowledge of Syracuse and its place in the world.

All of us who care for this institution will, I believe, be proud to add this book to our collections. It is, after all, about a man who taught us to cherish and defend Syracuse University.

Syracuse, New York   *Kenneth A. Shaw*
February 1996

Acknowledgments

THIS IS a commissioned work. Let's get that out of the way from the start. I was asked by, and paid by, Syracuse University to research and write this fourth volume of the university's history, dealing with the years covered by the chancellorship of William P. Tolley. Rather than attempt to downplay that fact (a strategy suggested by several of my colleagues, who argued that "protesting too much" is unwise), I am quite grateful for my alma mater's trust and support, and I little mind saying so publicly. I am grateful to the late William P. Tolley and his family, particularly his daughter, Katryn Tolley Fritz, for their unchecked access to his administrative papers, deposited in the Syracuse University Archives. I thank Chancellor Kenneth Shaw for his generosity and for making technical and office space available to me, which sped the work of both research and writing. Most of all, however, I want to thank Chancellor Shaw and the Tolley family for leaving me alone. No one ever once told me what to write about or how to write it. Any mistakes that the reader may find in this book are mine—as are the book's tone, theme, detail, and conclusions.

That is, of course, not to say that I received no help in writing this book. Quite the contrary. I had the assistance of an extraordinary research assistant, whose work is as integral to the completion of this book as was my own. Karrie Anne Baron was a student of mine at Cazenovia College, and after reading just one of her papers, I knew that I had met an undergraduate of singular talent. Karrie and I researched as a team throughout the summer of 1994, and her ability to analyze that vast mass of materials made available to us, as well as her uncanny ability to find a needle in haystacks as tall as Bird Library itself, were invaluable. She provided the material that allowed me to draw conclusions more sophisticated than I ever expected. She also planned many of the hundred-plus interviews that we conducted for this book, and conducted several of those interviews on her own. I am proud of Karrie—this book is as much hers as it is mine.

I am particularly grateful that Chancellor Emeritus Melvin Eggers sat down with us for a series of interviews just before his death in 1994. He was a gracious gentleman who was very interested in this project and spoke candidly with us on a number of subjects. His interviews, as is the case for all the interviews in this project, have been donated to the Syracuse University Archives (see "A Note on Sources"), as has been an annotated copy of this manuscript, so that interested researchers may check my sources. The lion's share of the research for the Eggers interviews was undertaken by another outstanding research assistant, Matthew Sharp, who also conducted several of the interviews with the former chancellor.

We directly benefited from the hard work of another scholar, one of the university's closest friends. Michael O. Sawyer, vice chancellor emeritus, made all his notes and interviews on the Tolley years available to us. They were a remarkable record—Michael researched this period with care and detail. I am also thankful for his gracious invitation to share his office on the sixth floor of Bird Library. His well-known nickname—"Mr. Syracuse"—is indeed a fitting one; the respect and admiration with which he is held by his students is both legendary and deserved. I am also grateful to Alexandra Eyle Mitchell, who allowed access to her research work on the Tolley years, also on deposit at the Syracuse University Archives.

I was unbelievably fortunate to have two of my closest professional friends right next door when I was framing this book. James Roger Sharp and David H. Bennett, two historians who served as my mentors while I studied at Syracuse University, provided encouragement and support throughout these past two years. How can one put it to give them my highest possible compliment . . . ah—they were my *teachers*.

The list of people at Syracuse University who assisted me is too long to mention. Four groups of individuals, however, stand out. The support that came to me from the chancellor's office—from Vice President Eleanor Gallagher, and from Loretta Nowicki and Marlene Carlson—was indispensable. The staff at the Syracuse University

Archives is, for my money, one of the best on the nation—and I have used many. Amy S. Doherty, Mary O'Brien, and their remarkable staff made the research phase of this project as easy as it could be. Syracuse University Press is a top-flight house. I thank Robert Mandel and Cynthia Maude-Gembler for their efforts, as well as every person at SUP, too many to mention by name here, who shared their talents with me and helped make this a better book. And finally, to all the members of the Syracuse University family who allowed us to interview them for this project: many of your names are listed in the essay at the end of this volume; I thank you all.

I also had the support of my friends, colleagues, and students at Cazenovia College, who have consistently encouraged my scholarly endeavors for the past seventeen years. I particularly want to thank President Adelaide "Van" Titus, Vice President Margery Pinet, and Dean Dolores Weiss for fostering an academic climate where one can produce and teach, and enjoy doing both. Christopher Wilson provided helpful research into the acceptance of Japanese-American students at Syracuse during World War II. Several students in an independent research seminar at Cazenovia College produced a lengthy paper in the spring of 1993 on "Syracuse University in the 1960s." This first-rate work was based on primary sources, and I used it with profit during my own research. I thank those students: Shelly Kazukiewicz, Vanessa Lapre, Louise Mongelluzzo, H. J. Refici, Gina Ruggierio, Jolene Sears, Chani Taub, and Jennifer Zasa.

And finally, a truly personal note. This book was written during a particularly challenging time for my family, to whom this book is—as always—dedicated. My wife and children understand how important my writing is to me, but no more so than over the past year and a half. It was often difficult to write, but it often helped. So did the support of our family in Syracuse, Olean, LaFayette, Horseheads, and Black River, New York, and Simsbury, Connecticut, as well as all our friends in Chittenango, particularly the Eisenberg family. In the end, however, we owe everything to Crouse-Irving Memorial Hospital's Neonatal Intensive Care Unit and Step-Down Nursery. The daily efforts of those extraordinary people make writing a book look like child's play.

Chittenango, New York   *John Robert Greene*
September 1995

SYRACUSE UNIVERSITY

The Tolley Years

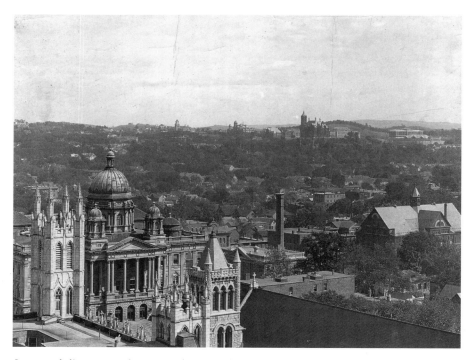

Syracuse skyline, as seen from Onondaga Hotel

PREVIOUS SPREAD: *Campus view, c. 1962*

CHAPTER I

New Leadership

The next chancellor can make or break Syracuse University.
There is no doubt about that.

—William P. Tolley, *Syracuse Post-Standard,* May 24, 1942

IT HAD BEEN almost a year since Pearl Harbor, but by the fall of 1942 the nation had only begun adjusting to the hardships of war. Prices had soared throughout the year, but it was not until November that President Franklin D. Roosevelt was given the power to regulate wages and prices. He set them at September 1942 levels and those controls had stopped prices from climbing. In November 1942 nationwide gasoline rationing was first established, and by the end of the fall all gasoline distributors were required to pump only regular-grade gasoline. Virtually all household commodities had been rationed since midyear, those that were not were in short supply, and drives for scrap iron and rubber had become commonplace. Few, if any, Americans felt it, but the national debt was climbing, as the administration borrowed money to pay for the war effort—by the end of the war, it would stand at $260 billion.

While sacrifice typified the home front as 1942 drew to a close, the sacrifices on the battlefield were only beginning. By the summer of 1942, Allied planes had begun to bomb Germany. In mid-October, Adolf Hitler had abandoned his attempt to take the city of Stalingrad; by that fall, the Soviet army had begun to push the Germans back to the west. In early November, Lieutenant General Dwight D. Eisenhower was named the commander in chief of Allied operations in Northern Africa; on November 8, Allied forces landed at Casablanca, Algiers, and Oran. The news from the Pacific theater was as encouraging. That summer, the Americans had regained the initiative in the Pacific at the Battle of Midway, when they sank four Japanese carriers and shot down some three hundred airplanes. But the war was far from over—in October 1942 the Congress voted to lower the draft age from twenty-one to eighteen.

As it was in the rest of the country, Central New Yorkers were coping with fear, waiting, and rapid change as best they could in the fall of 1942. Many Syracuse housewives were infuriated on Mondays when they took their washing off the lines and found it covered with oil, spillage from the planes flying overhead to land at the newly built Hancock Field, where they would refuel for the final leg of their trip to Gander Bay, Newfoundland—and Europe. Some people interviewed for this work remembered other childhood inconveniences: Boy Scouts who had to hike the entire distance to the camporee at Willow Bay because their leaders could not get gas for their cars; kids who had to peddle their bicycles out to Park Street by the Regional Market to buy a treat at the city's only soft ice cream stand. To be kept up to date, most Syracusans turned daily to WSYR radio to catch E. R. "Vadeboncoeur and the News." Later that fall, many Syracusans found themselves exposed to a new form of news service, as letters from their boys overseas came home accompanied by clippings from *Stars and Stripes,* which had begun publication that November as the first daily newspaper for the armed services since World War I. They also shared a new wartime leader: that fall, New York district attorney Thomas Dewey won his first term as the state's governor.

Yet Syracuse also shared diversions from the wartime tension with the rest of the nation. While they waited for news to come from a loved one in Africa or the Pacific, Syracusans may have gone to the opulent Loew's Theater (now the Syracuse Area Landmark Theater) and saw the fall's newest hit, Mickey Rooney's *A Yank at Eton,* or they may have devoured Erle Stanley Gardner's latest Perry Mason mystery, *The Case of the Careless Kitten.* Jukeboxes at Child's restaurant jumped to three new war tunes: Hoagy Carmichael's "The Cranky Old Yank," "Der Fuehrer's Face," the first hit for drummer Lindsey Armstrong "Spike" Jones, and Frank Loesser's "Praise the Lord and Pass the Ammunition!" Yet it was radio that held the community together, as it did everywhere in the nation. Along with the regular fare of soap operas, sporting events, and nighttime comedy shows that they shared with the nation, Syracusans had their own favorites. Many Central New Yorkers tuned in on Saturdays at noon to *Grand Central Station,* a show that opened each week with the sound of a train traveling down the Hudson and into Manhattan, followed by a story about one of the souls who lived in that city. On the local scene, Syracusans would come to respect and rely on a new morning voice that fall, and Robert F. "Deacon" Doubleday would be "swinging on the fence of the wired woodshed" of WSYR Radio for close to three decades. They also listened to Jim Deline's orchestra on WSYR or Dean Harris on WHEN. Most Central New York sports fans wanted to destroy their radios earlier that fall, however, when they listened to the mighty New York Yankees being beaten in the World Series by the upstart St. Louis Cardinals.

The fall of 1942, both for the nation and for its forty-first largest city (population 205,967), was a time of both exhilaration and apprehension. For the most part, the destruction of the depression had ended, and by the end of 1942 both the nation and Syracuse were wheeling toward full employment. Yet at the same time, the front page of the *Syracuse Herald-Journal* was beginning what would become a regular feature for the next two and a half years—the names of local war casualties. Into this atmosphere of hope and tension, one of the city's largest employers made an enormous change. The entire city sat up and took notice when it learned that the new chief executive officer of Syracuse University was, at forty-two years of age, the youngest chancellor of any university in the nation.

* * *

William Pearson Tolley was born on September 13, 1900, into a family steeped in the traditions and faith of the Methodist Church. Tolley grew up in Binghamton, New York, with two brothers and two sisters. His father was a shoe salesman who had emigrated from Cornwall, England, and his mother, whom Tolley credits with most of his development as an adult, is simply described in his memoirs as "the most saintlike person I shall ever meet." Tolley's upbringing reflected not the rapidly changing mores of the early twentieth century, but rather the strictness of his Methodist faith. His father was president of the board of trustees of the Centenary Methodist Church in Binghamton and his mother saw to it that the house was free of liquor, tobacco, and card playing.

Clearly a child of prodigious intellectual talents, Tolley felt himself to be beyond the educational system when he started, remembering that he did not study things that were new to him until the fourth grade. Indeed, elementary and secondary school bored the youngster; Tolley remembered that the "only difficulties I encountered" in his childhood were with the educational system, and reflected that "in looking back I wonder whether the silly rules I did not like as a boy made me more tolerant when I myself became a dean and a college president." Yet Tolley wrote in glowing terms of the curriculum in the public schools at the turn of the century, a period he would later remember as being the "golden period for the bright students in the public schools of New York State. . . . The goal was liberal education"—Latin, English, French, German, Spanish, history, sciences, and math—and that curriculum "was designed for bright students who were college-bound." His primary extracurricular activities were debate and public speaking, and he met his future wife, Ruth Canfield, while in high school. Tolley graduated in 1918 as valedictorian of his class, and that fall enrolled at Syracuse University.

In 1918, the school that the Methodists referred to as "Piety Hill" was little more than a small liberal arts college. Its total enrollment was 3,067 students; there were sixteen faculty members. The chancellor was James Roscoe Day, a man Tolley remembered as being "a majestic, overpowering figure." The United States had been involved in World War I for about a year at the time of Tolley's enrollment and, desperate to make a contribution to the war effort, Tolley lied about his age and signed up for the draft. He saw no active duty, however. He stayed at Syracuse and served in the Student Army Training Corps (SATC) as a supply sergeant. While a student, Tolley pledged the Delta Kappa Epsilon fraternity, debated, sang in the Glee Club and the University Choir, played sax in a jazz band—the "Synful Syncopators"—and worked part-time selling shoes at the Endicott-Johnson shoe store on Salina Street. In his senior year, Tolley edited the campus yearbook, *The Onondagan,* and was named the president and general secretary of the local chapter of the Young Men's Christian Association (YMCA). He and Ruth were married in 1925. They would have three children: Nelda, William, Jr., and Katryn.

Tolley graduated in 1922 with his bachelor of arts degree and a Phi Beta Kappa key. He could easily have become a national figure with the YMCA. However, he had decided to follow in the footsteps of his brother Earl, also a Syracuse grad, who had entered the ministry. Tolley entered Drew Theological Seminary in Madison, New Jersey, that fall on a full scholarship. At the same time that he attended Drew, Tolley took graduate classes at Columbia University, finished his Master's degree at Syracuse, and worked part-time at a settlement house on East Eleventh Street in Manhattan. Tolley obtained his master's in philosophy in 1924; that same year he was ordained a deacon, and the following year he took his bachelor's of divinity from Drew. He received a second master's degree from Columbia in 1927 and his Ph.D. from Columbia in 1930.

In 1928, two donors established Brothers College, an undergraduate college for men at Drew. Rather than take a ministry of his own —one was offered to him near Coney Island—Tolley, then twenty-seven, accepted a position as acting dean of Brothers College in spring 1928 and was promoted to dean of the college in 1929. While Tolley taught philosophy on the side at Brothers, he had found his niche in academic administration. When Allegheny College, a small liberal arts college in Pennsylvania that had been seriously hurt by the depression, offered Tolley the presidency—for the yearly salary of $8,000—Tolley accepted. He was at that time the youngest chief executive of a college or university in the nation.

At Allegheny, Tolley established a reputation as a doctor of sick institutions. With small colleges closing their doors throughout the thirties, and with large colleges and universities facing severe cutbacks simply to make their payroll, Tolley achieved the extraordinary accomplishment of not just saving but improving the lot of Allegheny. Not afraid to adjust course offerings, cut popular programs to save money—one of his first acts was to suspend football—nor to borrow money, Tolley brought the college out of debt, acquired $1,300,000 in endowment, and developed an innovative program in vocational and educational guidance. By 1940 the college had a balanced budget, faculty salaries had actually been increased, dormitories were being built, and the college was acquiring real estate around its borders. None of this could have been accomplished had Tolley not developed into a master fund-raiser, a job that he professed to have hated originally.

Soon, Tolley's influence transcended the Allegheny campus. As chairman of the Academic Freedom and Tenure Committee of the Association of American Colleges, he was the guiding light behind the drafting of the 1940 document on Academic Freedom and Tenure, which promised job security after a trial period of no more than seven years. He also served as president of the College Presidents of Pennsylvania, and president of the Association of American Colleges (1942 and 1943). Even more important for the future history of his alma mater to the north, Tolley was one of a group of college administrators who were instrumental in drafting what would become known as the Servicemen's Readjustment Act of 1944, or the "The GI Bill of Rights." He was also active in the hierarchy of his church. In 1932 he was appointed to the University Senate of the Methodist Episcopal Church, a seat he would keep for almost forty years, serving as its president from 1960 to 1970.

*   *   *

In 1936 William Pratt Graham had been the first alumnus to be chosen chancellor of Syracuse University, as well as the first nonclergyman. However, his influence was to be slight, as he proclaimed himself to be a lame duck before he even accepted the position. Graham told the board that he planned to serve only for a year or so, or "until my successor shall be appointed," and he instructed the search committee to continue its search. For all intents and purposes, then, Graham was an interim chancellor. They were difficult years as the nation became embroiled in World War II. In mid-April 1942 he informed the board that he was stepping down, explaining that "it is time that a younger man assume my position." This was not a decision that was met with universal approval. Despite a rise in tuition, enrollment had increased during his chancellorship to 6,641, and one member of the board of trustees remarked that "there is universal regret that he has requested to be relieved of his present responsibilities." Even some of the students were disappointed. The *Daily Orange,* the university's student newspaper, remarked that "the students have found Chancellor Graham a true friend with an open ear and an open mind; the faculty members know him as a trusted and capable counselor."

The nominating committee of the board of trustees was chaired by Dr. Gordon Hoople, and included trustees Lewis C. Ryan, Judge Edmund Lewis, George H. Bond, and Henry Phillips; alumni trustees Neal Brewster and Mrs. James D. "Sadie" Taylor; Harold Coon (president of the Alumni Association); Mrs. Hurlbut W. Smith; and faculty representative William M. Smallwood, professor of comparative anatomy. This committee sought nominations from alumni, educators, and other colleges. It also consulted the 1936 list of candidates. On that list was William Tolley, who had been invited to interview, although he was not offered the position.[1]

The nominating committee originally screened a list of 264 nominations and applicants. After several meetings at which the committee determined the qualifications it would seek in a chancellor, it chose a subcommittee of four to make a preliminary survey of the resumes. After hearing the recommendations of this subcommittee, the full committee cut the list, first to thirty names and later to ten. This list of ten names was submitted to the directors of the Rockefeller and Carnegie Foundations—then the two largest grant contributors to the university—who met with members of the committee and added their input. A final group of six educators was interviewed by the entire committee; Tolley's interview was at the home of Lewis C. Ryan.

It was Hoople, who had attended Syracuse with Tolley's brother, who visited Allegheny College. A force at Syracuse University throughout the Tolley years, Hoople would play a major role in both the beginning and the end of the Tolley years. Tolley remembered that when Hoople went to talk to him, "Gordon made his pitch, and I said 'look, I know I ought to say yes, but I just don't feel like deserting the ship for the sake of a little more honor. I know what I can do here.'" Hoople's response included a heavy dose of guilt: "I know you love this place, and I think the place loves you. But Syracuse is your alma

---

1. Tolley had also been offered the presidency of Pomona college in 1940.

mater. You don't say no to your alma mater. Syracuse gave you your beginning . . . you owe this to Syracuse." Tolley remembered that by the time Hoople was done, "I was almost in tears . . . and I finally said okay."

Tolley ended up being the unanimous selection of the nominating committee. The reasons, as offered by Hoople to the full board, were the outstanding character of the men who had supported Tolley's nomination; the fact that Tolley was an alumnus who had gained national recognition in higher education; the prestige that Tolley would bring to the university; his proven fund-raising ability, and his "acute understanding" of the problems that were facing Syracuse. The committee felt that "in general, Dr. Tolley, in the judgement of the committee, is peculiarly adapted by his philosophy and his personality to the Syracuse tradition of tolerance, of democracy, and of progressivism in higher education." The full board unanimously agreed, and on August 9, 1942, Hurlbut W. Smith, the president of the Board of Trustees, announced Tolley's selection as Syracuse University's seventh chancellor.

Tolley asked that his inauguration, scheduled for November 19, 1942, be marked by simplicity. In deference to wartime rationing, which had bred the slogan "Is This Trip *Really* Necessary?", he wanted very little in the way of transportation for his guests. The event was instead characterized by the university as a "family party." Nevertheless, in the fashion of a true alum, the inauguration was held in the morning, preceding that year's Syracuse-Colgate football game (Syracuse lost, 14–0). Held at Hendricks Chapel, the main speaker was Edmund Ezra Day, president of Cornell, who, along with outgoing chancellor Graham, received an honorary degree. Bishop Charles W. Flint, the fifth chancellor of the university, was also on hand. In his inaugural address, Tolley took a sweeping tone, speaking of the postwar world in terms of changes that he felt to be necessary, such as "changes in pre-college guidance, in admissions procedures, in methods of teaching, training in reading and communication, education for leisure, family life, and responsible citizenship."

        *   *   *

Formal inauguration of Tolley by Hurlbut W. Smith, chairman of the board of trustees, November 14, 1942

William Tolley had proven the equal of the crisis of the depression, but that was as head of a small college with a small endowment. Now he would once again be called upon to serve as a university's crisis manager, but the university was larger, and the crisis—the full impact of World War II on higher education—was a pivotal one for the history of both the nation at large and Piety Hill.

THIS IS THE ARMY

At Syracuse University

1944

CHAPTER 2

The Challenge of World War II

*The changes of war hit our class first and hard. We came back to campus
already aware that there were many familiar faces missing.*

—1943 senior class president Jamieson S. Reid

*Of course we can do it. We are in a war, and this is
our opportunity to do our part.*

—Gordon Smith

THE CRISIS that World War II wrought upon higher education
was acute. The November 1942 decision to extend the draft to
all eighteen-year-old males hit hard at schools like Syracuse University
that had actively recruited men who were already in the reserves.
Early in 1942, Dean of Men A. Blair Knapp was able to promise that
the vast majority of the school's 1,003 male students who were also
reservists would finish out the school year.[1] However, by January
1943 Knapp conceded that with the new draft law, one-half of the
college's reservists would be called up after March 1. This loss of
more than a third of its total enrollment was part of a nationwide
trend; by November 1943, 585 American colleges and universities
reported a 38 percent decrease in their enrollment. Students were not
the only ones leaving school. Believing, according to one federal

---

1. *Syracuse Herald-Journal,* Sept. 17, 1942. The story reported that 147 Syracuse
students were in the Naval Reserves, 70 in the Marines, 188 in Army Air Corps, 450
in General Reserve for the Army, 18 in the Signal Corps, and 130 in the advanced Reserve Officers Training Corps (ROTC).

report, that they were "giving little or nothing to the war effort," many professors either retired or, if of age, enlisted.

The Roosevelt administration was not caught unaware by the crisis in higher education. Early in 1942, it announced the creation of two programs that were largely designed to meet the needs of universities facing a loss of young men. The navy's V-12 Program and the Army Specialized Training Program (ASTP) would send qualified men to college, mostly in programs in the sciences or foreign languages, and then later draw them out for combat duty. However, the vast majority of colleges refused to accept servicemen onto their campuses, citing concerns that ranged from their inability to maintain social order with thousands of soldiers living in such close proximity to their coeds, to an inability to house the soldiers so that they might live on campus at all.

For reasons such as these, Graham had refused even to consider adopting either V-12 or ASTP. His solution to the impending enrollment crisis was the introduction of several specialty and vocational programs that were designed to attract men who would never serve, either because of age or physical condition. In August 1941 the College of Applied Science began offering Defense Training Classes. Not part of regular academic training and given with no tuition expense, the courses included elementary mechanical drawing, elementary machine tool design, design of jigs and fixtures, foreman training, and the like. In January 1942 the university offered a school for bomb reconnaissance agents taught by the officers of the Ordnance Department, Eastern Defense Command, which accepted local police and firemen. The Fine Arts school even offered a course in the theory and practice of camouflage.

While Tolley would continue these programs, he had no doubts as to the wisdom of welcoming servicemen to campus. He had actively lobbied the government for programs such as the V-12 and the ASTP while at Allegheny, and his position did not change when he came to Syracuse. Tolley's decision to open the doors of Syracuse University was a purely economic one; he remembered later that "I knew we could not survive without students, and that meant boys in uniform."

Thus began what was the most important development at Syracuse University in the second half of its history—the influx of soldiers: first World War II cadets, and then the returning veterans. The V-12 and ASTP program were set up immediately, and Tolley made it clear to Washington that Syracuse University welcomed servicemen to its campus, regardless of how long they would be able to stay. When the air force called saying that they had 550 cadets on a train—another college had promised to take them, but reneged—Tolley accepted them as students over the phone, even though he had no immediate idea where they would be housed. Daring decisions such as these moved Syracuse to the top of the War Department's list of cooperative institutions. This paid large dividends when the air force sent 2100 cadets to Syracuse for an academic program combined with military training. Over the war years, the university accepted some two hundred officers of the Women's Auxiliary Army Corps, and a training program in Russian and Slavic languages. By war's end, there were about eight thousand service people on campus, about four thousand of them making up the largest air force contingent in the country.

The most pressing issue was where all these soldiers would live. In 1943 there were only three dormitories—Sims, Winchell, and Haven Halls—a few cottages, and the Greek houses. The immediate relocation of more than 790 students (the vast majority of them women) into doubles, triples, or off-campus housing to accommodate the influx of servicemen was but a drop in the bucket. Tolley needed rooms, and he solved the problem with the skill of a real estate entrepreneur. In a strategy that had already become a fundamental part of Tolley's managerial style, he worried less about running up a debt than he did about moving quickly. To house that trainload of air force cadets, he purchased nearby Auburn Theological Seminary. Tolley then began to purchase large quantities of housing around the campus, beginning with several withered fraternity houses. Themselves facing a great loss with the outflux of men, many frat houses leased their houses to the armed services. The crunch lasted until 1944, when the size of the army contingent decreased. By then, fifteen of the women's cottages were vacant; in the spring of 1945 there were still six unoccupied.

As with housing, there were not initially enough classes to accommodate the servicemen, and the university had to provide and staff an increased number of sections. Eric Faigle, dean of the College of Liberal Arts, talked many members of the faculty into teaching much longer hours, but the demand of students consistently outraced the supply of instructional material and personnel. One of the many examples will suffice: on one Sunday, word was received by Prof. George B. Cressy, chairman of the Geography Department, that thirty-four hundred soldiers would arrive on the following Thursday, and all had to include geography in their program. Cressy was also informed that no sections would exceed thirty students. It quickly became necessary to recruit a staff of several dozen people from related departments overnight and train them to teach map reading, meteorology, and geographic principles.

The instant registration of servicemen swelled classrooms to record numbers. It was only a matter of time before many on the faculty began to voice concerns for the quality of students who were being turned out of these programs. Estimates were that the student/soldier only had one hour to study for each class hour. With the concentration on math, physics, and chemistry, the humanities were often neglected. The Selective Service Act said that local draft boards could defer students until they completed their current academic year, and also defer students preparing for "essential occupations"—students of engineering, medicine, dentistry, or one of the natural sciences. As a result, academic advisors tried to steer students away from the humanities and toward the sciences. It was also difficult to gauge the value of the credits earned by the ASTP. Jokes abounded: the story of the army trainee who looked out the window during his mathematics course and missed trigonometry; and the V-12 trainee who, upon returning from a short walk, was told that he had missed his sophomore year.

A word should be said about the spirit of the students during this period. While all concerned agreed with Tolley when he praised the "patience and good sportsmanship of both men and women who were forced to move on short notice in the middle of the term," the students had nevertheless moved into substandard and overcrowded accommodations. Fraternity men and sorority women vacated their rooms with just five days notice that the houses had either been leased or purchased, to allow the university time to refurnish and redecorate. Throughout, there was little dissention from the students. There was, however, a great deal of dissension on the part of the conservative elders of the Syracuse area business and journalism community, when they found that their new chancellor had a surprising liberal streak.

*   *   *

Immediately after Pearl Harbor, residents of California, Oregon, and Washington lashed out against their sizeable Japanese-American population. Racism mixed with a fear of sabotage; neither was abated when the residents read stories such as the Japanese-American truck farmer who was alleged to have planted tomatoes so that they formed an arrow pointing to an air training field. California politicians, most notably Governor Earl Warren, pressured Roosevelt to do something. Roosevelt complied by issuing Executive Order 9006, which gave the army the power to deal with the problem. The army's solution was relocation. Beginning in early 1942, some thirty-four thousand Japanese Americans were resettled in camps located in remote desert regions of the western United States.

Yet the War Relocation Authority (WRA), which had set up the camps, set out to do what many felt could not—and should not—be done, as it actively encouraged churches and other groups to help transfer Japanese-American students of college age to institutions of higher learning outside the exclusion zone. Coming as it did at a time of Japanese victories in the Pacific, the plan was met with a combination of skepticism and scorn. Many felt that this program would be ultimately unsuccessful, and many more agreed with the assessment of Mississippi congressman John Elliot Rankin: "Once a Jap, always a Jap. . . . You cannot regenerate a Jap, convert him and make him the same as a white man any more than you can reverse the laws of nature." Arkansas passed a bill "barring members of the Mongolian race from attending white schools," and both state houses unanimously passed a resolution denouncing the War Relocation Authority's policy of allowing internees to attend colleges in other states.

Only a handful of colleges and universities accepted Japanese-American students. Tolley did not hesitate. When he was asked by the

American Society of Friends to offer scholarships to at least five American-born Japanese Americans, who would then be released from the relocation camps, Tolley sent a telegram offering to take one hundred. After learning that Syracuse University would be sent sixty-five Japanese-American students, Tolley remembered thinking, "My God, what have I done," and asked the editors of the *Daily Orange* not to announce the arrival of the Japanese-American students. Students came from each of the ten internment camps. Scholarships from church groups paid for their expenses. Mary Okmura Watanabe went into the nursing program and remembered that "it was a joy just to be in a place where you could walk on the sidewalks, have clean clothes, and see green grass instead of being surrounded by towers with guards and machine guns."

Clearly, Tolley was not using so small a group of students to bolster his enrollment. The acceptance of Japanese-American students to Syracuse University in 1943 was a commendable example of educational altruism. It was also an act of some political courage on the part of the new chancellor. When the story leaked out, Tolley was attacked in the pages of the Syracuse *Post-Standard,* by no less an editorial writer than that paper's editor, William Rogers. Tolley was also derided by local chapters of the Veterans of Foreign Wars and the American Legion, both of which sent delegations to Hurlbut W. Smith, president of L. C. Smith Corona and then chairman of the university's board of trustees, to complain. Part of that resistance was silenced by Smith's agreement not to oppose Tolley on the issue. Part of the opposition was quieted by the actions of one of the Japanese-American students, Frank Watanabe, who had won a January 1943 contest sponsored by the university for designing the best patriotic poster. The $100 award was presented to Watanabe by Tolley during the annual review of the university's ROTC cadets, who gasped when they saw that the award's recipient was Japanese American. Watanabe turned the tables, however, when he presented his check back to Tolley, asking that it be given to the American Red Cross. Watanabe left the reviewing stand to the applause of the ROTC Cadets. Many of the city's more conservative leaders never fully forgave Tolley for allowing what one remembered as being "the enemy" to matriculate onto Piety Hill.

*   *   *

Both the war in general and the influx of servicemen to the campus had a profound effect on the university's female students. For those young women who were able to pursue their education rather than having to work in defense factories as "Rosie the Riveters," colleges nationwide introduced a number of courses designed to give their coeds a feeling of participation in the war effort. In January 1942, Syracuse coeds began signing up for twelve training courses, the nature of which—air raid training, a mechanics course (if the coed owned a car), child care, communications, knitting, shorthand, typing, and home nursing—showed that although Syracuse was willing to offer its coeds some training in the manly pursuits, the rigors of war had not dimmed the perception that there was still a necessity to study that which was charitably referred to as "women's work." It is clear that Syracuse, like the vast majority of coed institutions during World War II, did not give serious thought to the vocational education of its female students. In fact, as much thought was given to the social separation of soldiers and coeds as was given to their education. Very clear regulations were set. Coeds were not allowed to say hello to a cadet between 6 A.M. and 6 P.M. Monday through Friday, "unless it was common courtesy." For their part, military students were not allowed in the waiting room of a coed's dorm or house unless they were calling on that coed, or unless they had leave papers. Yet the absence of civilian men on campus, men who had previously monopolized the leadership positions in the student body, opened new opportunities to women. For example, in 1944 the *Daily Orange* boasted its first all-female staff.

This temporary empowerment of women played a large role in the first attempt by the Syracuse University student body to democratize student government. The Men's Student Government (MSG), an independent organization, set the political and social agenda for the entire student body. Dominated by the fraternities, the MSG had a General Assembly, which represented each dorm and fraternity, and a Civil Service section, which administered and supervised the school and class elections. The Women's Student Government (WSG) fell under the purview of the dean of women, and in the words of one campus leader, "our attitude was that they were simply an adjunct of the Dean of Women's office . . . [and] did what the Dean of Women told them." The WSG had two houses of government, which were largely responsible for the issuance of "permissions"—passes so a coed could stay out past her assigned curfew.

In April 1943, student activists sparked an attempt to bring men's and women's government together. This group of men and women drew up a constitution that called for a Single Student Government (SSG) with a Coed General Assembly, an enlarged civil service, a Student Court, and a Student Discussion Board. The activists scheduled a campus-wide election, but before it could be held, their plan was attacked in the *Daily Orange* by three top administrators: Vice Chancellor Finla Crawford, Dean of Women M. Eunice Hilton, and Dean of Men A. Blair Knapp, who argued that not only had the new constitution not been submitted according to established procedure but that, because of the war, "this is certainly not the time for a revolutionary change in student government." As Grafton Willey, one of the activists, remembered with a smile, "we did not respond mildly." Two days after the deans' letter appeared, the students responded with their own editorial—"We ask this of the deans: What is the purpose of a University if not to prepare men and women for postgraduate civic responsibilities; the responsibilities which loom greater for this generation than ever before?" For his part, the new chancellor stayed above the fray, remarking in a letter to the *Daily Orange* that "having been on campus so short a time, I do not feel that I know enough about the history and strength of student government on the campus to express an informed and intelligent opinion on the subject." In the ensuing election, the activists were defeated. Student government would remain a segregated system for several more decades. Remembering the battle some fifty years later, Willey remembered that the student body had been "decorously uproarious."

＊　　　＊　　　＊

Women on campus also figured prominently in the most important curricular development of the wartime period. The shortage of trained nurses had become acute by the end of 1942. The services would eventually employ twice as many nurses in World War II as

Edith Smith, with students of the School of Nursing

they had taken in all of World War I; in the spring of 1943, the army was taking some three thousand nurses into duty each month. The market need was obvious, and Tolley moved to acquire a school of nursing for the university. He asked Edith H. Smith, then with the National Nursing Council for War Service, to serve as the school's first dean. Smith was clearly the catalyst for the development of the new school. Students from its first class remembered her as a "powerful woman" who was very close to each of the nursing students. One student remembered taking one of the required nursing classes taught by Smith. When she failed most of the students because of their poor grammar, she reminded the disappointed nurses that "you are professionals representing nursing and SU—your English has to be top notch." She was also a favorite of Tolley, and had his ear as few members of the upper administration did.

It was for her support of the nation's newest and most innovative nursing curriculum that Smith is best remembered. Smith wanted to join the very few schools who had taken the chance and developed a bachelor of science degree in nursing. Such a program would take a student four or five years to complete but would allow the student to have both clinical and classroom experience.[2] However, Smith was pressured by many to offer the normal three year program toward earning a registered nurse (R.N.) degree, which would not only offer a potentially larger enrollment, but would send nurses into the field immediately. Recognizing the pressing need to offer the R.N. program, Smith nevertheless saw it as only a "wartime expedient," and insisted that the "collegiate option," as she now called the extended program, be emphasized in the college's literature. The admissions office protested, believing that only a select few women would attend Syracuse if they knew that it might take them beyond the normal three years to graduate. Yet building an elite, prestigious school was always Smith's major goal. She carried her case to Vice Chancellor Finla Crawford, arguing that "if we didn't begin at once building the collegiate program, the end of the war, when it came, would find us with no students in it."

Smith prevailed, and the School of Nursing opened its doors on June 28, 1943. It offered both the R.N. and the B.S. options, with the admissions literature emphasizing the bachelor's programs. It quickly became the preeminent training facility for nurses in upstate New York, swallowing up the programs of both the University Hospital of the Good Shepherd[3] and Syracuse Memorial Hospital, which both discontinued their nursing programs to cooperate with Syracuse (indeed, when the university school found that it had no library, save what it could borrow from the university's medical school, the two hospitals donated their entire collections to the new school of nursing).

2. To earn a bachelor of science in nursing, the student spent two years of academic preparation in liberal arts and in the social, physical, and biological sciences, then spent two and one-half years in clinical instruction and intern experience. Upon completion of the degree, the student could take the state board exam (*Alumni News,* July 1945).

3. In 1874, Bishop Frederick D. Huntington founded the University Hospital of the Good Shepherd as a temporary nursing care facility. It eventually became the teaching hospital for the university's medical and nursing schools. In 1964, it was renamed Huntington Hall and renovated for classrooms and office use.

Only days after the School of Nursing opened, the War Department, now pressed for nurses as never before, announced the creation of the U.S. Cadet Nursing Corps. Sensing a way to increase the military population on campus, Tolley made it clear that he wanted the Cadet Corps on campus, and Smith acquiesced. The lot of the cadet nurse was a particularly grueling one. The program crammed the normal thirty-six months of work into thirty months, including two summer sessions. During that period students received basic training on nursing techniques, followed by six months in a civilian or a military hospital as an intern ("Senior Cadet Period"). One student remembered her difficult schedule and that the nurses were used as "slave labor" in already understaffed wards. During the 1944 polio epidemic, their services were invaluable. The students also learned psychiatric nursing, as they spend a six- to eight-week rotation at Willard State Hospital. They also took a turn at morale boosting, as every Friday night they were urged to go to the USO Club at the Community Chest building on Salina and James Streets and dance with the soldiers. As compensation for this exhausting schedule, cadet nurses received their tuition, maintenance, books, and uniforms for free, and were paid $15 per month for the first nine months, and then $20 per month. The cadets had to promise to serve in a branch of nursing vital to the war effort until after the war, and after the war the university made it clear that they were expected to return to school and complete their B.S. in nursing.

It was difficult for Smith to continue to sell her B.S. program to the administration in the face of such success at both attracting to and graduating students from the R.N. program. Asking nursing students to attend school for one and a half to two years longer than it would normally take them to earn their R.N. was a risky business for a small school concerned with declining enrollments. Smith held her ground, however, and the program thrived. Smith would later boast of the pluck of her students—living first in Memorial Hospital, then in the Washington Arms Apartments, and for a time sleeping on army surplus cots. And her students returned the compliment, remembering Smith's dedication to her program and students. The success of the nursing school continued throughout the postwar period. A Department of Nursing Education was established in 1948 to train teachers

and administrators of nursing, and in September 1949 the National
Committee for the Improvement of Nursing ranked the Syracuse program in the top 25 percent of the nation's programs.

*   *   *

As it did in nursing, the war had a profound effect on the university's medical school. The college had originally existed as Geneva
Medical (a part of Hobart College) from 1834 to 1872. It was established at Syracuse University in October 1872 and was the oldest
division of the university. The medical school was one of the university's true success stories of the depression. One explanation for that
was a new physical plant, completed in 1937 and conceived with an
ultimate physical connection in mind between the med school and
Memorial Hospital. The other key was the college's dean, Herman G.
Weiskotten. Born in Syracuse in 1884, Weiskotten received his Ph.D.
(1906) and his M.D. (1909) from Syracuse University. After a resi-
dency at the University Hospital of the Good Shepherd, he moved to
academe. He began teaching pathology, and was made full professor
in 1917. In 1922 Weiskotten was named dean of the Medical School,
and also director of University Hospital. Few people on the hill during the Tolley years had the respect of both colleagues and students,
as Weiskotten did. A superb classroom instructor who continued to
teach as dean, Weiskotten also served as chairman of the Council on
Medical Education and Hospitals of the American Medical Association. Weiskotten's reputation was unparalleled in the Syracuse medical community. It was a good thing—for the first seventy-five years
of its existence the college had been staffed completely by practicing
physicians of the city; it was not until 1947 that the college hired its
first full-time faculty members in its clinical departments.

Although an integral part of the college, the medical school was,
nevertheless, distant, carrying on its academic work apart from the
rest of university life. The 1943 *Onondagan* remembered the college
as "a mysterious abode where students in white hurry back and forth
bent on a grim, silent mission." That mission changed with Pearl
Harbor, when the government made it clear that they needed doctors.
As happened in the nursing school, the medical school adopted an ac-
celerated program, known to the students as the "fast track." The

pressure was even greater than had been the case for the nurses. Medical students were in school twelve months out of the year, with one week off for vacation. One student remembered that students not chosen for an internship were shipped to the military. The pace was so frantic that in 1943 and 1944 two classes of M.D.s were graduated each year.

*   *   *

To say that campus life changed during the war years is an understatement of mammoth proportions. Much of campus culture reflected the national spirit of wartime sacrifice. The *Daily Orange* appeared four times a week instead of five because of the paper and labor shortages, and Slocum Auditorium was transformed into a PX for the army. The Chapel Association ran war bond drives, the 1943 Pan Hellenic Banquet was cancelled, and the women of the class of 1944 sponsored a "Junk Jewelry" drive, collecting their finery for the natives in the South Pacific.

The most publicized area of sacrifice in student life was Tolley's May 1943 announcement that intercollegiate athletics had been suspended for the duration. Tolley told the trustees that he had come to his decision as a result of transportation difficulties, the shrinking enrollment of civilian students, and the decision by the War Department not to allow army and air corps training units to participate in extracurricular activities. By late 1943, the sports page of the *Daily Orange* became a news section for the army air corps men at SU, and the university made arrangements for the students to be admitted to high school football games that were played in Archbold Stadium.

Not everything was cancelled. Movie star Phyllis Brooks made a visit to Zeta Psi house, and the class of 1944 danced at the Junior Prom to the music of Charlie Barnett. But the spirit of sacrifice overshadowed every event—even commencement. On August 28, 1943, the university convened what was its first commencement in Hendricks Chapel, its first summertime commencement, and the first in many years where the candidates received their degrees individually. In a moment that symbolized for many the war years at Syracuse, the diploma of Lt. Robert E. Genant, killed in action in the African campaign, was given posthumously to his parents.

*   *   *

Having prospered, not merely survived, during the war years, Syracuse University had cause to celebrate that April, as it marked its seventy-fifth anniversary. The opening event was a faculty dinner, during which 125 faculty members were honored for serving the university for more than twenty-five years. Freeman Galpin, professor of history, and President Alan Valentine of the University of Rochester were the speakers. The next day featured an anniversary concert in Hendricks Chapel. The formal commemoration ceremonies, held on Saturday, April 28, included an address by Dr. George Stoddard, New York State Commissioner of Education, and was followed by a lavish banquet at the Hotel Syracuse.

Before the summer was over, the entire nation had cause to celebrate. The announcement of the fall of Nazi Germany on May 7 led to muted celebrations in Syracuse; the entirety of the formal civic remembrance was a brief retreat service held on May 8 at the Soldiers and Sailors Monument in Clinton Square. The streets were deserted, and everything was closed, but a sign in the window of the Addis Department Store said it all— "The War is Not Over—Remember Pearl Harbor!" The moment for explosive catharsis came to Central New York on August 13. When the formal surrender of Japan was announced, hundreds of Syracusans headed downtown. South Salina Street was a mob scene, with good-natured but increasingly tense policemen moving the crowd back onto the sidewalks. Streams of ripped paper fell from the Chimes Building, and the Drum and Bugle Corps, which had been conducting its weekly rehearsal, offered the crowd impromptu, but welcome, music. The next day—VJ Day— was more sedate, with church services, like the interdenominational service at St. Paul's Episcopal Church, the order of the day.

Some 18,000 alumni and former students of Syracuse University had been in uniform during World War II. Of these, 195 were reported killed and 51 missing. Six Syracuse graduates earned the Distinguished Service Cross; 427 others received various other commendations.

Finla Crawford

CHAPTER 3

Tolley and His Administrators

I've got to be the chancellor.

—Tolley to George Hopkins Bond

WHEN TOLLEY came to Syracuse, he found that under Graham, all routine financial matters were referred to former trustee George Hopkins Bond, senior partner of Bond, Schoeneck and King and a former member of the college's board of trustees. Such service did not come cheap. Tolley's immediate reaction to the situation says a great deal about him as an administrator, as he moved quickly to wrest the institution's direction away from its lawyers. Tolley took Bond out to lunch, and he remembered telling him: "Regent Bond, I've got a problem. . . . I know that I can't do it as well as you can, but I've got to be the chancellor."

Tolley had cut his administrative teeth in small academic environments where the chief executive officer was responsible for a myriad of areas. This could, and in Tolley's case did, breed a manager who was attuned to the slightest details, as Tolley candidly reflected in a 1981 interview with Syracuse University professor Michael O. Sawyer:

> Before I was dean of Allegheny, I ran the bookstore, the alumni
> office, and the news bureau. I knew what was going on in public
> relations and in admissions. But when I came to Syracuse, I had to
> remind myself that it was a university, not a college, and that I
> shouldn't administer it as I had this small college. But there was an
> inevitable tendency to know what was going on in every aspect of the
> university, and to assume that you could tell the bookstore manager,
> as I did, that he didn't know how to run a bookstore.

In many ways, Tolley remained a small college administrator, even after he took the reins of Syracuse University. As Clark Ahlberg, one of Tolley's top administrators, remembered, "It was his university. He had the keys to all the doors. He worried about the litter on the grounds and he knew who was the janitor in every building—so he had an enormous capacity for detail." They were details that he rarely shared with others, even his board of trustees. Referring to himself as a "do it yourself kind of guy" in a 1992 interview, Tolley admitted that he viewed the chairman as "the only important trustee. . . . I never had any secrets from the Chairman . . . [but] I'm afraid I did withhold [some information] from the Board as a whole." Such attention to detail often irritated those who had become accustomed to a less proactive chancellor who left the management of the institution to the administration and its deans. One faculty member echoed the belief of many when he grumbled that Tolley "ran the place like a feudal lord."

William Tolley understood power, radiated it in his personal mannerisms, and delegated it sparsely. Although recognizing that his fund-raising duties should necessitate his having confidence in an administrator who could make decisions as he would make them, he nevertheless reserved the ultimate ability to effect change to the institution—a classic definition of power—for himself. He expected that his administrators would take care of the day-to-day details not by following their own instincts but by predicting what Tolley would have done in that situation, had he been responsible for making the decision. In his more than two decades of administering Syracuse University, Tolley entrusted such authority to only three such men.

*   *   *

Born in Andover Mills, New York, in 1894, Finla D. Crawford received his bachelor's degree from Alfred University in 1915, then moved on to the University of Wisconsin, where he received his master's in 1916. He served during World War I as a machine gun private; by the time the war ended, he had risen to first lieutenant. Crawford was assigned to the war plans division of the general staff at the close of the hostilities, and was stationed in Camp Dodge, Iowa, and Camp Hancock, Georgia. Crawford came to Syracuse University in 1919 as an assistant professor of political science. He was promoted to professor in 1921, finished his Ph.D. at Wisconsin in 1922, and was made chairman of the department in 1925. Crawford was a founding staff member of the Maxwell School in 1924, and from 1934 to 1935 he was the acting director of the School of Citizenship. In 1938, he was appointed dean of the College of Liberal Arts, a position in which he served until 1950. He also served as acting dean of the College of Business Administration from 1943 to 1946, and acting dean of Maxwell from 1945 to 1946.

While George Bond looked after the university's finances during Graham's chancellorship, Crawford ran virtually everything else. Acting as a provost without portfolio, Crawford made decisions on faculty salaries, appointments and promotions, and teaching responsibilities. He was clearly qualified in 1942 to run the entire university, and he just as clearly wanted to be Graham's successor. However, his politics and his religion got in his way. One of the leading lights in the Syracuse Democratic party, Crawford was the Democratic candidate for mayor of Syracuse in 1929 (he was defeated by Rolland B. Marvin), a delegate to the Democratic National Convention in 1932, and a member of several gubernatorial committees and commissions. Tolley remembered that Crawford's politics angered the predominantly Republican, conservative board of the university. Crawford's son Richard remembered in a later interview that his mother believed that Crawford would have been chancellor, except for the fact that he was not a Methodist minister.

Recognizing both his influence and his knowledge, Tolley immediately promoted Crawford to vice chancellor in 1942. For the next seventeen years, Crawford carried out much the same responsibilities as he had done under Graham. Clark Ahlberg remembered that "all the deans were responsible to [Crawford] and he controlled the academic budget for the university. He controlled it in a very detailed, personal way. He kept it in the lower left hand drawer of his desk and he almost kept books. . . . He was Mr. Inside, and Dr. Tolley was Mr. Outside." Richard Crawford admitted that his father did not have the fund-raising ability that Tolley had, but that did not lessen his influence. The younger Crawford likened Tolley to the chief executive officer of the university and his father to the "chief operating officer" of the corporation, remembering that "nobody moved on that campus without my father being involved." And Crawford was no pushover. Guthrie Burkhead, soon to have his turn as dean of the Maxwell School, remembered that Crawford was "as hard as nails when he wanted to be"; the student body knew him as "the old man of the mountain."

Put most simply, Crawford was indispensable. As future chancellor Melvin Eggers, who would join the Maxwell faculty in 1950, remembered:

> The transition that it went through in his time as chancellor was from a time when there was one chancellor, there was one vice chancellor and there were some other people that worked for them, but there was a chancellor and a vice chancellor and that's all you really needed to administer a university . . . and then that sort of [bogged] down as some of the functions took on greater importance. . . . [Tolley] wanted to do the external stuff himself and he let Finla Crawford do it and then he had to split it because it was too big.

When Crawford retired in 1959, Tolley's administration underwent a significant change. When it was done, two names emerged that had been given a combined authority that exceeded that held by Crawford. Together, they became known as the "A and P Company."

*   *   *

Clark Ahlberg came to Syracuse in 1939 as a graduate student in political science. He earned his M.A. in 1944, served during the war in Panama, then spent a year traveling the country as assistant director of the sixteen-man planning committee for the Veteran's Administration. In 1947 he accepted a post as director of the Maxwell School's Washington Research Office. Ahlberg had two responsibilities while in Washington—conducting research projects and developing sources of financial support for graduate education and research on the campus. Ahlberg developed a close friendship with Crawford, who felt that someone should facilitate the flow of federal money for the university. As a result, in 1951 Ahlberg was brought back to the hill as assistant dean of the College of Applied Science, then the hotbed of federal funding. Ahlberg's job was to get the university's share, and he succeeded beyond Tolley's wildest dreams. From 1955 to 1959, Ahlberg served as Deputy Director of the Budget for the state of New York, a political appointment that ended with Governor W. Averell Harriman's 1958 defeat at the hands

Clark Ahlberg   *Frank Piskor*

of Nelson Rockefeller. As part of his general reshuffling following the retirement of Crawford, Tolley invited Ahlberg back to the university as Vice President for Administration and Research, with primary responsibility for university research and the resulting new relationships between the university and the government. As will be seen in chapter 6, Tolley had no higher priority than the establishment of Syracuse University as a research institution; Ahlberg was not only present at the creation of that institution, he, more than any other administrator save Tolley, was responsible for its long-term success. From 1959 to his departure in 1968, it was Clark Ahlberg who ran the research side of the institution.

Ahlberg's administrative colleague, Frank P. Piskor, ran the institution's academics. A native of Turners Falls, Massachusetts, Piskor earned his A.B. from Middlebury College. He joined the administrative staff of Syracuse University in 1939, when he was named personnel counselor with an academic appointment in political science. He was made acting dean of men in 1943 and the same year was made chairman of Maxwell's Citizenship Program.[1] When he was appointed dean of men in 1947, he was but thirty years old. He quickly earned the chancellor's confidence—Tolley described him as

1. For a discussion of the evolution of the Citizenship requirement, see chapter 15.

"the best dean of men Syracuse ever had"—and in 1953 he was promoted to Vice President for Student Affairs. When Crawford retired, Tolley passed over Eric Faigle, who had succeeded Crawford as dean of the College of Liberal Arts, and promoted Piskor once again, this time to the position of Vice President for Academic Affairs and Dean of Faculties.

In a letter to Ahlberg, Tolley described Piskor's new job as "the building of academic excellence in the campus colleges of both the undergraduate and graduate level." Piskor did a better job of describing his responsibilities to a *Daily Orange* reporter: "I am responsible for all matters having to do with faculty members." Piskor's mandate in the academic area surpassed even that of Crawford, and he made the most of it. A workaholic by nature, Piskor insisted on being a part of every academic decision, right down to the departmental level.

*   *   *

Tolley had several other administrators whose financial and fundraising skills aided the financial growth of the college in the first two decades of his tenure. F. Gordon Smith was known as much for his flashy diamond ring and his natty dress as for his skill as a fundraiser; it was Smith who negotiated the federal loan for the medical school, and he assisted in the construction of the Maxwell School. In the 1950s, he was Tolley's right-hand man as the school entered into the Building and Development Fund drive. Smith convinced Newell Rossman, a former dean of men, to return to the university after spending the war at the Research and Service Bureau of the personnel division of the Panama Canal Administration. Rossman took over the Alumni Fund and became Vice President for Development in 1957. After Smith's death in 1964, Rossman accompanied Tolley on virtually every fund-raising trip of substance.

Tolley's business managers did more than keep the books; they assumed important advisory roles in the chancellor's inner circle. Tolley got Hugh C. Gregg from Albion College in 1945. A former high school teacher, Gregg served Syracuse as its business manager until his retirement in 1959. When Gregg left, Tolley promoted the university comptroller, Francis (Frank) Wingate, to the position of treasurer. A colonel in the army reserve, Wingate was more than adequately trained for his position, holding a B.A. from Bowdoin College and an M.A. from the Harvard Graduate School of Business Administration. Wingate's role cut beyond mere accounting, as he served as Tolley's financial representative on virtually every important committee. In 1961 he was promoted to vice president and treasurer; his responsibilities included campus security, the bookstore, food services, married student housing, and the treasury of the university's Research Corporation.

But Syracuse University between 1943 and 1960 was Tolley's domain. He enjoyed his rare moments of personal, informal contact with members of what he often referred to as "my family." Ahlberg remembers that "in many ways he behaved like a Dean of Students himself. He did go around, he used the chapel, he used the fraternities, he used student government as a way of developing personal relationships and he got a kick out of that." There are many who worked both for and with Tolley who praise his people skills, and have nothing but scorn for those who view him as imperious. But although Tolley could often motivate those who worked for him, it was never his sole purpose to do so. In the pre–Human Resources style of management, Tolley preferred to administer by edict, reaching a consensus with his vice presidents and faculty only when necessary. In this Tolley resembled his contemporaries from the business world. His private secretary, Eleanor Webb, remembered for an interviewer: "even though he had a treasurer or comptroller, whoever it was that prepared the budget, it came to him. I can remember when he used to go through the budget line by line."

This type of administrative strategy was far from singular in the higher education of the postwar period; indeed, it was the norm. Yet Tolley deviated from this norm by not being satisfied with being a mere manager of the institution. He wanted to shape it. He held a comprehensive and far-reaching vision for the future of Syracuse University. Like most visionaries, Tolley's plans for the future were grandiose, often contradictory, and always expensive.

The new classroom, 1948

CHAPTER 4

The "GI Bulge"

Who would have ever come to college if it hadn't been for the GI Bill?

—Luke LaPorta, Class of 1948

*I remember asking a young veteran I met on campus where his dormitory was.
He said "I'm not sure where it is. It's called Baldwinsville."*

—William Tolley

IN 1947, the Report of the President's Commission on Higher Education was published. Concerned with the quality of higher education, it argued that "the educational attainments of the American people are still substantially below what is necessary either for effective individual living or for the welfare of the society." The report estimated, using test scores, that at least 49 percent of the population "has the mental ability to complete fourteen years of schooling"; therefore, it estimated that in 1960 the total college enrollment *should* be 2,924,000.

The report turned out to be a classic understatement. By 1947, enrollment in the nation's colleges was already 2,300,000. Nearly half were veterans.

*   *   *

Upon their separation from the service in 1919, veterans of World War I were given $60 and a railroad ticket home. Feeling cheated out of fair compensation for putting their lives on the line in France, discontent bubbled among veterans groups during the 1920s and exploded in 1932 during the poignant march of the "Bonus Army" on Washington in July 1932. Neither Congress nor President Herbert

Hoover would grant the depression-ravaged veterans an early payment of their promised salary bonus, due in 1945—$1 per day for each day served, and $1.25 for each day spent overseas. Their frustration led to a bitter and ironic protest, as Americans were appalled to find that their own army had been called in by the president to forcibly evict starving veterans from squatter's shacks set up immediately behind the Capitol Building.

Franklin Roosevelt meant to see to it that he would never have to face such a confrontation. On October 27, 1943, the same day that he announced the lowering of the draft age to eighteen, he announced that he was forming a committee of educators to study the problem of the interruption of education. From that committee, upon which served William Tolley, came a proposal that Tolley later characterized as "legislation born of the fear of long unemployment lines." Their proposal was drafted into a bill by Senator Champ Clark of Missouri, and it was quickly passed by both houses on June 22, 1944.

The Servicemen's Readjustment Act of 1944—better known as the GI Bill of Rights—provided one free year of college for each ninety days of service and one additional month of paid education for each month of service up to forty-eight months. Veterans would receive free books, their student fees would be paid in full, and they were given a living allowance of $50 a month for lodging and an additional $25 per dependent. The GI Bill was popular; 83 percent of the public was in favor of educational assistance for returning vets. However, the War Department did not believe that many men would take advantage of this offer. In 1944 a War Department survey estimated that 1,280,000 men intended to go back to school after the war.

The War Department was wrong. Between 1945 and 1950, some 2.3 million students used the GI Bill. Between the spring of 1946 and the spring of 1950, veterans made up anywhere from 33 to 50 percent of all matriculated college students. Although no serious study has been done of these students, it seems fair to conclude that most of the veterans who took advantage of these new benefits—most of them males between the ages of 23 and 30 who had seen combat—would never have been able to get a college education without the GI Bill.

Most of the nation's universities, while they certainly would not refuse a qualified veteran or his government stipend, simply refused to recruit veterans, for many of the same reasons that had led them to refuse having cadets on campus during wartime. This trend bothered Governor Thomas Dewey, who, in 1946, called a conference of the colleges and universities in New York, and asked them to expand their facilities to accommodate the influx of veterans. Tolley needed no urging from the governor; he had long planned to actively recruit veterans. In an interview with the *Syracuse Herald-Journal* on March 7, 1942, Tolley had made it clear that "there will be programs for these men to come home to; programs that will fit their needs and interests," and the university announced its first plan for Veteran's Programs as early as December 1943. The basis of this was what some wags called Tolley's "uniform admission program." Tolley simply promised each man entering the service that a place would be there for him when he returned. He did not even require that they have high school diplomas, just that they passed entrance examinations — and arrangements were made with local high schools so that courses taken in the army could be applied to the high school diploma. The rest of the high school courses were taken on campus. Veterans received credit for courses of college grade taken in schools, camps, or stations when certified by the USAF Institute, or work in the educational programs of the armed forces at accredited colleges and universities. Tolley's justification to his trustees for this radical departure from the stringent admissions policies of the past was simple — "these boys feel they are coming home. We can't let them down."

It is inconceivable that Tolley's decision to adopt what was essentially an open admissions policy for veterans was not enrollment driven. Despite the influx of cadets on campus during the war, enrollment had fallen in 1943 to the dangerous low of 3,838 students. It was also the most important decision of his tenure as chancellor. Within the space of four years, the number of students enrolled at Syracuse University quintupled. In the fall of 1945, 247 veterans enrolled at Syracuse University, out of 1,124 men enrolled (total enrollment of 4,391). In January 1946 total registration reached an all-time high of 7,405 students,[1] with more men than women for the first time in three years. By the fall of that year, total registration had almost doubled, as the number of veterans on campus had swelled to

1. This topped the 1938 civilian student record of 6,601 students (*Alumni News,* Jan. 1946, 10).

7,649 out of 10,516 men (total enrollment of 15,228), and during the academic year 1947–48—the height of what became known as the "GI Bulge"—there were 9,120 veterans on a campus of 14,344 men (total enrollment: 18,456). By the end of 1947, SU ranked seventeenth in the nation in veteran enrollment.

*   *   *

Veterans, often still in uniform, faced the same problem in 1946, although on a much larger scale, that the cadets had faced in 1943: a lack of space. The first rule throughout the years of the GI Bulge was that if a veteran had family living in Syracuse, he had to live at home. Beyond that, the university improvised. Only two additional housing areas were ready for habitation in the fall of 1946. The first would become semi-affectionately known by its residents as "Mud Hollow." In early 1946, 175 trailers were purchased from the navy and delivered to the university with the help of Roderick Burlingame of Drumlins Country Club. Those trailers were assigned to married veterans without children.[2] Located in a DeWitt apple orchard near Drumlins, Mud Hollow housed about two hundred people. The second area, also for married students, was located at the northeast corner of the university farm along East Colvin Street—now Skytop and Slocum Heights. But space was in short supply, and families were housed in twenty-five two-family prefabricated house units purchased from a war workers colony in Massena. Rental for a Mud Hollow trailer was about $26 per month; rental for a prefab house was $35 a month.

Neither Mud Hollow nor the prefabs would house all the veterans, however. The Yates Hotel made parts of two floors available for the balance of the 1945–46 school year. The Westminster Lodge 778, International Order of Odd Fellows, also provided space. By the time school started in September 1946, other emergency sites had been set up. Two barnlike buildings at the army air base in Mattydale housed 170 students; eight more buildings were acquired in Baldwinsville, on Route 31 (near today's suburb of Radisson). An additional 750 men bunked at the New York State Fair Grounds in converted animal

2. The trailer camp, which had become its own small "town," complete with "streets," and a "mayor,"—officially closed in June 1951 (*Alumni News,* May 1951, 9).

stalls, what was then the Boys and Girls Building, and the Women's Building.

By the end of 1946 the situation had stabilized, as a more permanent form of housing was near completion. Governor Thomas Dewey was so grateful that Syracuse had admitted so many veterans—clearly the largest class of veterans in New York State—that he sold Tolley close to seven hundred Quonset huts, many of which had been obtained from North Carolina and Camp Upton, for the price of one dollar per building. Two hundred of them, rebuilt to house 2,000 men, were located on a twenty-three-acre tract leased by the university from Morningside Cemetery. Twenty-two more units, housing 532 students, were built in a vacant lot on East Colvin Street and called Collendale. One hundred of the buildings were on the main campus, behind Crouse College—near where the Heroy Geology Building is today—serving as classrooms and laboratories. The rest went up to Skytop, which would eventually boast some six hundred prefab houses, old barracks, and Quonsets that would eventually house some 3000 students. The last of these buildings was razed in 1991.

Life in the temporary housing became synonymous with what became known as the university's "Can-Do Spirit," documented so well in Alexandra Eyle's 1987 article for *Syracuse University Magazine,* which featured interviews with many students of the period. One remembered sharing his living quarters with ninety-two other veterans—a "cozy little room" in the cow barn at the fair grounds; others remembered trying to catch one of the "Blue Beetle" vans to and from Baldwinsville, a forty-five-minute trip each way. One alum remembered Mud Hollow as a trailer camp dotted with privies, as there were no indoor toilets, and since there was only cold running water in the 7-by-22 foot trailer, everybody brought a small electrical device to heat up water. Yet all those interviewed remembered the time with a mixture of patience and fondness; all hastened to add that it was a far sight better than the conditions that they had recently experienced in combat.

The curriculum and classrooms were no more ready for the influx of veterans than was dormitory space. Thanks to the innovative University Veteran's Educational Program, the veterans were given the

option of when they wanted to graduate—1947 was the last class
that graduated in the winter (with 1947W on their transcript). Teaching that number of veterans became easier thanks to a provision of
the GI Bill, which financially helped teachers return to their positions.
But the classrooms were crowded. William Fleming, centennial professor emeritus of fine arts, remembered for Eyle that the classrooms
were "wall-to-wall students. . . . I had to spell out the names of artists
and composers because I could not get to the blackboard to write
them down." With the exception of the packed laboratories at
Thompson Road, the genesis of which will be described in chapter 6,
the classrooms were the most crowded in the School of Education, as
teaching was the second most popular curricular choice of the veterans. Harry Ganders, who had been dean of the school since 1930,
had to do some fast staffing work, and by 1950 the college was offering courses and workshop programs for teachers in some eighteen
different New York communities.

Perhaps this veteran's invasion was helped by a university policy
to limit the enrollment of women during the first two years of the
bulge. The board was told in the fall of 1945 that

> to make more room for veterans we are discouraging the admission
> of women in January or May if they require dormitory accommoda-
> tions. The freshman class of women to be admitted next fall will be
> limited to the approximate number in residence during the year. Since
> this number is likely to be under 500, we shall report next fall the
> smallest freshman class of women to be admitted for many years. . . .
> Thus our alumni and trustees should not be surprised if high ranking
> women students are denied admission on the grounds that there is no
> more room.

As a result, the number of women in the residence halls between 1945
and 1947 dropped dramatically. By 1947 the assistant dean of
women could report that "at all times during the present academic
year there have been vacancies for undergraduates in the women's
centers. This is a condition not obtained in recent years." Nevertheless, despite the "greater selectivity," as the university called it, in
1947–50 there was a record rise in the number of men in the residence halls.

*   *   *

Before the end of 1946, Tolley came to the conclusion that Syracuse had swallowed all the students that it could. He called Dewey and proposed an inexpensive solution—a program run by a consortium of area college presidents at the abandoned army barracks at nearby Camp Sampson. Dewey liked the idea, and by April 1946 the appropriate legislation had been passed. Sampson was opened immediately, enrolling some three thousand students. The "Associated Colleges of the State of New York" was thus born, including Syracuse University, Cornell, Colgate, the University of Rochester, and Hobart College. Joining Sampson in this consortium of what Syracuse's *Alumni News* called "three temporary emergency colleges" were one other empty army camp at Plattsburgh, New York, which enrolled some nineteen hundred students, and Mohawk College, which took some twenty-five hundred students. The key to the success of the Associated Colleges was the man Tolley chose to head the program, Asa Knowles, who had been dean at Northwestern University. According to Tolley, the Associated Colleges "never cost the state of New York a penny," and when they closed, "we returned a substantial balance" to New York.

But Tolley had substantially grander plans for extending Syracuse University than the temporary expedient of the Associated Colleges. The university had begun extension schools in both the Binghamton and Utica areas during the depression, primarily to offer graduate work for high school teachers. Students started their work there, and then went on to either Syracuse or to another college for their degrees. Both schools helped the local areas get through the depression. But with the veterans in mind, Tolley decided to take the step of establishing full colleges in both cities.

In 1932, Syracuse had established a university extension program in the Susquehanna River Valley at Endicott, New York, eight miles west of Binghamton and five miles west of Johnson City. Known together as the "Triple Cities," Endicott was the home of both Endicott Johnson shoes and the International Business Machines Corporation (IBM). Although most of the extension classes met at Union-Endicott High School, classes were also held at Binghamton North High

School, Binghamton City Hospital, Johnson City, and Vestal. From the depression years to 1941, the academic work of the Endicott Extension Program was supervised from the main campus in Syracuse. In February 1941 Syracuse sent Benjamin Hopkins-Moses to Binghamton to manage the extension program as its resident director. During World War II extension classes in Endicott actually grew—in 1946 more than 225 students were enrolled for their first classes toward their degrees. The Endicott Program, centered in a population of 200,000 and fifty miles from the nearest major college, seemed ripe for expansion.

The question arose as to whether the expanded college would be moved from Endicott to the more populous Binghamton. Hopkins-Moses wrote to Tolley that "the university has fairly deep roots in Endicott. I anticipate that a withdrawal from here in favor of Binghamton would create a considerable resentment on the part of several people of influence in Endicott." One such "person of influence" was Thomas Watson. A native of the southern tier, Watson had turned the National Cash Register Company and several other cast-off companies into IBM. On its way to becoming one of the nation's top ten largest industrial concerns, IBM had computerized the nation—introducing the first electronic computer, the ENIAC, in 1946—and had revolutionized managerial techniques with Watson's brand of sales and managerial evangelism. Watson's IBM, with its huge conglomeration of subsidiaries, its commitment to staying ahead of the cutting edge of research, its exhortation to "Think" on every office wall, and its huge payroll, represented the type of institution that Tolley wanted Syracuse University to be. More important, Watson liked Tolley's style, once asking him to leave Syracuse to head up what Watson visioned as the International Business Machines College at double his salary. A university report on the background of the Binghamton project noted that Tolley made "only one [donor] request" when financing the southern tier project—Watson. In January 1946 the Colonial Building (formerly known as the Bowes mansion) in Endicott was donated to the university by Watson. It became the school's College Administration Building. Three months later, the university purchased a small parcel of land adjacent to the Colonial Building from the New York State Electric and Gas Corporation, and the erection of temporary classrooms and alterations to the Bowes mansion began in July.

On June 7, 1946, the Triple Cities College (TCC) was formally inaugurated with a dinner held at the Arlington Hotel in Binghamton. TCC opened that September with 957 students (819 full-time and 138 part-time) enrolled. A faculty of fifty-five assembled under Dean Glenn Bartle, a former geology teacher and dean of Liberal Arts at the University of Kansas City. By November, in addition to the Colonial mansion, eighteen aluminum buildings had been added. By the spring semester, the colonial mansion and the aluminum prefabs housed fourteen classrooms of varying size, two lecture rooms, three labs, a cafeteria, a library, faculty offices, a bookstore, and two student lounges. TCC also made money. At the end of 1947 it had an operating balance of $96,153. On January 27, 1948, Bartle announced that the college was assuming four-year status.

The expansion of the university's extension school in Utica was planned no less as a permanent college. Clearly there was a large amount of community commitment. The July 18, 1946, announcement that Syracuse was enlarging its Utica operation was met with an outpouring of community support—the registrar began receiving applications only eleven days later. The Utica College of Syracuse University was formally established in September 1946 as an academic division of Syracuse University. Tuition was the same as on the home campus, $450 per year. Like TCC, students who finished two years at Utica College with satisfactory grades were promised transfer privileges to the SU main campus. Also like TCC, Utica soon moved to four-year status and began granting baccalaureate degrees in 1949. Winton Tolles served as Utica College's dean in 1946–47. A graduate of Hamilton College (A.B. and M.A. in English and public speaking) and Ph.D. from Columbia University in 1940, Tolles had taught at Washington College in Maryland. He entered the navy in 1942, where he served as the executive director of the naval training school at Hollywood, Florida, and later plans officer at Okinawa.

Fully certified under the GI Bill, 90 percent of Utica College's students were veterans. Designed to accommodate about 500 students in liberal arts and business, Utica College, like its main campus counterpart, quickly outgrew its own expectations. During its first year, it had an enrollment of 675 students in the day division and 320 in the evening division; that increased to 970 day and 1,321 evening in 1947–48. The college opened at the Plymouth Congregational Church at Oneida Square, using the Sunday school as classrooms. On the first day of classes, students sat on chairs borrowed from a local undertaker—the college's chairs had not yet arrived. The church's assembly space became a lounge and study area. The old Francis Street School, two blocks away, became the other half of the campus—the city made it available for a lease of one dollar a year. The basement of the building housed the bookstore, run by the legendary Harry "Pop" Adams. Owen Roberts was the first faculty member; he resigned from Utica Free Academy to teach literature and freshman English there.

*   *   *

In 1948 the Baldwinsville dorms closed. By the following year, all freshmen were living on campus. In 1949–50, the number of enrolled veterans dropped to 8,611; the following year, it dipped to 5,368. That same year, 1950–51, total enrollment dropped some 3,500 students, to 16,007. The "GI Bulge" was over, and the university would have to search for new ways to expand. But a new university had been created, one that would develop and thrive along the lines prescribed by Tolley in the 1946–48 period—ironically, not always to Tolley's satisfaction.

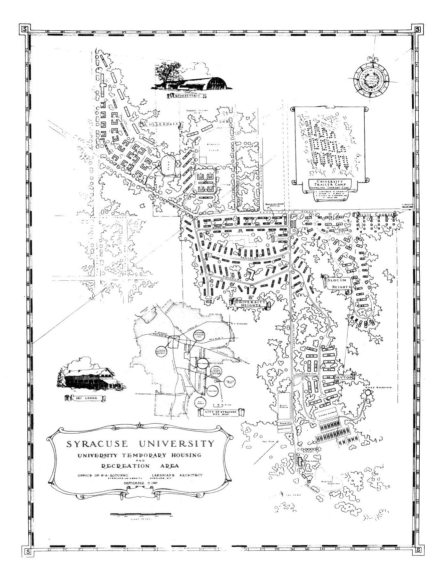

Syracuse University campus, 1948

CHAPTER 5

The Building Bulge, Part One
The Building and Development Fund

The building of a university takes endless patience and time. . . .
We must take the long look. . . . We should not permit ourselves
to be hurried. We must be concerned only with quality. We must
have a passion for excellence. This is not a mushroom
we are growing. This is a sturdy oak.

—William Tolley

I N THE LAST MONTHS of the war, Tolley served as the general chairman of the Syracuse-Onondaga Post-War Planning Council. Established by Mayor Thomas E. Kennedy on January 1, 1943, in co-operation with *Fortune* and *Architectural Forum* magazines, its purpose was to create a detailed plan ("a program of immediate action") for the reconversion effort in Central New York. Their report, submitted on December 15, 1945, had an almost evangelical tone ("Success in making a better community and world will come only if consideration of the supreme maker is placed first, and if his grace attends man's efforts"). The report covered all areas of social and economic life, but for our purposes, the section on Syracuse University is the most important, as it gave a revealing hint as to the direction that Tolley intended to take the college after the war. It was a direction that seemed to belie the maxim, quoted in the report, that "wise planning is conservative planning." Assuming a decline in employment, the report recommended the creation of an Industrial Research Institute and a Business Research Service at the university, as well as the

49

"acquisition of a number of desirable industrial sites, to be improved and kept in readiness for use by new industries." This Institute of Industrial Research "will cooperate with industry not only in advancement of fundamental research projects but in more specific industrial studies as well." In academics, the report predicted the establishment of the Institute of Aeronautics and the Institute of Applied Arts and Sciences. However, it also said that "the development of instruction in Art is to be emphasized, because the University believes it has a special field of service here, in as much as the state has provided no school for instruction in this field." Noting that "two year terminal vocational courses" will be in "great demand" in the postwar period, Tolley announced plans to set up a division of the college in that field, reminding his readers that "even in wartime the Extension School had 1500 students." He also predicted a "broad expansion in the field of radio and television." To house all this, the report predicted that the University would erect "some 20–30 buildings in addition to those already mentioned for the arts and forestry to meet needs expected to arise in the next 50 years."

As a forecast of the future, the report was remarkably accurate. Of those buildings listed in 1945, most were completed. By 1960 Tolley had a research program intact, and it was operating as one of the most innovative in the nation. Most of the academic programs listed in the report were inaugurated by 1969. Yet it is the breadth of the vision that impresses the historian. Taking the long view is the task of any successful administrator; Tolley's vision of the long view for Syracuse University was stunning in its imagination, its accurate reading of the marketplace, and its creativity.

*   *   *

Soon after he took office, Tolley discovered that Graham had borrowed heavily against the university's rather small endowment. This not only created a debt that the university had to pay to *itself,* but it also was in danger of making the university a bad risk for banks. It was soon clear that Tolley was not going to let the university's debt stand in the way of his dreams of expansion. Several years before the GI Bulge had made it necessary, and several years before it was even financially feasible, Tolley decided to build the university into na-

tional prominence. This was a chancy move in 1943 — the endowment was small, and most institutions, fearful of a postwar recession,
were consolidating rather than expanding. However, no such qualms
bothered Tolley, as he bemoaned the fact that "college presidents and
boards of trustees are notorious for their failure to take the long
view." Clark Ahlberg remembered Tolley as "a great land speculator
. . . he had a vision that these land values would rise and they did and
that real estate was a good investment. It required a long vision because often it did not return income currently. Then you had other
desperate needs and it took a pretty hard nose to say buy this or do
that. He did it."

The university was cash-poor in 1945. Moreover, it had never undertaken a serious national development campaign. The Centurion
Club, a group of $100-plus donors created by Gordon Smith, was a
worthy beginning. However, Tolley's plans called for a more serious
commitment to fund-raising. Newell Rossman remembered that
when Tolley informed his cabinet that the university was going to
launch a campaign for $30 million, "the stomach distress that went
through that room! Two of them almost fainted." After the idea had
been thought through and staffed out, it was scaled down to a still-
imposing $15 million campaign, which would be dubbed the Build-
ing and Development Fund.

Begun in 1948, the drive, planned for five years, almost met with
disaster. The university had engaged the services of Charles W. Gamble and Associates, a New York City public relations and fund-
raising firm, to run the drive. However, the firm did not meet Tolley's
expectations. Two years into the campaign, goals had not been met,
and Tolley was furious. He wrote Gamble in May 1950 that

> as far as I can see, we are exactly where we were in February except
> for some modest contributions through the Special Gifts Committee.
> . . . I am reluctant to concede failure, but it is obvious that unless we
> reverse the tide promptly we are looking at defeat in the face. What
> disturbs me is that there is no excuse for failure. The alumni expect
> to give and give generously. They are simply waiting for someone to
> call. . . . The situation is critical.

Gamble asked that his firm be allowed to represent the university for
one more year, but Tolley had had enough. He released the Gamble

Organization in June 1950, made Newell Rossman the director of the Alumni Fund, and authorized Rossman to increase his staff as much as necessary. Three years later, Tolley established the University Fund Council, composed of Smith, Gregg, Rossman, and Vice President of Public Relations Kenneth G. Bartlett, "for the purpose of extending and coordinating the University's fund raising activities." Thanks to the efforts of this committee, and the timeliness of a major Ford Foundation Grant in December 1955, the fund drive met its goal.

The Building and Development Fund drive was important, as Rossman remembered, because it "changed the thinking, the attitude of the whole community at Syracuse in those days, got us used to the fact that we could achieve." This was clearly the case, as the drive would be cited by many as testimony to Tolley's fund-raising wizardry. It also set the stage for Tolley's crowning achievement in fund-raising, the Syracuse Plan, discussed in chapter 12. However, funding the endowment had never been Tolley's first goal—$12 million of the Building and Development fund was earmarked for building, and the rest for scholarships and endowment. Indeed, when Tolley retired in 1969, he left behind a small endowment for an institution of its size. Clearly, Tolley had not become chancellor to save money for the future. He had become chancellor to build a bigger institution.

*   *   *

No facet of the development of the institution had Tolley's rapt attention as did its physical growth. The school needed to grow; it was bursting at the seams. Treasurer Hugh Gregg told the trustees in 1947 that thanks to an enrollment that had tripled over two years, "our physical plant is taxed to 150 percent of its normal capacity . . . [it] has become one of our major worries." Tolley had prepared for this with much purchasing during the war years—by 1946 the university owned all the frontage along University Place from Irving Avenue to Walnut Avenue, except the area still held by the Corner Store. He had also purchased along Waverly, University, and Ostrom Avenues. The question now became how to make the best—and most rapid—use of this new land.

Late in 1947, the trustees authorized a the creation of a University Design Board, whose task was "to formulate and develop a Univer-

sity land use plan. It shall study and review all building site proposals, plans for all buildings and landscaping; and make recommendations of the [*sic*] Chancellor upon matters of physical development of
the University related to architectural and land-use planning." The
Design Board was chaired by L. C. Dillenback, former director of the
School of Architecture and presently serving as dean of the College of
Fine Arts, and it included Vice Chancellor Finla Crawford and seven
other experts. It was renamed the Design Committee and written into
the university bylaws in 1953.[1]

The real head of the Design Board was William Tolley. He reveled
in making plans for the building of the university, and no detail was
too mundane for his attention. The Design Board in particular, and
building in general, was, in the words of one faculty member, a
"recreational outlet" for him. Tolley traversed building sites and cor-
responded not only with architects but with contractors, discussing
everything from paint color to the overall plans for a building's sub-
structure. This correspondence makes it clear that Tolley had more
than just a passing knowledge of architecture. His questions are
probing, and the discourse that he carried on with his architects went
deeper than mere amateur meddling. Indeed, Tolley once spent in the
neighborhood of $15,000 for a scale three-dimensional model of the
university.

Tolley's first university architect was Lorimer Rich of Brooklyn. A
graduate of Syracuse's School of Architecture, Rich had achieved national renown as the designer of the Tomb of the Unknown Soldier
for the national cemetery at Arlington, Virginia. But there was soon
trouble between the thoughtful artist and the impatient chancellor.
Rich had been commissioned to do three buildings that were high on
Tolley's list of improvements: a Women's Building, a new women's
dormitory, and an on-campus building for the College of Law. By
September 1950 the construction of all three buildings had been delayed by a mixture of Rich's slow development of plans and delays in
his bidding out for contractors. Tolley angrily wrote his chief architect that "I cannot say earnestly enough that we need speed and more

1. Along with Crawford and Dillenback, the original Design Board included Professors N. A. Rotunno and D. Kenneth Sargent, Trustees Harry Smith and Gordon
Hoople, Mrs. John W. Brooks, William B. Marquis, and Lorimer Rich.

speed. There is no evidence that we have had anything remotely re-
sembling speed since January when the go-ahead signals were first
given for these three buildings." By May 1954 Tolley was refusing to
pay Rich's bill, and when the architect complained, Tolley shot back
that "there is a feeling here which may or may not be justified . . . that
we have been taken for a ride on architectural fees. The feeling is particularly strong in connection with the charges made for preliminary
studies and the finished plans of buildings not yet built. . . . The sen-
timent here is that if the . . . dormitories and the law school are not
built, a substantial refund seems to be due the University."

Although there does not seem to have been a formal parting of the
ways between Rich and Tolley, by the mid-1950s Tolley had shifted
the bulk of the university's business to Harry A. King and Curtis
King. More conservative in their building style and quicker to respond to bids and contractual arrangements—both areas that pleased
Tolley—King and King would maintain a close relationship with the
university throughout the Tolley era. The system was simple; Tolley
bought real estate at a breakneck speed (between 1942 and 1969, he
had added between nine hundred and one thousand acres to the university), consulted the Design Board as a pro forma courtesy, and
turned the physical development of the campus over to his trusted architects. The result was a blizzard of building—a true "Building
Bulge"—that was experienced by few other universities during the
postwar period.[2]

*   *   *

The first postwar structure erected on the main campus—a new
wing adjoining Sims Hall, which housed a new dining hall—was
built in 1948. The following year a warehouse was erected on Ains-
ley Drive, complete with garage, maintenance shop, and storage facilities for the university food service. Early on-campus renovation
had focused on the addition of Quonsets and trailers to house veterans temporarily, prefab buildings that would offer more long-term
housing solutions, and the $2,000,000 renovation of the Archbold
Gym following the January 12, 1947, fire that destroyed the rear

2. For a complete listing of construction and acquisition during the period, see
appendix C.

portion of the structure with most of its contents. The remodeling of the gym was one of the projects that Tolley felt had been delayed by Rich; not until 1951 was the remodeling completed, and Tolley dedicated the new gym in February 1952.

The first completely new building on the Syracuse campus since World War II was the Lowe Art Center. The building was the gift of Joseph Lowe, the president of Joseph Lowe Corporation, a manufacturing and import firm that manufactured, among other things, popsicles, fudgesicles, and creamsicles. Lowe and his wife, Emily, an artist of some reputation, were also known for their aid to young artists and students who wanted to continue their education at Syracuse. Their gift of $150,000 was the foundation for the new art center, built to house the expanding art program. Designed by the King Brothers and Lorimer Rich, construction of the building was particularly sticky, and led to some interesting delays. For example, when construction began it was essential that the builders locate a sewer pipe that was twenty-four feet under the ground. There was no map in either the city or university files, so construction was delayed while workers tried to locate the pipe. When the pipe was found it showed that early plans of the city called for a street to cut diagonally through the bookstore. No one knows if that street was ever built.

The Lowe Center was contemporary in style, made of red brick and limestone, with glass dominating the north and south sides and terraces to the east and north that served also as outdoor galleries and open-air classrooms. The first and second floors contained studios with moveable portions to convert the classrooms to whatever size and form the program required. It also contained studios for all advanced drawing and painting classes, as well as offices, student lounges, and lithography rooms. In his comments at the May 14, 1952, dedication, Dillenback tied his discipline to the frenetic action of the Building Bulge: "Fine arts are the inevitable consequence of growth and are the manifestation of the principles of their origin."

The Lowe Art Center was a spectacular addition to a university that was very close to becoming one of the preeminent art programs in the nation. However, the GI Bulge demanded that the lion's share of Building and Development Plan monies be spent on dormitories. Early in the history of the university, there had been *no* dormitories;

students had been housed by private householders and fraternities. Chancellor Day saw the need for dorms, and borrowed from the endowment to build Winchell Hall (for women) in 1900, Haven Hall (for women) in 1904, and Sims Hall (for men) in 1907.[3] No new dorms were built during either the Flint or Graham administrations, but a number of frame cottages had been acquired (in 1941, there were forty-one cottages used for the residences of undergraduate women). During the war, Sims was converted into a freshman women's dormitory; it would not be returned to male occupancy until 1956. The rapid multiplication of trailers, cottages, and Quonset huts that accompanied the veterans to Syracuse made the need for further student accommodations abundantly clear.

In November 1949 Tolley accepted what was to that point the largest single contribution ever presented to Syracuse: a $1.5 million gift from the estate of the late Mary Margaret Shaw. The gift was to be used for a women's dormitory, dedicated to her late husband, Robert Shaw. Shaw Hall was to have been the first dormitory built on the parcel of land to the university's south, which rose one hundred feet above sea level, and whose nickname had changed from "The Elephant's Back" in the 1930s to "Mount Olympus" in the 1940s. However, Rich's delays in the project, as well as his coming in with a $4 million estimate when Tolley specifically stated that the project cost was not to exceed $1.3 million, led Tolley to cancel Rich's contract for the job. The money and the Shaw name were transferred to a dormitory that was already under construction on the corner of Euclid and Comstock Avenues. Shaw Hall opened on September 16, 1952, housing 335 coeds, with kitchen facilities and a dining hall. It was followed in September 1954 by Watson and Marion Halls, which had been financed through gifts to the Building and Development Fund from Thomas Watson, chairman of IBM, and former university trustee Frank J. Marion. The U-shaped complex, located at 405–415 University Place, featured two four-story brick buildings that held 498 men—half freshmen, in the west wing, half upperclassmen, in the east wing. One of the more innovative housing

3. Winchell hall was demolished in 1984; Haven Hall was razed in 1962 to make room for the Newhouse Communications Center; Sims Hall was converted to classrooms in 1963.

projects was the Morris W. and Fannie B. Haft Cooperative Dormitory for Women, dedicated in 1956 on the corner of Ostrom and Euclid Avenues. Financed in part by a gift from Mr. Haft and in part by a $100,000 loan from the National Life Insurance Company, the co-op cottage held twenty-six coeds and a head resident. It highlighted a living arrangement where the coeds did all cooking and house-cleaning for themselves on a rotating basis.

More anxious than ever to begin construction on Mount Olympus, Tolley turned the job over to King and King. The result was Flint Hall, dedicated in 1956 and named for Bishop Charles Wesley Flint, the university's fifth chancellor. A four-story dormitory with two wings, Flint housed 530 coeds and was built at a total cost of $2,200,000. Its companion hall, named for Chancellor James R. Day, was opened in the fall of 1958. Day Hall was an eight-story dormitory that housed 455 women, built at a cost of about $3.4 million. Graham Dining Hall was added in the fall of 1958 and was connected to Day and Flint Halls by a specially constructed corridor. Although students would groan for years to come as they traversed the reinforced concrete walkway (five ramps and seventy-nine steps) up the side of the hill to "the Mount," new housing for almost 1,000 women had nevertheless been added.

Other dormitories followed in the wake of the swift development of the Mount. A $3 million loan to the university for an eight-story dorm was approved in September 1957. Located on Stadium Place, it was dedicated in 1960 and named in honor of John W. Sadler, an alumnus and former surrogate judge of Onondaga County. DellPlain Hall, which faced the garden of Thornden Park and occupied the entire block of Ostrom, Waverly, Comstock, and University Place, was dedicated the following year. The development was named after Morse DellPlain of the class of 1905, who was the chairman of the board of Welsbach Engineering and Management Corporation in Philadelphia, had chaired the Syracuse Building and Development Campaign in the Philadelphia area, and was a university trustee from 1956 to 1962. Featuring an odd configuration with eight floors on one side and nine on the other—due to the slope of the land—DellPlain housed 482 men. September 1962 saw the dedication of Claude Kimmel Hall, a small (129 men) dorm on Waverly Avenue that emphasized the mixing of freshmen and upperclassmen on the same floor of a dorm for the first time in the university's history.

Along with dormitories to replace the trailers came classroom buildings to replace the Quonset huts. More students meant more classes, which meant the need for more space to study, do research, and hold lectures. The story of many of these academic buildings—the purchase of the Thompson Road facility; the building of Hinds Hall for the College of Applied Science; the refurbishing of the old Medical School into University College's Reid and Peck Halls; the purchase of the Regent Theater under the auspices of University College; and the completion of the George L. Manley Fieldhouse—are discussed in the following chapters that deal specifically with their disciplines or schools. It should be thus, as Tolley always believed the growth of classroom buildings should follow closely from the growth of an academic or extracurricular program. Hinds, for example, was not built on the main campus until engineering had grown out of the Thompson Road campus. Manley, one of the cornerstones of the Building and Development Fund, did not become a reality until the championship football season of 1959 promised a sports revenue that would help to pay for the new fieldhouse.

Many at the time—and since—have criticized Tolley for having a shortsighted view of the beauty of the campus, destroying the "Old Oval" with new buildings that had little aesthetic quality. This was, indeed, an issue debated by the Design Board, but all concerned agreed with Tolley that utility, as well as location, were more important than long-term aesthetics. The main campus soon became dotted with cranes, steam shovels, and backhoes; William Tolley's vision was taking brick-and-mortar form.

The biggest classroom project of the period, the Huntington Beard Crouse Classroom Building, was testimony to the steady growth of the College of Liberal Arts. Named after a former trustee who had died in 1943, and dedicated on October 22, 1962, the three-story building, which students would soon dub "HBC," featured seventy-seven offices; two auditoriums, Gifford (442 seats) and Kittredge (218 seats); classrooms; language labs; and a cartography and photography studio. It also carried the distinction of being the first completely air-conditioned building on campus—all at a cost of about $1.6 million.

Increasing program enrollment also prodded another change that had been promised for some time, as the College of Law was moved from downtown Syracuse to a new home on the hill. The law school had had more than its share of homes. From 1895 to 1898 it was located in the Bastable Building; from 1898 to 1904 it was in the University Block, second floor; from 1904 to 1926 it was located at the John Crouse Residence at the corner of Fayette and State Streets; and since 1926 the school had been housed in Hackett Hall, located at 400 Montgomery Street, across the street from the County Court House. One alum liked Hackett because at lunch she could sit in on court. Nevertheless, Hackett was old; it could no longer hold the number of students that the school was attracting—in the post–World War II period enrollment grew gradually, from about 100 to 240 in 1964—and the students were separated from the university proper. The law school celebrated its fiftieth anniversary in 1945, and Tolley used the occasion to launch a fund-raising drive to finance a new building on the hill for the school. The Ernest I. White Building, named after the Syracuse lawyer and president of the *Post-Standard* company, who gave the university $424,000 toward their $500,000 goal, was announced in 1947, but Tolley once again became infuriated with construction delays, which he blamed on Lorimer Rich. The formal ground breaking was not held until June 1953, after the project had been turned over to the Kings. The total cost of the building was $922,000, and it was dedicated on December 11, 1954.

Regardless of program enrollment, the time had come for one particular building. The first donation for the fund for a Women's Building had been made in 1910, when the Cleveland alumni donated $10. Since then, university women had raised small sums through bake sales and craft shows, all being set aside for a future building that would house women's athletics and governance. The decision finally to build the Women's Building was spurred by the 1949 purchase of eighteen acres from Oakwood cemetery for $64,000. The November 15, 1950, ground breaking was an emotional affair. Katherine Sibley, a leading proponent of the project who had retired that spring after forty-seven years as director of physical education for women, turned over the first spadeful of earth. Dedicated on November 17, 1953, the building, which covered a full acre of ground, boasted a swimming pool, library, three gymnasiums, six bowling alleys, a recessed dance studio unit, and offices for both the dean of women and the director of physical education for women.

Tolley had also acquired a pastoral retreat that became the envy of all Central New York schools. In September 1948 Carl M. Loeb, president of a New York City investment firm, presented the university with fifty-three acres of property on Gilpin Bay in the upper Saranac Lake region. Included in the gift was a summer estate, Pinebrook Camp, which consisted of twelve buildings and six hundred feet of waterfront. The beautiful East House had been erected by Levi P. Morton, a former governor of New York. Christened the Pinebrook Continued Studies Center and placed under the administrative supervision of University College, the facilities soon got a lot of use. Pinebrook was made available to university faculty and administrators for summer vacation use. In 1947, rates were $6.00 per day for a family, and in the summer of 1950, more than two hundred university families spent vacation time there.

Perhaps best known, however, were the Student Leaders Conferences that Tolley hosted at Pinebrook. Once each year, beginning in 1949 and lasting until the end of his chancellorship, Tolley invited the presidents of the various student organizations to go to Pinebrook to discuss issues of campus importance (a student went for two years in a row—once as incoming president, and once in the year of presidency). The chancellor and all his top administrators were in attendance, and the small group sessions often yielded useful fruit. As one student leader remembered the Pinebrook meeting she attended, she offered that it was "before its time."

However, Pinebrook really cost the university a great deal of money. During the first year, for example, the total income was $105.00 and the expenses were $18,188.25; in the second year, the property produced $5,000 income against $15,000 in expenses. Nevertheless, as a campus retreat, Tolley remained convinced that Pinebrook was more than worth it.

*   *   *

Two stories from the years of the Building and Development Fund show the convergence of Tolley the fund-raiser and Tolley the builder. The first—Tolley's relationship with Joseph Lubin—is vintage

Tolley, acting as his own chief development officer as he courted the New York City business leader. The second — Tolley's relationship with George Arents — is no less an example of Tolley's fund-raising skill. However, the story of the building of the Arents Rare Book Room in Carnegie Library also is testimony to Tolley's desire to do more than erect utilitarian buildings; it shows his true desire to preserve knowledge at Syracuse University.

At age fourteen, Joe Lubin worked as a page at the Astor Hotel. Eventually he would own that hotel and several others. A graduate of Pace University, and New York University Law School in 1923, Lubin was a founding member of Eisner and Lubin Certified Public Accountants in New York. His specialty was real estate — he owned the land on which the United Nations was built — but his second calling was philanthropy. A donor to several eastern universities, Lubin was also one of the nation's most consistent supporter of Jewish causes.

Lubin was first brought to Tolley's attention by Lionel Grossman, a major Syracuse sports booster who had informed the chancellor that the financier and his daughter, Ann, were coming to look at the school. Tolley met them and was smitten by the girl — he described her as "breathtakingly beautiful" — and told her, without even checking her grades, that she was admitted (Tolley later remembered for his memoirs that Lubin "had a long succession of friends that he wanted to get into the university and I got them all in"). Tolley was also smitten with Ann's father, a fact that he describes in a 1987 interview with writer Alexandra Eyle in no uncertain terms: "It's fair to say that of all the friends I've had in 85 years plus, I never had a better friend than Joe Lubin, and I was never closer to any human being than I was to Joe Lubin. I loved him as a brother and I was closer to him than any of my brothers." Lubin was as captivated by Tolley, and he began to send some of his largesse toward the university. The first dealt with the housing of Beta Chi Alpha, a sorority that Ann Lubin had formed with her friends toward the end of her sophomore year in a cottage on University Place. Only three Jewish sororities existed on campus at the time, and when the national sorority accepted the girls, Lubin bought the Chappell mansion for them to use. In 1955 Lubin provided funds for the purchase of the former Sigma Chi fraternity House at 129 College Place, across from Sims Dormitory. It became known as Lubin Hall, and it housed part of the School of

Business Administration. It was hardly the end of Lubin's generosity, but it was certainly enough to warrant his 1952 honorary degree and his July 1953 appointment as a university trustee.

*   *   *

Books were William Tolley's passion. Tolley's collection of Rudyard Kipling first editions, as well as imprints and letters from the English master, was world-renowned. He had also acquired an original second leaf of the Gutenberg Bible, which contains the first printing of the Twenty-third Psalm (only forty-seven copies of the Bible survived at that time, not all of them complete). Every fund-raising trip would include a stop at a bookstore of substance (his favorite dealer was James Drake of New York), and Tolley purchased thousands of volumes. The correspondence between him and library director Frank Yenawine regarding book purchases—either Tolley himself doing it or ordering it done—is voluminous. No detail, no matter how minute, missed Tolley's attention regarding this subject. A large portion of Tolley's personal library, now located in the Visiting Scholar's Room on the sixth floor of Bird Library, is devoted to the study of books, and an entire chapter of his memoirs discusses "Collecting Rare Books."

It was, perhaps, inevitable that Tolley would eventually plan for a repository for his collection, which he fully intended to donate to the university. For this, he approached New York financier George Arents, Jr. Arents had inherited his money from his father, a co-founder of the American Tobacco Company. Tolley hoped that Arents could be persuaded to donate to one of the chancellor's pet causes —the building of a new library to replace the antiquated Carnegie Library. However, despite the fact that he had served as a chair of the university's board of trustees, Arents was far from an easy fund-raising mark. First, Tolley remembered that his "primary loyalties" lay with the New York Public Library and the St. Thomas Episcopal Church. Second, Arents was a particularly shy man who needed to be approached carefully. Yet he and Tolley shared a love for bibliotheca (in 1954, Arents sponsored an award for the best undergraduate book collection), and it was from this common interest that Tolley was able to cultivate Arents as a rather regular donor, usually in the form of stock certificates.

Tolley and George Arents

In mid-1955, Tolley pitched the idea of a Rare Book Room to Arents. Tolley's original estimate was $25,000. By the end of the year, Arents had presented Syracuse University $14,000 to establish an "oak-paneled, air-conditioned rare book room on the third floor of Carnegie Library." The room was completed in September 1956 at a final cost of $32,000.[4] The formal opening of the room was on April 30, 1957. The room was state-of-the-art; to protect the collection, the atmospheric humidity was kept constantly between 50 and 55 percent and the temperature was always 68 degrees. Arents also continued to donate books to the collection throughout the late 1950s on a regular basis—the George Arents Stephen Crane Collection and the George Arents Collection of Books about Books were the largest such compilations. On December 13, 1960, Arents died, leaving the school some $2 million for a completely new library.

4. Immediately upon learning of the final cost of the room, Arents wrote Tolley: "The stock I gave you brought approximately $14,500, so I will send you after the first of the year enough common stock to cover the difference" (Arents to Tolley, Sept. 27, 1956, Tolley Records, box 13, Arents folder 2).

T-Road

CHAPTER 6

The Research Institution

*At Syracuse, research has brought the professor face to face with
the industrialist, the businessman, military and federal government agencies, plus contacts with foreign governments in
the Middle East and Europe.*

—*Syracuse Herald-Journal,* May 29, 1958

T HE GROWTH of Syracuse University between 1945 and 1960—
driven by the GI Bulge and accommodated by the first phase of
the Building Bulge—was both a reflection and a cause of the transformation of the university into a major research institution. The
laurels of this new institution no longer rested solely on its undergraduate programs, but also on research and graduate programs that
had achieved national prominence—particularly, but not exclusively,
in the sciences. Over the period from 1942 to 1952, academic research expanded to the point where two-thirds of the professional
staff published, and contract research increased from $50,000 per
year, largely in the field of medicine, to $2 million, exclusive of med-
icine and forestry. The story of this growth of Syracuse University
into a national research institution, both in the arts and in the sciences, is the focus of the next two chapters.

*   *   *

It was only natural that growth would begin in the sciences. During World War II the federal government had contracted for the first
time with universities for military research. The residual effect of this
research, as well as the advent of the atomic and space races in the

1950s, led to an increased demand for scientific output from academe. This research would not be undertaken solely for its intellectual worth, but also for its military worth, to help the nation keep up with the Khrushchevs. It was the beginning of a whole new purpose for American higher education—as policy and scientific think tanks for the federal government. For colleges whose physical plants and mission statements allowed them to accept federal research, the compensation was superb. But the competition for federal grants was keen, and only those colleges that had the best facilities would receive the grants.

In January 1946 the State of New York announced its intention to build its Material and Testing Laboratory on a plot donated by Syracuse University. When announcing the decision, Governor Thomas E. Dewey opined that Syracuse might well become one of the great research centers of the nation. Tolley had long been planning for that very achievement. Later that same year, he and a group of local industrialists anted up $750,000, and in July 1946 founded the Institute for Industrial Research (IIR). Designed to deal with faculty-directed projects, the IIR was neither a division separate from the university, nor was it affiliated with any one division or school. As Tolley explained it to the alumni, the IIR had three functions. Fundamental, or pure, research would be undertaken by the personnel of the institute under contract with specific businesses and industries; applied research, relating to commercial production, would also be undertaken on a contractual basis; and the institute would train scientists and technicians for employment in business and industry. Tolley might also have added that the IIR was designed to be a huge magnet to attract the prestige projects and the accompanying monies needed to establish Syracuse as the East's leading research institution. This the institute did. By the end of only two years of operation, the IIR was engaged in fourteen different projects totaling $210,000.

The first director of the IIR was Ralph Montonna, of the university's class of 1916. Montonna had been the director of the Research Institute at the University of Minnesota since 1943, where he was also a professor of chemical engineering. His administrative assistant, W. C. Wheadon, joined the staff of the Materials Engineering Department in 1947 as an instructor and as a research associate. On leave from General Motors Corporation, Wheadon was appointed acting director of IIR when Montonna resigned in August 1950, a position that now reported directly to Tolley.

*   *   *

The growth of the IIR was contemporaneous with, and occurred for many of the same reasons as, the growth of the College of Applied Science. Founded in 1901 as the fifth college of the university, the school was named after Lyman Cornelius Smith, a pioneer in the typewriter industry, who donated the funds for the new building. The dean of the college since 1951, and the overseer of much of the research development during the Tolley years, was Ralph Galbraith. Galbraith had earned his B.S. from the University of Missouri in 1933, and his Ph.D. from Yale in 1937. He had worked as a researcher for the Detroit Edison company, then taught at the University of Texas. During the war Galbraith was on the Massachusetts Institute of Technology Radar School staff, and immediately following the war he went to Georgia Institute of Technology. Tolley brought him to Syracuse as the chair of the Electrical Engineering Department in 1946; he became dean of the school in 1950–51. One former student described Galbraith as a "laid-back, slow guy," a description echoed by most of Galbraith's contemporaries. Yet Galbraith was a proactive dean, wedded, as was Tolley, to the goal of instant growth in the research sciences. Galbraith was noted for recruiting faculty who already had positions at other universities, whether or not they were tenured.

Galbraith's job was made easier by the fact that the national push towards scientific achievement had made engineering *the* growth curriculum of the 1950s. More than 25 percent of the veterans returning to college asked for engineering training. One of the reasons was the plethora of job openings in the field, and Central New York was one of the fastest growing areas of the nation for electronic engineering. In 1946 General Electric (GE) decided to headquarter its electronic division in Syracuse. The company asked the university to develop graduate programs in engineering suitable for the many engineers they would be bringing to Syracuse plants. The university happily responded to the call, aided by Galbraith's keen understanding of the field, which had been his area of research interest before entering academic administration. Enrollment in electrical engineering skyrocketed, but the whole of the College of Applied Science was affected. As demand grew, the university supplied. In the first forty years of its existence the College of Engineering awarded 2,024 bachelor's degrees and approximately fifty master's degrees. Over its next twenty-seven years it awarded 3,566 bachelor's degrees, 1,052 master's degrees, and 169 doctorates. Galbraith's faculty recruiting became easier with every passing year of record enrollment and increased graduate-level involvement. He could promise his staff a stable classroom environment, graduate-level work to stimulate their teaching, and the IIR to facilitate their research. But Tolley was once again faced with the pleasant predicament that had come to symbolize the postwar decade—where was he going to put everybody?

*   *   *

Once again, Tolley's plans were ahead of the need. Tolley had been looking to expand the plant for Applied Science since September 1945, when a $1,150,000 fund-raising drive had been kicked off under the chairmanship of William Lawyer Hinds, the president of Crouse-Hinds Company, who was then serving as the chairman of the university's board of trustees. On April 27, 1946, Tolley was able to announce that Hinds's drive had yielded fruit; $750,000 had been pledged toward a building or buildings to house the new IIR and had been invested in government bonds. Tolley knew right away how he wanted to spend the money. Sometime in late 1946, the university began negotiations with the federal government's War Assets Administration to acquire a part of the Naval War Plant on Syracuse's Thompson Road, which had housed General Electric's research work on turbines and generators during the war. Both the university and the Carrier Corporation had bid for it—the university's bid, placed in July 1946, was $20,000,000.[1] From the start of the bidding, Tolley flooded the press with statistics showing how many engineering students he would be able to train at the facility. He also announced that there would be vocational training at the center (Hugh Gregg

1. The Autolite Corporation of America, also involved in the early bidding, seems to have dropped out quickly (*Syracuse Post-Standard,* July 1, 1946).

explained: "In this way veterans who do not desire to attend school for four years can obtain training to fill such positions as foremen and technicians in commercial engineering plants"). And along with housing the IIR, the facility would be the new home of the College of Applied Science and the ROTC program. The campaign for the purchase was particularly bloody. One person close to the negotiations remembered that at times Cloud Wampler, the president of Carrier, and Tolley would not even talk to one another; Galbraith was used as the go-between.

On September 3, 1946, the War Assets Administration announced that it had made a Solomon-like decision—Syracuse University and Carrier would *share* the plant. The university's portion came at a bargain-basement price. Representing a real value of $8 million, the War Assets Administration assigned it a fair value of $2,130,000. However, Tolley applied for and received an educational discount of 70 percent, thus making the real cost to the university a paltry $669,368. The Carrier Corporation obtained the rest of the plant—a turbine factory and power plant—for $4 million.

The way to a clear title was a complicated one. Many objected to the university's acquisition of a working plant at a 70 percent discount. But a more real problem was the fact that GE was still performing research for the government at Thompson Road. As a result, the Reconstruction Finance Corporation told the university that it could not obtain title until 1948. Tolley solved this problem by developing a plan where GE could use one of the major manufacturing buildings and two of the small wooden radar buildings for up to two years. The plan was accepted, and the university began to remodel the facilities.

Syracuse finally received the title to the plant on October 1, 1947. Yet Tolley's dream was a wider one than just the acquisition of the building itself. Hoping that this would be the beginning of a north campus, with housing and playing fields, tennis courts, and gymnasium facilities, Tolley purchased a fourteen-acre plot located to the south of the university's new property and sixteen acres along its eastern borders from the Syracuse Land Development Corporation.

By the end of 1947, both the IIR and the College of Applied Science were using the Thompson Road property; full occupation occurred by March 1948. The IIR was using two of the five buildings: the lab building and the former Impregnation Building. But equally important was the fact that the growing College of Applied Science had found a new home. The woodworking shops of the Engineering College were in the Impregnation Building. The Department of Aeronautical Engineering used the former test cell building. The Department of Electrical Engineering and the ROTC used one of the wooden radar buildings, and the building called Radio II housed the offices, classrooms, and labs of the College of Applied Science. The purchase of the facility also attracted thirty new faculty members and spurred the college from a prewar enrollment of less than four hundred students to a 1947 enrollment of nineteen hundred, 72 percent of whom were veterans.

However, the students disliked the daily grind of driving from their temporary housing twelve miles away to the facility they had, with only lukewarm affection, dubbed "T-Road." The infamous "Blue Beetle" buses dragged the three upper classes of engineering students to the new facility every day (freshmen continued to have their classes on the main campus, most of them in Smith Hall). One student remembered it bitterly as "a drag . . . [we] lost an hour a day" in travel alone. The faculty grumbled as well, but Galbraith's memories were more sanguine: "Nobody on the faculty was happy at being out there but they had things they never would have had otherwise. But we were isolated, no matter what we said."

The IIR was also having its problems. The research dollars that had been so plentiful at the Institute's beginnings were now drying up, as more and more schools, most with even better research facilities, entered the competition. Galbraith's success at faculty recruitment turned out to be a double-edged sword, because the university was having to strain to meet T-Road's inflated payroll. The overworked faculty, many of whom were conducting contracted research while teaching a full load, were grumbling. These troubles were publicly dismissed as "growing pains," but the need for change at IIR was acute.

When Wheadon became director of the IIR following Montonna's 1950 resignation, he made a number of recommendations to Tolley. Wheadon observed that the concept of a service organization to business and industry had never been discussed with the faculty, and many faculty resented being "rented out" by businesses. Wheadon also argued that investing in a building for research made no sense, as it would quickly become outdated. Wheadon argued that the institution should invest in equipment to strengthen the departments. He also mentioned that faculty resented the IIR name, as it did little to reflect on Syracuse University as a whole. Last, and most important, Wheadon concluded that the research dollars would soon be drying up, as large companies could now afford to do their own research in-house. His recommended first step was to sell the Thompson Road facility and build a new, on-campus home for the College of Applied Science. Tolley agreed, and in November 1952 he told the board that while the buildings were serving their purpose in terms of increasing the university's research capability, the cost of maintenance was high, and students were losing a good deal of time in travel to and from the campus. He suggested that the university sell T-Road, and Carrier, already owning half of the plant, was the logical buyer.

The immediate problem was that General Electric had leased part of the Thompson Road facility from the university, so that it might continue several projects that it had contracted with the government—a deal that allowed the university to apply GE's rent money to the amount that university had borrowed from the government to purchase T-Road. The original agreement was that GE would vacate by 1949, but its government contracts had not yet been completed. But Wampler showed interest in buying Tolley out, and despite GE's lease, negotiations between the university and Carrier commenced seriously in June 1952. The university made it clear that it could transfer the property only on terms that would allow IIR and the College of Engineering to continue functioning until such time as they could move without disturbing any ongoing research. Agreeing, Carrier offered a price of $3.5 million. The deal was submitted to the board on June 27, 1952.

Once again, however, relations between the university and Carrier took a nasty turn. A dispute arose over what personal property the university could legally remove from the buildings, in particular a million-volt x-ray machine. There was also a question about when GE would evacuate the premises. Indeed, Wampler said that he would make the university pay a quarter-million-dollar penalty if Tolley could not dispossess GE immediately. Believing that Wampler had welshed on their deal, Tolley was enraged. On his way to Europe for a vacation, he wired Wampler: "Inexpressibly shocked. Original terms of sale so advantageous to Carrier and reflect such credit on your skill as a negotiator. Your greatest embarrassment would be failure to honor them as agreed. Sail Soon. Regards."

Despite Tolley's anger, he was over a barrel. It seems that he had not told Wampler in the original negotiations that they could not get rid of GE, and Carrier had always insisted upon occupancy of Radio III by December 31, 1954. The university's interest was finally sold for $3.5 million. Carrier also agreed to pay $100,000 for two x-ray machines and adjoining lands and to let Syracuse keep the rents from the GE lease. However, the university had to pay a substantial penalty ($250,000) in case Carrier could not take possession of Radio III from GE by January 1, 1955. The decision to sell Thompson Road to Carrier was made within the Executive Committee of the board, and announced to the full board on November 14, 1952. At that time, arrangements had been made to have Carrier take possession of the Radio III building. Syracuse would also have to pay the U.S. government $556,348.18 for the cancellation of the educational restriction on the portion of the plant under lease to GE.

When they returned to the main campus, the College of Engineering—the new name for Applied Science—took over four two-story barracks at Collendale, which had been converted to laboratories and office space. There the college awaited completion of its new home. There had been some debate over whether it would get more than one building, and whether a large research complex should be located on the campus quadrangle. As noted in the previous chapter, many university supporters were firmly opposed to any large, modern-style structure intruding on the beauty of the Old Oval. They made it clear that even if they lost out on the on-campus location, they would not tolerate more than one research building to mar the hill. Even King and King, who supported a two-building approach, originally argued for an off-campus site for the new engineering facility.

But Tolley was firm. Utility, close proximity to the campus at large, and the ability to house all research branches of the university won the day. It was decided that there would be a two-building engineering complex, built at a projected cost of $1.5 million, located on the quad. The first building, to be named for William Hinds, would be constructed immediately.[2] Galbraith was in constant touch with King over the project, which was funded in part by monies raised by Hinds (only after Tolley had agreed to name the building for Hinds did he make a $25,000 contribution, matched by a $75,000 Crouse-Hinds pledge), and in part with the revenue realized from the sale of the Thompson Road facility. The $940,000 building, which would serve some six hundred engineering students, was dedicated in October 1955. It was the tenth building to be erected under the Building and Endowment Plan.

*   *   *

Relocation alone would not solve the problems that ailed IIR. Money problems persisted, and in September 1953 Wheadon and university comptroller Frank Wingate suggested that Tolley change the institute's name and that it be brought under the closer control of the university by including the comptroller and the dean of the Graduate School on the institute's board and having the institute submit its budget to the comptroller and the vice chancellor for approval. Tolley agreed, and on February 1, 1954, the IIR formally changed its name to the Syracuse University Research Institute (SURI). The university moved quickly to bring its research division under tighter rein. On June 4, 1954, the trustees passed a resolution stating that "in order for Syracuse University as a corporation to engage in security agreements with the Department of Defense . . . no member of the Board with the exception of Chancellor William P. Tolley shall be granted access to any classified research project in progress with the University," unless other members of the board have an active security clearance or are given permission. Tolley was now the line officer in charge of institutional research, and he was about to branch out in still another direction.

Since about 1950 Tolley had had a friendly correspondence with

2. The second building, Link Hall, would not be completed until 1970.

Frank Wingate, Chancellor Tolley, and W. R. G. Baker

Dr. W. R. G. Baker, the vice president of General Electric. A communications pioneer, Baker had received the army's Medal of Freedom citation in 1953 for advice given to the army on the problems of utilization of electronic devices to the maximum extent in modern warfare. Perhaps his most important contribution, however, had to do with the new innovation of television. Baker organized and directed two national television system committees that recommended engineering standards to the Federal Communications Commission, paving the way for commercial monochrome telecasting and color television in 1953. A Schenectady station owned by GE bore his initials (WRGB). From 1941 to 1956, the period during which GE had become entrenched at Syracuse's Electronics Park, Baker had directed GE's electronics division as its general manager. Tolley addressed him fondly as "Doc"; for his part, Baker had provided the university with research machinery and material at a discount. In the spring of 1957 Wheadon proposed to Tolley that the position of Vice President for Research be created and offered to Baker, who was scheduled to retire from General Electric in November 1957. An offer was made to

Baker in March 1957; Baker accepted and had his salary ($25,000) turned back over to the university.

In the spring of 1957, the new vice president convinced Tolley to open a new research division of the university—the Syracuse University Research Corporation (SURC). While SURI would continue to handle faculty projects, SURC would deal with research projects from outside contractors, particularly in the growing area of electronic intelligence communications and military electronics dealing with radar and sonar. But this did not mean that the university and its programs would not benefit from SURC. Its research programs would support the university's academic programs and be as closely related to them as possible. Graduate students and faculty would be used whenever possible to supplement the efforts of the career personnel. Not wishing to have a repeat of the organization problems of the IIR, the president of SURC would also be the president for research at the university, with the chairman of the board and the chancellor sitting as ex officio members of SURC's board.

Tolley took the proposal to the board during its May 31 meeting. He made it clear to the board that he did not expect SURC to make a profit, but that he was convinced that SURC would draw to the campus a heretofore untapped source of research revenue: "It is true that the focus of this immediately may be in a relatively narrow field: government and defense contacts, but Dr. Baker, Dean Galbraith, and Mr. Wheadon think it will not stay there. There will be opportunity for a good many defense contracts. We haven't the slightest intention of losing our work at [SURI]. Certain contracts should go to the Institute, others to the Corporation." After hearing Tolley's proposal, the board committee, which had studied the issue, reported that "the standing and prestige of eminent scientists who will supposedly be engaged by the corporation will attract many young assistants of great promise." The committee estimated that SURC would need $250,000 in start-up money for the first six months, and that it might cost an additional $750,000, depending on the contracts received. However, it also reported that "the entire sum of $750,000 is now available." At the end of the meeting, the board approved the creation of SURC, and Baker was named chairman of the institute's board of governors and the chairman of its executive committee.

Only days after the board agreed to charter SURC, Baker suffered a stroke. Promised that Baker would soon return to duty, the board decided to go ahead with the project. SURC was set up in the Collendale prefabs, and for the first six months money was tight—a worried Tolley often told Galbraith to be careful. In October, however, the Army Signal Corps signed a $94,000 contract with SURC and another contract for a scientific intelligence center was by then under negotiation. By 1959 a solid SURC consisted of three units. The Defense Systems Laboratory, under Dr. Andrew Longacre, was concerned with the applications of electronics to military use—their work was classified. The second division, the Scientific Intelligence Center, under Vice Admiral Robert Rice (USN, ret.), engaged in research in scientific areas with which the nation's intelligence sources were vitally concerned. The third was the Microbiological and Biochemical Research Center.

Baker never fully recovered from his stroke, and by late 1959 he was seriously ill. Partially because SURC's leadership was in flux, and partially because of cuts in defense spending for research toward the end of the Eisenhower administration, SURC hit a slump in early 1960. Even before Baker's death on October 31, 1960, there was some discussion about combining SURC and SURI to consolidate the load; there was also some talk about turning the entire research operation over to Wingate. However, Galbraith recommended that Tolley give the research operation to Clark Ahlberg. Tolley agreed and named Ahlberg to the newly created post of Vice President for Administration and Research of the University; after Baker's death, Ahlberg assumed the presidency of SURC.

*   *   *

The velocity with which the university sped through its change into a major research institution was astounding. The entire face and scope of the institution had changed in less than a decade. By the end of the 1950s, Syracuse ranked twelfth nationally in terms of the amount of its sponsored research, and it had over four hundred professors and graduate students engaging in that investigation. At the turn of the decade, the university was engaged in some 249 sponsored research programs, with a total net worth of $9 million.

Ivan Mestrovic, working on Croatian Rhapsody

CHAPTER 7

The Professional Schools, Adult Education, and the Liberal Arts

An impressive transformation

—Tolley describing the postwar School of Art

I N 1940–41, there were 601 graduate students at Syracuse University, the vast majority of whom were in programs in the College of Liberal Arts. In September 1948 there were 2,052 graduate students, a bare majority of which came from the College of Applied Sciences. As we have seen, the growth of graduate programs that followed the introduction of research centers on campus was little less than astounding. Yet despite this growth, the other professional schools in the fine arts and the social sciences, as well as the College of Liberal Arts and the university's continuing education programs, were hardly ignored. In fact, although he received advice that argued that the university should downplay its nonscientific programs and perhaps jettison a few of those programs that attracted but a handful of students, Tolley simply refused to do so. The growth of the university in the 1950s was remarkably symmetrical, as all arms of the university expanded their offerings in the 1950s.

✳   ✳   ✳

The College of Fine Arts—the first degree-granting college of fine arts in the United States—was established in 1873. Two former directors of the School of Architecture, L. C. Dillenback (1945–58) and D. Kenneth Sargent (1958–69) served as deans of the college in the Tolley period. But for all intents and purposes, Tolley was "co-Dean." In fact, more so than at any other school save Applied Science, Tolley personally influenced the growth of one of the schools of the College of Fine Arts—the School of Art. As a result, it quickly evolved into a nationally known professional school that had taken on a look that was the distinctive creation of William Tolley.

Although it is true that the college's School of Art began, in Tolley's words, an "impressive transformation" during the postwar years, it was a slow beginning. Following the resignation of Charles Bertram Walker as the school's director in 1946, Tolley overrode the decision of the search committee (prompting the resignation of Marjorie Stuart Greenfield, who went to the University of Iowa), and hired Norman Rice. Trained at the University of Illinois, Rice had been head of the Art Institute of Chicago and in charge of the Institute's School of Drama. It was Rice who oversaw the building of the Lowe Art Center, but even a new building could not end dissention within the school. Upon his arrival, Rice had infused the program with the ideals of modernism and contemporary art. Many on the faculty felt Rice had taken this development to extremes. The imbalance in the program was felt by the students as well. In April 1954 sophomores petitioned Tolley with their grievances: they believed their classes to be too large; they wanted better trained models; and they argued that "Realistic Art should be taught on an equal basis with abstract art." In July Rice resigned to take a position at the College of Fine Arts at the Carnegie Institute of Technology. Tolley was disappointed with Rice's resignation, charging Dillenback that "we should be looking for a person with ideas, not afraid to experiment and with a clear sense of direction regardless of its popularity. The ambition of the director must be to establish the finest university art school in the United States. . . . I do not think we should set a salary limit. Our first job is to identify people of talent."

In Laurence Schmeckebier, Tolley found talent. Schmeckebier earned his Ph.D. at the University of Munich in 1931, majoring in art history and psychology. He had taught at the University of Wisconsin from 1931 to 1938, and then at the University of Minnesota from 1938 to 1946. From 1946 to 1954, he had been the director of the Cleveland Institute of Art. Schmeckebier made waves from the start. He was no less committed to contemporary art than Rice, and his personal interest in faculty work was interpreted by many as interference. By the spring of 1955, there were eleven faculty resignations. But Schmeckebier had the unqualified support of Tolley, and under his auspices the school began to blossom. In 1955–56, the school's loose curriculum was replaced with a two-year core curriculum that compelled students to take basic drawing, painting, design, English, and art history. A new Gallery Program was established, with a series of regular exhibitions by nationally known artists such as George Grosz, Rico Lebrun, and Karl Zerbe, and exhibitions by prominent local artists, such as the memorial exhibition of Gordon Steele.

One of Schmeckebier's best known innovations was the Mural Program, an idea that began in 1958 when the university acquired Lebrun's *Crucifixion* from the Whitney Foundation.[1] In 1960 Schmeckebier inaugurated a program under the aegis of French muralist Jean Charlot, a French artist who had been one of the major movers in the Mexican mural movement. As a visiting artist for six weeks, Charlot muraled a 9 by 45 foot wall in the dining hall of Shaw Dormitory. Both undergraduates and graduate students had the opportunity to apprentice with a master—a practice virtually unheard of at that time. Even the film department got into the act, shooting a documentary of Charlot at work. Other murals were painted by nationally known artists, including Ben Shahn, Kenneth Callahan, Adja Yunkers, and Marion Greenwood, as well as Syracuse alum Anthony Toney and faculty member Robert Marx.

The Mural Program, actively supported by Tolley, was an example of the chancellor's guarantee that the School of Art would become a player on the national stage by hiring internationally renowned talent for its faculty (it was in conjunction with his acquisitions for the School of Art that Tolley was quoted as saying "in my experience the best people are cheap at any price"). Tolley absolutely reveled in the story of the hiring of Ivan Mestrovic. It is one of Tolley's favorite yarns, and he often recounts with glee how he "broke every rule on the book" to get the Yugoslavian sculptor away from European exile and onto the Syracuse University faculty as head of a new department

1. Originally installed in the main reading room of Carnegie Library, the mural is now in Heroy Hall.

of sculpture in the College of Fine Arts. The Mestrovic story is a story of Tolley the micromanager at his most wily, as he built a new department from scratch, virtually on his own whim.

Born in 1883 to a Croatian peasant family, Mestrovic studied under Auguste Rodin (who would later write "your Mestrovic is greater than I") and attended the Academy of Fine Arts in Vienna, but only after he had lived for several months with a Czech family so that he might learn the required German language to be admitted. He studied there from 1900 to 1904, and before he was thirty-one had had twenty-nine European exhibitions. Yet there was another cause in Mestrovic's life; he became a leader of the movement for Yugoslav national unification and independence. Between the wars, the now world-famous sculptor became a target of interest for the German Nazis. Enamored of Mestrovic's work, Adolf Hitler offered to open an exhibition of his work in the Reichstag if the artist would attend; Mestrovic declined. The collapse of Yugoslavia in 1941 led to Mestrovic's arrest by the ruling Italian Fascists. He remained in prison for four months, and was released only through the intercession of the Vatican. For the three years before he was offered the job at Syracuse, Mestrovic lived in exile in Switzerland. Tolley was clear about his motives in his memoirs: "When the opportunity came to attract him to a professorship at Syracuse University, I was moved as much by the concern to rescue a great artist as by the desire to make an eminent addition to the faculty of the School of Art."

In the summer of 1946, Tolley and his wife were in New York City visiting Thomas Watson. Tolley went into Manhattan to see a sculptress, Malvina Hoffman, who was executing a bust of Watson. Hoffman told Tolley how distressed she was about her friend and mentor Mestrovic. According to Hoffman, he was quite ill. She said that she had been to Columbia University to try to get him a teaching position but had failed. Tolley told her that she should cable him: "You have appointment as professor of sculpture at Syracuse University effective September this year [1946]. Will pay all expenses for you and your family to come to the states."

Tolley received little or no criticism for his blatant interference into the faculty hiring process. Not only had he landed a truly international superstar for the Syracuse faculty, but Mestrovic soon became a university institution. One student who was a friend of the Mestrovic family remembered that the professor, whom she described as a "wonderful, sensitive man," was not really a "teacher," but more a sculptor-in-residence who took on only a few graduate students. His 1947 one-man show at the Metropolitan Museum only added to his fame. It was this growing fame that caused the university to lose Mestrovic to Notre Dame. Commissioned to build a Jewish Memorial that would require the expansion of his Marshall Street studio, Mestrovic asked Schmeckebier for the money. Pressed for funds, Schmeckebier could only promise Mestrovic space at Collendale. Disappointed by this and other slights, Mestrovic resigned in July 1955 after being offered a higher salary and a larger studio by Notre Dame University.

Although Syracuse lost Mestrovic, before his tenure was completed Tolley had purchased much of the sculptor's collection for the university. Next to book collecting, acquisition of works of art—and the display of same—was Tolley's great intellectual passion. Newell Rossman remembered for an interviewer that Schmeckebier "had an acquisition fund that was sweet. . . . I want to tell you, it was the greatest acquisition committee you ever saw: Rossman, Schmeckebier and Piskor. I went along to vote yes. I didn't know anything about art but I learned about it. He bought new paintings . . . art, [and] tapestries." By about 1960 the university had built a collection of approximately twelve thousand art works with an insurable value of over $2,000,000. Tolley gave Schmeckebier most of the credit— something that Tolley's records certainly support.

But there was no place to put it. The Lowe Art Center was a worthy addition to the university, but it was hardly a large enough facility to house the size collection that Tolley was accumulating. As per one of the great themes of the period, Tolley had expanded the university beyond its physical capabilities, and it was time once again to build. This time, however, Tolley's efforts would result in one of the greatest disappointments of his chancellorship.

One of Tolley's deepest wishes was to have the university affiliated with a yet to be built Syracuse Museum of Art. Indeed, Schmeckebier referred to that dream when he accepted Tolley's offer as the director of the School of Art. Tolley tied his dream to the estate of Helen

Everson, one of Central New York's most dedicated patrons of the arts. In her will, Everson established the Everson Museum Fund to establish and maintain an "Everson Museum of Art" in the city of Syracuse. She also established a board of trustees charged with the creation and maintenance of that museum. When Everson died in 1941, she left about $1 million for that purpose, and First Trust and Deposit Corporation was appointed as the fund's trustee. In 1943 three of Everson's cousins contested the will; the question in probate revolved around whether she intended to have the museum built in the *city,* or at the *university.* The surrogate court instructed First Trust that it might assign the fund *either* to Syracuse University or to the Museum of Fine Arts, or it could create a new corporation, the trustees of which would build a new museum.

On the day that the court's decision was announced, Tolley, wasting not a nanosecond, was quoted as saying that he hoped that the university would be chosen as the site for the museum. He later wrote to a First Trust official that "because a museum is now a teaching institution and no longer a repository of art it should be related to the other teaching institutions of the community." The Everson board strongly opposed Tolley's move and an intense battle ensued. It was summarized in one piece found in Tolley's files: "If it had been Miss Everson's desire to endow the present facilities of either the Syracuse Museum of Fine Arts or the Syracuse University College of Fine Arts she would logically have mentioned one or both by name. This she did not do." Giving up for the moment on his attempt to acquire Everson's estate outright, Tolley floated a second proposal: that the Syracuse Museum and Syracuse University "*cooperate* in the use of the Everson trust through 'The Everson Museum of Fine Arts at Syracuse University.'" Tolley even offered to hit the trustees up to "match dollar for dollar any funds provided by the Trustees of the Everson Estate for the erection of the Everson Museum." The trustees of the Everson Museum apparently took Tolley up on his offer and announced in June 1955 that it intended to build an $889,000 facility on the Syracuse University campus.

But Tolley had lost the war. The battle over the Everson had soured his relationship with the community and had enraged several of his key donors and alumni. Plus, pressure was put on the Republican city administration to give a major building project to the downtown area, about to undergo a process that the nation would come to know as "urban renewal." Pressure mounted on Tolley to drop the idea, and, although the details of the decision are sketchy, in 1960 planning began for the Everson Museum of Art, located in downtown Syracuse.

One area in the College of Fine Arts where no immediate improvement was necessary was in the School of Drama. Sawyer Falk was one of the university's most widely known and respected faculty members; some have argued that he was the most influential teacher of the dramatic arts in the nation. Falk had been appointed head of the Drama department in 1927, with the title of Director of Dramatic Activities. Falk's reputation cut a wide swath; he served as president of the National Theater Conference and was a member of the Board of Directors of the American National Theater and Academy. In 1957, he took over the direction of the Broadway musical *Shinbone Alley*, and in the spring of that year, he served as a consultant specialist in drama to India, on behalf of the Department of State. In the summer of 1960, Falk directed a summer drama course at Stratford-on-Avon for Syracuse University. One of Falk's most famous students, comedian Jerry Stiller, remembered that Falk "made Theater Arts part of the curriculum not just of SU but of the country. . . . [He was] born a Methodist, but his religion was the theater. . . . By the breadth of his acting, he could change the human condition." Stiller also remembered that Falk took it upon himself to call around and find jobs for students.

Falk was also able to take advantage of the university's 1958 purchase of the Regent Theater. Up to that time, the university's drama productions were held in Machinery Hall—the seating capacity was about two hundred people. Located at 820 East Genesee Street, the Regent, which had been running as a movie house right up to the time of the sale, had a seating capacity of eleven hundred, had been remodeled only fifteen years before, had wide screen projection capability, and had air conditioning. In 1957 Schmeckebier suggested to Comptroller Hugh Gregg that the university purchase the Regent. Tolley agreed, but he decided to place the theater under the control of University College, the adult education arm of the university, apparently in an effort to have Dean Alexander Charters develop a film series that would pay for the building.

A classic academic turf war developed between Charters and Falk. In March 1959 Falk had asked Tolley to referee the problem with the Regent, but the problem of authority was never fully resolved. Nevertheless, both University College and the Drama Department turned the Regent into a combined classroom for the arts and functioning movie house and theater. At the end of 1961, over two hundred thousand people had attended approximately four hundred separate events at the Regent Theater. Falk's death in France on August 30, 1961, did not stop the development of the Regent, but it most certainly brought to an end an era in the College of Fine Arts.

*   *   *

In 1919 the university began offering journalism courses out of the School for Business Administration. A department was established in 1926, and the School of Journalism was founded in 1934. The school originally occupied Yates Castle, a gothic structure built by Cornelius Longstreet, a wealthy Syracusan who wanted to reproduce a Rhine Castle—moat included. Yates was designed by James Renwich, the architect of St. Patrick's Cathedral in New York City, and it was rumored to be one of the stations of the Underground Railroad prior to the Civil War. Acquired by Syracuse University in 1905, it was one of the most venerable buildings on campus. It was as well known for its grand stairway—which led to a floor-to-ceiling mirror that had been imported from Italy—as for its poor ventilation and crowded workspace.[2]

The school's first dean, Matthew Lyle Spencer, served in that capacity until 1950. The son of a Kentucky preacher, Spencer worked as a reporter for the *Milwaukee Journal*, where he won a Pulitzer Prize for "disinterested and meritorious public reporting." In World War I, he served in military intelligence. After the armistice, he was named dean of the School of Journalism at the University of Washington, where he served from 1919 until 1926, when he was named that school's president. Spencer gave up that position in 1937 to accept the challenge of organizing a new school of journalism at Syracuse.

One of the most celebrated developments under Spencer's tenure

2. The Castle was razed on Apr. 1, 1967, to make room for an extension of the State College of Medicine.

was the expansion of the curriculum in radio and television. The school's Radio Center (WMAC) had been organized in 1930 with the help of Syracuse radio station WSYR. From 1930 to 1937, the Radio Committee had a contract with WSYR for seventeen hours a week, when it produced shows that were aired on that station. In 1937 the school developed a Radio Workshop, and in 1946 it expanded this workshop into a student broadcasting group, built with state funds earmarked to aid veterans' education. Located in the basement of Carnegie Library, the new Radio Workshop originally went by the name of WORK, which continued to supply programs to WSYR and now WFBL—one of which, "Syracuse on Trial," won the Peabody Award for excellence in public service programming.

The school then took a step that would place it at the forefront of broadcast education. Thanks largely to the efforts of radio professor Kenneth Bartlett, and with the cooperation of General Electric, the university became the first college in the nation to have its own low-power (two-and-one-half-watt) FM broadcast station, WJIV-FM, which was established in October 1946 and broadcast its first program in April 1947. Called "Jive" by the students, the voices of the announcers reached out for about a mile from the makeshift water-pipe antenna on the roof of Carnegie Library. As a result of this experiment, the Federal Communication Commission (FCC) decided to amend its rules and permit special broadcasting with power of ten watts or less as one of its established services. Three months after WJIV's initial broadcast, the FCC granted the station one of these special experimental licenses. WJIV immediately changed its name to incorporate the letters Alpha Epsilon Rho, the journalism national honor society, and its motto: Always Excellent Radio. After two years of experimental broadcasting by WAER, the FCC agreed to give broadcast licenses to other institutions. By 1950 some thirty additional colleges had been granted low-power radio station licenses.[3]

WAER's first studios were in one of the prefabs; the station was then moved to the basement of Carnegie Library. WAER alumnus Dick Clark remembered the format as being "a little bit of every-

3. In Sept. 1950 WAER raised its power to 1,000 watts—the first college station to broadcast at such a high wattage. It was also the first college station in the nation to boost its power to 40,000 watts, in Sept. 1961.

thing." Classical shows were programmed alongside interview shows at the chapel with foreign-speaking students; the students produced and wrote their own dramas, and bands were brought in to perform. It was, in the words of Clark, "like old time radio of yesteryear."

The school was also a national pioneer in the field of telecommunications. In August 1948 General Electric donated to the university a low channel (five kilowatt) television transmitter. In April 1950 university students and faculty broadcast a slate of television programming, which was simulcast over WSYR-TV thanks to a novel transmitter link. Students were trained by General Electric personnel in Studio A in Carnegie Library—formerly the main studio of WAER (which had been moved to the prefab Radio House). Syracuse became the first university to offer graduate training leading to a master of science degree in television.

As radio and television grew, the print component of the program, long one of the nation's best, continued its ascendancy. It had spawned the *Daily Orange* (known to the campus as the *DO*), one of the nation's preeminent student dailies, in 1904. In the immediate postwar period, the *DO* was unquestionably the most influential extracurricular activity on campus. The *DO* shared office space in Prefab 7 (better known as the "Hellbox," a testimony to both the level of heat and the level of student activity in the building) with two other student publications, the student yearbook *Onondagan* and the *Syracusan*. The *DO* of 1949—its forty-fifth year—had a circulation of sixteen thousand, as well as a paid senior editor.

In terms of graduate study in journalism, the university offered a program singular in the nation—a degree in religious journalism. The program grew out of the ideas of Frank Laubach, who inspired the school to launch a literacy journalism program in 1949. Roland E. Wolseley, who came to the university in 1946 to head the Magazine Program, headed this master's level course, the only one of its kind in the nation. The curriculum was designed for men and women from foreign countries interested in Laubach's World Literacy and Christian Literature Movement. Trained in the rudiments of magazine journalism, these students would be able to go to their mother countries and set up training workshops for their people. Ahead of its time, the religious journalism program reminds one of future Peace Corps programs, members of which would also be trained at Syracuse.

It was left to Wesley C. Clark, a member of the journalism faculty since 1941 who succeeded Spencer in 1950 and would be dean of the school throughout its most exciting period, to oversee the construction of a new building to accommodate the growing school. The story of the building of the Newhouse School of Journalism will be told in detail in chapter 12. However, the first phase of that story was a particularly unhappy one for journalism alumni and faculty alike. As part of the deal in which the university's medical school was sold to the state university system, Yates Castle was taken over by the state in the spring of 1953 to eventually make room for the new Upstate Medical Center. The journalism school was temporarily relocated to the Women's Gymnasium, next to Archbold Gymnasium. The sixty-two-year-old gym was a shabby building, and there was much protest from the students and alums that the relocation would hurt the program. The gym was remodeled, but several prefab buildings also had to be used to accommodate the school's programs. Clearly a new building was needed—but Sam Newhouse's dream was a little over a decade away.

*　　*　　*

George Maxwell's dream has long confounded observers who seek to place the Maxwell School of Citizenship into a flow chart of the university's structure. The school began in 1924 as the basis of a citizenship course for college freshmen and a graduate training program in public administration. At its undergraduate level, Maxwell served as the social science division of the College of Liberal Arts, including, in 1945, six academic social science departments—anthropology, economics, geography, history, political science, and sociology; and ten interdisciplinary programs—public administration, international relations, social science, metropolitan studies, comparative national planning, Eastern African studies, South Asian studies, Soviet studies, Latin American studies, and American studies. It had always been murky where Maxwell belonged at the graduate level. A 1959 report said that it was a "special social sciences school operating as a division of the Graduate School." However, as professor of economics and future chancellor Melvin Eggers admitted, "there has always been an ambiguity at this university about Maxwell." The Maxwell School was seen as, and behaved as, an independent college, rather than as an arm of either the College of Liberal Arts or of the graduate school.

With the 1945 retirement of William Mosher, who had guided the Maxwell School since 1924, former political science professor Finla Crawford served as acting dean for one year. It was Crawford (who, in the memories of several faculty members, treated his former college as a particular favorite during his tenure as vice chancellor) who was the guiding force behind the hiring of Paul Appleby as dean in 1947. Appleby had begun his career as a journalist, but he soon gravitated to public administration. He served as undersecretary of agriculture from 1940 to 1944, was chief of the U.S. Food Mission to Great Britain in 1941 and 1942, and was special advisor to the Lend-Lease administrator in 1942–43. A specialist in India, Appleby took three extended trips there while dean. Guthrie Burkhead, a future dean of Maxwell, remembered Appleby as a "small town newspaper editor—not a highly verbal man . . . laconic . . . midwestern. . . . He was a story teller all his life."

Appleby's major contribution as dean was the beginning of formal links between Maxwell and Washington, D.C. In 1949 the Research Branch of the Maxwell Graduate School was established in Washington. In 1951, Appleby also established the first Russian language training program run by a civilian institution for the air force in the postwar period. As a result, Slavic became the fastest growing language program at Syracuse. He also oversaw the beginning of a graduate program in public administration in Albany, undertaken with the cooperation of New York University and at the request of Governor Dewey. The program allowed professional training of personnel currently employed by the state and other government agencies.

One of the most innovative of the university's curricular developments was a part of Maxwell and another of Tolley's pet academic projects. As Tolley fought with the state over the creation of the SUNY system, he began to realize that with SUNY there would be a tremendous market for well-trained college teachers, particularly in the social sciences. The problem was that in 1950 no school, including Syracuse, was turning out enough Ph.D.s to meet this upcoming demand, as many candidates dropped out of the program before completion. Tolley turned to Roy A. Price, who had come to Syracuse in 1935 with a dual appointment to Maxwell and the School of Education, to develop an innovative doctorate-level program that would train college teachers in the social sciences. With the formal adoption of the Doctor of Social Science (D.S.S.) degree in 1945, aided by a small ($7500) grant from the Carnegie Corporation, Syracuse became the first major university to offer advanced work leading to a doctor's degree based upon an interdisciplinary approach to the development of college level teaching skills. Where the program was particularly inventive was that each successful candidate had actually *taught*—either in the required freshman course in responsible citizenship or in one of the introductory courses in history, economics, geography, sociology, or American government. Critics argued that the D.S.S. was simply a way for Tolley to get reasonably qualified teachers for free. Perhaps, but its popularity cannot be denied. The program was an instant success, and the university had surprisingly little trouble placing its graduates in college-level teaching positions.[4]

Despite the success of the D.S.S., much of Appleby's tenure as dean, although not a public part, revolved around his defending himself against charges made by the House Committee on Un-American Activities (HUAC) that he had communist sympathies. Appleby resigned in 1956 to become Director of the Budget for New York under Governor Averell Harriman.

Appleby was succeeded by Harlan Cleveland, who served as Maxwell's dean until 1961. A Rhodes Scholar from Princeton, Cleveland entered government through the National Institute of Public Affairs. During World War II, he had worked for the Department of Agriculture and the Board of Economic Administration. Following the war, he served as acting vice president of the Allied Commission in Italy, and on the Economic Cooperation Administration (forerunner of the Mutual Security Agency) from 1948 to 1952. He left government service in 1953 to become a journal editor. In March 1956 Appleby heard Cleveland give a paper at the Woodrow Wilson Cen-

4. Several of them were hired by Syracuse University: Donn Hart (Department of Social Science); Kenneth Kindelsperger (School of Social Work); Robert Smith (Department of Marketing); Ralph Ketcham (American Studies and Political Science); Robert Pickett (College for Human Development); and Malcolm Schlusberg (Law and Public Policy), to name but a few. In 1968 the Doctor of Social Science was changed to a Ph.D.

tennial Celebration at Princeton and committed himself to making Cleveland his successor, despite Cleveland's lack of graduate degrees. Tolley communicated that this was "not necessarily an insuperable handicap," and agreed to meet with Cleveland. After that meeting, Tolley reported that "we were completely captivated by . . . Cleveland," but "as the matter stands at present, the academicians would welcome him as a colleague but not as a dean. This situation, however, may change." With Appleby's sudden resignation, the situation indeed changed, and Cleveland accepted the deanship.

Where Appleby had succeeded in using his contacts to link Maxwell with the Washington establishment, Cleveland used his background to make Maxwell a truly international school. Ambitious, with an eye toward future government service, his legacy was the Maxwell Overseas Programs, which began with a $10 million Ford Foundation grant for a program in Pakistan. Before his tenure was completed, Cleveland had engineered programs abroad in Italy and Kenya and a master's program of study abroad in foreign consulates, and he had joined a university consortium (Syracuse, Princeton, Yale, Stanford, and Penn) in working in foreign government offices. Cleveland also strengthened the metropolitan studies area and was able to bring in amounts of government grants previously unheard of for Maxwell.

*   *   *

Perhaps the most startling development of any college during the postwar period, outside Applied Science, occurred in continuing education. Evening classes had been established at the university in October 1918 and expanded through the 1920s as part of the national trend towards "extending" the offerings of the university to nontraditional students and on a nontraditional schedule. In the 1930s, the new School of Extension Teaching and Adult Education established thirty-three extension centers around the state. As we have seen, two of these—at Endicott (Triple Cities) and Utica—would mature into full colleges and become a major part of the story of the 1950s in their own right.

In August 1946 the School of Extension Teaching was reorganized into University College (UC). It moved into the Fayette Street buildings vacated by the medical school, which had only recently been sold by Tolley to the State University System. Kenneth Bartlett, who along with other duties had been acting director of the School of Extension Teaching from 1943 to 1946, was made the new dean of UC. Discussed above as the driving force behind the expansion of the radio program at the university, the multitalented Bartlett had been with the university since 1929, when he was made an instructor in speech. In 1939 he was appointed assistant professor of radio education in the College of Liberal Arts and became chairman of the Department of Radio in the School of Journalism in 1942.

Under Bartlett, the concept of institutional branches was expanded beyond the extension centers of the 1930s. Through UC, the university took its courses and programs to major companies that had requested master's-level work for their employees, most notably in electrical engineering. The company paid part of the tuition, and the university, through UC, provided faculty and staff. Between 1951 and 1954, three off-campus graduate centers were founded: one in engineering and sciences at Rome (drawing students from the Rome Air Development Center of the air force and the General Electric Company in Utica); a second in Endicott-Owego (drawing from IBM, General Electric, New York State Electric and Gas, Ansco, Bendix, and the Link Division of General Precision); and a third in Poughkeepsie-Kingston (also drawing from IBM). Faculty members commuted from Syracuse, taught seminar classes, and conducted thesis research and advanced courses for some eight hundred students.

In 1953 Tolley tapped Bartlett as his new dean of Public Relations (a position that would turn into Vice President and Dean for Public Relations in 1956). Bartlett's assistant, Alexander Charters, was promoted to dean of UC. A native of Vancouver, British Columbia, Charters had taught school for a few years in Canada before attending the University of Chicago. During World War II, he served in the Royal Canadian Navy as a landing craft operator, seeing action at such battles as Salerno, Anzio, and Normandy. After the war, he returned to Chicago for his Ph.D., during which time he served as an educational consultant for the International Harvester research project in adult education. Tolley was a great admirer of the adult education curriculum at Chicago (he hired Charters and his eventual successor, Clifford Winters, from there), and Charters was hired as Bartlett's assistant.

As dean, Charters would continue UC's growth spurt. A grant of $250,000 from the Fund for Adult Education led to the 1959 introduction of the Humanistic Studies Center, which developed short courses for adults who no longer needed or desired formal academic credit. The grant also funded a Discussion-Leadership Center, created to help adults operate more constructively in these two types of communications settings.

Yet one cannot escape the belief that Tolley saw UC as a vast receptacle for programs and ideas that did not seem to fit anywhere else in the university. This was due in equal measure to Tolley's respect for Charters's talents as an administrator, and Tolley's belief that the adult education arm of a university should be flexible enough to accommodate many different types of programs. An excellent example of this is the social work program, which had begun as a joint venture between the University of Buffalo and Syracuse University. But following the receipt of a Gifford Foundation grant, the cord was severed, and the program was assigned to Charters and UC. The story of the purchase of the Regent Theater has been told above— Charters explained the assignment of the theater to his UC domain quite simply: "A lot of things that Hugh Gregg bought passed over to UC." Charters was also charged in 1959 with developing a foreign studies program. The first program was a summer studies program in Mexico. (Charters remembered that since many faculty went there during the summers anyway, it was relatively easy for him to approach them to teach, and to pay them at the going summer sessions rate.) Charters joined forces with Maxwell's Harlan Cleveland, who, as noted above, was attempting to internationalize the Maxwell School. Together, the two men laid the groundwork for what later became the Department of International Programs Abroad (DIPA).

In 1943 the School of Extension Teaching had 813 students registered in college credit courses, including those enrolled at institutional branches; by 1958 UC was servicing 4,000 students in Syracuse alone. As the program grew, Tolley wanted to recognize that growth by renovating and renaming the old medical school buildings in which UC had been squatting for almost a decade. Tolley originally hoped to name the buildings after Finla Crawford; however, Crawford nixed the idea. Tolley then wrote Charters in February 1958 that he thought that Jesse T. Peck, one of the original founders of the university, and Dr. and Mrs. John Morrison Reid, who had provided the funds for the original administration building, had been inadequately honored by the university. In typical Tolley fashion, the chancellor told his dean that "if I had to settle the matter today, I would name one building Reid and the other Peck but I think you should be a party to the final decision." Charters agreed.

*   *   *

Many alumni and administrators quietly pushed Tolley to favor—with buildings, monies, and administrative emphasis—the scientific and technical programs. These patrons, however, misunderstood the depth of the university's heritage and misread Tolley's commitment to the College of Liberal Arts, the oldest college of the university, and the college from which Tolley had graduated in 1922. While his corporate common sense led him to expand the sciences in the 1950s, Tolley's heart was always with that mode of study that had begun with the Greek Sophists and was perfected by those Renaissance philosophers who professed that all educated men be exposed to the *studia humanitatis:* literature, the arts, history, and philosophy. Hardly neglected, these curricula grew as the sciences and contract research grew. The result was the creation of an institution that was on the national cutting edge of scientific research, but still wedded to its professional and humanistic roots—by 1960 Syracuse was a university in every sense of the word.

To go through every discipline in the College of Liberal Arts would be an exercise in pedantry and would result in a list of departments, rather than a part of a story. It seems, however, that here the story can be told through several faculty vignettes: great teachers, as it were. There can be no doubt but that there were great teachers among the research and social sciences—several have been introduced above. However, the teachers at the College of Liberal Arts, by virtue of the fact that many of their courses were required across the university, touched more lives than did the instructors of any other college on campus. When alumni are interviewed and asked to reflect on the teachers who shaped them as adults, invariably the faculty of the College of Liberal Arts come to the fore. Allow the author the luxury of presenting three names to the reader for consideration.

*   *   *

Eric Faigle is first on virtually every alumni list. Faigle was a geographer and ultimately dean of the College of Liberal Arts, although administrative work was never his forte. Faigle received his B.A. from Syracuse in 1928. He stayed on at Piety Hill as an instructor while working toward the master's degree that he was awarded in 1930. Five years spent earning his doctorate at the University of Michigan were the only adult years that Faigle spent away from Syracuse University. Most who hear his name remember him as the "Mr. Chips" of the college—tough student cases were sent to him, and he gave them the individual attention that many teachers found all too time consuming. Tolley mentions Faigle's commitment to teaching in his memoirs, as well as in a later interview: "if I didn't take care of [the tough student cases] personally, I had Eric take care of them. . . . He never lost a case." An admiring Clark Ahlberg also remembered: "He was respected and loved and sought after by those students for his personal association as well as counseling and to have that kind of man on a complex, large campus was a godsend. . . . He gave the university some of its heart that can sometimes be lost."

*   *   *

One faculty member defied even the byzantine organizational structure of the Maxwell School. Thomas V. "T. V." Smith's national reputation had long preceded his tenure at Syracuse. Smith had been a professor of philosophy at the University of Chicago since 1927. He was the author of twelve books before he came to Syracuse and had also served as Illinois congressman-at-large. A sought-after speaker, Smith wanted to move East for the final few years of his academic career. Tolley remembered, with some tongue in cheek, that when he extended an offer to Smith, "I learned that he might be interested if we offered a divan instead of a chair." In an unprecedented move, Tolley offered Smith professorships in poetry, philosophy, and public administration, and Smith accepted. It was a good buy, even if it was

Eric Faigle

Mary Marshall

T. V. Smith and Chancellor Tolley

for a short period of time. Students, particularly those who attended Smith's citizenship lectures, marveled at the erudition of the man whom they called the "Three-P Professor." After Smith's retirement in 1959, his multidepartmental position went unfilled.

*   *   *

Mary Hatch Marshall began teaching English at Syracuse in 1948. She retired in 1970, only to return in 1973 to teach some more. She earned her A.B. from Vassar in 1924, and her Ph.D. from Yale in medieval and Renaissance literature in 1932. At Syracuse, she was the first woman to be named a full professor in the College of Liberal Arts. One of the university's most dedicated patrons of the library, Marshall was honored for her service to both Carnegie and Bird on several occasions. But undergraduates remember the rigor and the imagination of her Shakespeare, Elizabethan drama, Renaissance poetry, and modern drama courses. Marshall turned her classroom into a theater, with dramatic readings of Shakespeare and his contemporaries. Of her classroom presence, a colleague marveled: "She talks in arias." In 1974 Marshall was voted one of the *Post-Standard*'s all-time women of achievement for her contributions to the city's cultural development, and in 1978 an anonymous donor gave the institution $100,000 in her name. It was only fitting that in April 1978 Marshall re-retired by teaching the last class in the Hall of Languages before it was closed for several years of renovation.

*   *   *

As research and scholarship in all fields began to grow at Syracuse in the Tolley era, it was often disseminated to the world via another Tolley creation. What was described as a "casual train chat" between Tolley and Thomas Watson led to the founding of an organ of the university to publish its research. Tolley promised to organize a university press to publish IBM's *Precision Measurement in the Metal Working Industry.* Thus, Syracuse University Press (SUP) was formed in August 1943. Lyle Spencer, dean of the School of Journalism, was the first president of its board of directors, and Dr. Lawrence Siegfried served as the press's first editor. In its first year, SUP published the first volume of *Precision Measurement in the Metal Working Industry;* it was followed by a second volume in 1944.

In 1945 William Miller, formerly an assistant director at Rand McNally in Chicago, became SUP's first full-time director. In a cramped office located next to the printing plant, Miller and the fledgling press published fifty-eight scholarly books and monographs, compared to seven before Miller took over. Several of the press's books were quite successful. Robert T. Oliver's *Effective Speech Notebook* was in its fifth printing in 1948, selling about twenty thousand copies. The beautifully illustrated *Sculpture of Ivan Mestrovic* (1948)—called by one writer the press's "masterpiece"—was designed by Carl P. Rollins, printer to Yale University, and continues to serve as the definitive work on the subject. *A Critical Bibliography of French Literature,* a series, represented the efforts of hundreds of specialists in the field. The press also made a contribution through its publication of controversial studies of Russia and the Soviet Union, most notably Warren B. Walsh, *Readings in Russian History* (1948) and Wladyslaw Kulski, *The Soviet Regime: Communism in Practice* (1954), a book that in 1960 was in its third edition.

However, the press was as yet hardly self-sustaining, and the administration threatened on several occasions to either drop or sharply curtail its activities. It was left to Donald Bean, who replaced Miller in 1955, to put the press on a sounder financial footing. Formerly the director of presses at Stanford (where he published about four hundred titles) and Chicago (where he published about a thousand), as well as the founder of the American Association of University Presses, Bean, with the help of controller Frank Wingate, managed the press to an increase in income during each year of his directorship. In September 1956 publishing offices were moved to Brewster House, which held the distinct advantage of being on the opposite side of campus from the noisy printing presses. Critical and financial successes soon followed. *William Bulmer and the Shakespeare Press* won a 1958 typographical award for the press, and Ernst Bacon's 1960 *Words on Music* won rave reviews. A series begun in November 1960, entitled Men and Movements and dealing with nonconformist leaders, produced several critical successes. The initial volumes were Karl Schmidt, *Henry A. Wallace: Quixotic Crusade 1948,* and D. Joy Humes,

Oswald Garrison Villard: Liberal of the 1920's. The next year, books were released on Norman Thomas, Gifford Pinchot, and the hugely influential H. Wayne Morgan, *Eugene V. Debs: Socialist for President* (1962). Perhaps the most important offering of the press during Bean's tenure was Siao-Yu's *Mao tse-Tung and I Were Beggars* (1960), an account of his school days with the leader of the People's Republic of China. Yu was then director of the Sino-International Library in Montevideo, and his wife, a Syracuse alum, urged him to write the book and submit it to SUP.

In 1960 Richard Underwood, formerly of the University of Texas Press, replaced Bean and would hold the directorship for the next fifteen years. With the help of assistant director Arpena S. Mesrobian, who had been with the press since 1949 and would soon serve as the press's director, SUP made some major changes. In January 1961, SUP left the cramped quarters of the Brewster House and set up shop on the top floor of the Continental Can Building on Erie Boulevard. Now all the press's functions were under one roof. During Underwood's tenure, some of SUP's most successful volumes came from the Maxwell School. Stuart Gerry Brown's *Conscience in Politics: Adlai E. Stevenson in the 1950's* (1961) was, to that point, the best-selling work the press had ever had, and it stands today as the most thoughtful biography of the Illinois governor and perennial presidential candidate. The pathbreaking twelve volume series on Economics and Politics of Public Education (1962–63) evolved from a three-year research project by Jesse Burkhead, and was financed by the Carnegie Corporation of New York. Donald Meiklejohn's *Freedom and the Public: Public and Private Morality in America* (1965) argued that "present American thinking has been confused and blocked by the lack of clarity about our public and private interests and the moralities in which we try to organize those interests."

It was during the Tolley period that the first two volumes of the official university history, written by W. Freeman Galpin of the university's history department, were published. Tolley commissioned the studies as one of his first acts as chancellor in 1943; the first volume, *The Pioneer Days,* covered the first twenty-three years of the university, from its 1870 founding to the 1893 retirement of Chancellor Charles N. Sims. The second volume was released in 1960 as *The Growing*

Years, covering the chancellorship of James Roscoe Day from 1894 to 1922. Galpin, who had since been named University Historian for his efforts, began writing the third volume, which was to cover the period from 1922 to 1942. However, Galpin died in 1963, leaving the future of what many had come to call the "Galpin Series" in doubt.

The School of Forestry: left: Bray Hall; right, Marshall Hall

CHAPTER 8

The Challenge of SUNY

Can't Private and Public Schools Live Together in New York State?

—Title of a *Syracuse Herald-Journal* editorial, Mar. 5, 1956

*I found the officers of the State University difficult to deal with.
Everything was a one-way street.*

—Tolley, *At the Fountain of Youth*

D EVELOPMENT IN public higher education in New York had
come late. Although the administration of higher education in
New York began in 1784 with the creation of the Board of Regents
of the University of the State of New York, there was no state university system in New York—the only state in the union not to have one.
Despite the creation of Cornell University, the great state university
systems built under the Morrill Act (1862) were largely in the midwest.
To rectify the situation, in 1946 New York governor Thomas E.
Dewey set up a temporary commission on the need for a state university. The twenty-one member commission was headed by Owen
D. Young, the former chairman of General Electric. After eighteen
months of study, the Young Commission was stalemated. The biggest
issue of concern in December 1947 was whether the commission
would recommend a centralized or a decentralized state university.
The committee's staff had circulated reports that had concluded that
a decentralized state system, with new four-year state schools established in various localities, met the needs of New York State, as their
research had found that more students attended college in those areas
where educational facilities were provided locally. However, several

of the commission members called for a centralized system, beginning with the designation of one state university campus. The core of the debate was transparently political. The board of regents felt that a decentralized system, without one locus of power, would be easier to control; the Dewey administration felt that the decentralized system would be too expensive. Plus, Dewey was about to announce for the presidency against the embattled Harry Truman—he needed to show that his state was in the vanguard of higher education, and he wanted it done cheaply.

Syracuse University, and virtually all the other leaders of New York's colleges and universities, stood to lose from the decentralized system. Their enrollment would suffer, as prospective students could now choose a much less expensive local alternative to private education. Nevertheless, the reality of the situation was that Dewey would see to it that New York had a state university system in time to showcase during the presidential campaign. The only way that a private institution might benefit from the situation was if the centralized plan carried the day and its campus was named the state university.

This scenario came breathlessly close to happening to Syracuse University. In December 1947, in an attempt to break the stalemate, Dewey and his staff wrote what was termed an "alternative draft," designed to counter the expected recommendation by the committee staff for a decentralized university. The draft was presented by State Budget Director John E. Burton, a commission member, who urged that an existing university, preferably Syracuse University, be acquired for the purpose of being named the central state school. Republican legislative leaders gave their unqualified approval to Burton's plan. However, Democratic leaders in the Senate, led by Minority Leader Elmer Quinn—who called Burton's proposal a "fraud"—pushed hard for the Young Commission to recommend a decentralized approach.

When the story broke in the *New York Times* on January 3, 1948, Tolley was away on business in California, and Crawford had no comment. Tolley had never wanted a state system—it would end up costing the university money. But if there was going to be a state system, having The State University of New York at Syracuse was an irresistible temptation. In meetings with his administrators, Tolley let it be known that he was giving serious consideration to allowing the Burton plan to move forward without opposition from Piety Hill. The need to decide never arose, however. Worried that the impasse would drag on into the primary season, Dewey forced the Young Commission to a compromise. On February 16, the commission unanimously recommended the establishment of a state university system under the board of regents. Neither accepting nor rejecting the idea of Syracuse as the central state university, the commission concluded that "first consideration" had to be given to building colleges in areas of the state not yet served by higher education. Existing state-operated institutions would be brought under the state university umbrella, and community colleges, either on a two- or a four-year level, would be created. Capital expenditures were to be divided on an equal basis between the state and the community; maintenance expenditures were to come one-third from tuition charges, one-third from the community, and one-third from the state. The commission also called for the establishment of two teaching medical centers— one to be located in metropolitan New York and one in upstate New York. On March 12, 1948, the legislature passed a law creating the State University of New York (SUNY), effective July 1, 1948. Dewey signed the measure on March 30 and named Alvin C. Eurich the first SUNY commissioner.

If Tolley ever held any further hopes of Syracuse becoming SUNY's central campus, he never voiced them. As the building of the first state universities took center stage, the issue of the central campus died a natural death. But this was far from the end of Tolley's interaction with the state university system. Put at its simplest, Dewey had given Tolley unwelcome competition. There was bound to be a clash, and the first battle came over a situation that was made to order for conflict—the nebulous relationship between Syracuse and one of the handful of collegiate centers that had been subsidized by the state prior to the Young Commission—the New York State College of Forestry at Syracuse, New York.

*   *   *

By the turn of the century, the importance of the nation's forests had been etched into the American consciousness. None other than the president of the United States, Theodore Roosevelt, had made land and forest conservation a personal crusade. Partly as a result of Roosevelt's support, between 1903 and 1914 twenty-one schools of forestry were established, and in the same period there was a dramatic increase in the hiring of professional foresters. In 1898 a New York State College of Forestry had been established at Cornell University; it was abandoned, however, in 1903 as a result of the failure of state appropriations. The state had never, to anyone's knowledge, appropriated *any* money for the school. Syracuse chancellor James Day pounced on Cornell's bad fortune, and in July 1911 the New York State College of Forestry was established at Syracuse University. Its original goals were to conduct experiments in forestry and forestation, and to plant, raise, cut, and sell trees and timber so as to learn and refine the science of reforestation.

The relationship that developed between the university and the College of Forestry has been an extraordinary one. The college was a creation of the state, and the law provided for free tuition for any New York State resident—any other tuition or fee was to be sent to Albany, to be applied to the maintenance of the school. The college had its own board of trustees chosen by the state, on which sat Chancellor Day as an ex officio member. Yet its degrees were conferred at Syracuse's commencement, and its students were considered both students and alums of Syracuse. Indeed, the university ultimately deeded a two-acre plot to the state for a building. Faculty salaries were paid by the state, but the college's buildings were heated by the university.

When Tolley took office, the dean of the College of Forestry was Joseph S. Illick. He had graduated from Lafayette College (1907) and had served as State Forester of Pennsylvania. Illick had come to Syracuse as a special lecturer in 1931 and became head of the Department of Forestry Management the next year. In the fall of 1942 enrollment at Forestry was holding steady at 423, but the student body would be one of those hardest hit by the withdrawal of men into the armed forces. In 1944, only 104 undergraduates and four graduate students were registered, and the New York State Ranger School at Wanakena, New York, was forced to close for the duration. But Forestry was also one of the schools that picked up enrollment the fastest after the war. Part of this increase was due to the construction of a new $569,000 general forestry building, suggested by Illick and approved by the regents in 1943. In 1945, enrollment more than doubled, reaching 258.

In 1951 Illick retired. He was succeeded as dean by Hardy Shirley, who had joined the college faculty as assistant dean and professor of forestry in 1945. Prior to that appointment, he had taught at the University of Nevada for three years and then had been with the U.S. Forest Service for sixteen years. Shirley proposed a new emphasis on graduate training—a goal that, not coincidentally, was right in synch with Tolley's desire to emphasize the university's research and graduate programs. With this in mind, by the spring of 1957 the third major structure of the Forestry College, Baker Laboratory, was completed at a cost of some $4 million. By 1960, the college had become the largest forestry college in the country, with an enrollment exceeding seven hundred students.

Forestry's growth was overshadowed, however, by the fight between Tolley and SUNY for control of the college. There was never any question that Forestry would be named a part of the new SUNY system of schools; the Young Commission had so recommended in 1948. The fight revolved around differing interpretations as to who had ultimate *control* of the college—SUNY or Syracuse. The Young Commission had concluded that Forestry was one of nine colleges that had been operated for the state under contract by a private institution. This was how Tolley viewed the relationship, but the new SUNY board of regents quickly disagreed, arguing in 1950 that Forestry was a completely state-managed organization. Tolley told the university's board of trustees that the state had an ulterior motive in making this claim so late: "The State University Trustees have the feeling that they will never achieve an integrated State University unless all the powers reside in the parent body. We can understand this. They have an unwieldy structure. Their primary desire is coordination and integration." Nevertheless, the state was more than ready to act on its conclusion—on April 16, 1951, SUNY announced that all Forestry degrees would henceforth be offered by SUNY alone.

Virtually every official in the Syracuse University administration felt that this decision was a violation of the spirit, if not the letter, of the Young Commission report. It also angered Tolley that Syracuse was the only school where this was happening—the other eight contract schools were not being so attacked. Since commencement was upon them, the university agreed to run the ceremony as SUNY wished but refused to make any promises for future commencements.

That winter brought the second broadside from SUNY. On December 5, 1951, acting SUNY president Charles Garside wrote Tolley to inform him that a bill would be put forth in the state legislature to reconfigure the Forestry College Board of Trustees as a Board of Visitors, which would supervise the college in the name of the state and according to the guidelines of state law. Tolley was quick to see the danger—if adopted, the bill would, in effect, transfer the power to control the college from Forestry's board to SUNY. His response to Garside was immediate:

> It is a very grave shock to us to learn that of the three privately endowed universities with state colleges on their campuses (Syracuse, Alfred, and Cornell), Syracuse is suddenly and unexpectedly singled out for special legislation. The New York State College of Forestry at Syracuse University has been a contract college and an integral member of the family of colleges of Syracuse University for forty years. Now for the first time the State University proposes to separate the New York State College of Forestry at Syracuse University from the other contract colleges and to group it with the State teacher's colleges, the technical institutes, and the Maritime Academy. Our immediate reaction is that this is either an unintentional error, or one more step in a campaign to take over the direct operation and control of all the contract colleges.

The battle escalated over the next two months, as Garside accused Syracuse of profiting from their relationship with Forestry. Tolley's reply to that charge was even angrier than his first:

> No taxpayer or member of the legislature could say that Syracuse University as a privately endowed university has profited from the connection. To the contrary, Syracuse has provided the gymnasium, playing fields, infirmary, chapel, general education classrooms and laboratories, dormitories, dining halls, and land so that the State College could enjoy all the resources of a large university on a minimal budget and a minimal capital outlay. It is important to remember, moreover, that the fact of dual boards and separate fiscal controls has not meant separateness. Distinct in corporate structure they have nevertheless been two parts of one whole.

The fight got amusingly petty: Tolley wrote SUNY that "I see red" that the official stationery did not show the relationship between Syracuse and Forestry. Tolley ordered that no new stationery be ordered until the trustees had been consulted. The question seemed to be one of gratitude—who was responsible for the College of Forestry: New York State, who passed the legislation that created it, or Syracuse University and James Day, who built it? Tolley's view is clear on the matter, as he wrote to trustee Frank Marion in January 1952: "In time I think it will be apparent to the State University that the Forestry College needs Syracuse University's help much more than we need the College of Forestry." He referred to the bill that would create the Board of Visitors as the "bill of divorcement," and began to refer to the many things that would disappear—everything from library privileges to faculty discounts at the bookstore, residence on campus, and admission to frats—if the bill went through. By February, Tolley was also quoting Article 11, Section 4 of the State Constitution, which prohibited the use of state property, credit, or money in aid or maintenance of any school of learning "wholly or in part under the control or direction of any religious denomination."

The bill was finally introduced in the Assembly and the Senate in February 1953. It called for amending the State Education Law to read that the state schools, including Forestry, "have been, since July 1, 1948, or hereafter may be acquired, established, operated or contracted to be operated for the state by the state university trustees."[1] Thanks to the influence of State Senator John Hughes, long a friend of Syracuse, the bill was amended to exclude Forestry from its provisions and then passed. However, no one believed that this would be the end of the matter. The wrangling went on, and on March 2, 1954, a bill was put in front of the Assembly and the Senate that would dissolve the board of trustees of the College of Forestry, and extend the administration of the State University to the College of Forestry.[2] Once again, Hughes saw to it that the bill died in committee.

The grumbling continued throughout 1955, and in February 1956 Hughes submitted his own bill, which if passed would codify the original view of the Young Commission. The Hughes Bill called for

1. Assembly Bill Print No. 1811, Int. 1750; Senate Bill Print No. 1670, Int. 1588.
2. Assembly Bill Print No. 3440, Int. No. 3191; Senate Bill Print No. 3077, Int. No. 2752.

the classifying of the College of Forestry as a contract college of Syracuse University, abolishing the present board of trustees and having its operations paid for by the state but operated by Syracuse. The bill was opposed by Forestry's faculty, alumni, and the students as being too complicated, but Tolley saw it as the solution to his problems, announcing through his director of public relations that "it must be made clear that Syracuse University is not in an academic hotel business. Syracuse University should not be placed in the position of having to provide services to students and faculty who belong to a completely separate institution." Tolley began to talk about "dual enrollment" in both institutions—a more formal setup of the situation that had been in place since 1911.

Thus stalemated, in April 1956 the two sides agreed to what amounted to a cease-fire. A "General Policy Statement" on the working relationship between the two schools was agreed upon—Syracuse recognized that the College of Forestry was a part of SUNY and that SUNY trustees "have general responsibility for providing a broad coordinated program to public higher education for the youth of New York [including] all units of the State University." The board of trustees of the College of Forestry would hire deans, act on faculty issues such as appointments, promotions, and salary issues, and would invite to its meetings the president of SUNY or his deputy. For its part, the state agreed "not to take action on questions of major importance affecting the College [of Forestry] without first referring these to College trustees for study and recommendations." The new name of the college was even a compromise—heretofore known as the State University College of Forestry at Syracuse University. But questions regarding the status of the Forestry *student*—was the student dually enrolled at SUNY and Syracuse University? From which institution did the student receive his or her degree?—were never solved during the Tolley years.

*   *   *

After the State University was formed in 1948, it proposed a "master plan" that provided for several two-year community colleges and one or possibly two four-year liberal arts colleges. Almost immediately, there were hints that SUNY wanted to locate one of these colleges in Binghamton. A local committee was organized in Broome County in July 1949 to try to land a unit of the state university in the southern tier. That committee was headed by Glenn Bartle, then serving Syracuse University as the dean of Triple Cities College (TCC). Seeing the handwriting on the wall, during a September 20, 1949, public hearing in Albany, Finla Crawford announced that Syracuse was prepared to cooperate in the development of community colleges by making its TCC operation available to the state. However, Crawford made it clear that Syracuse's compliance in the matter would not come free: "The university has made very substantial investments in its branch colleges for which it should be reimbursed if and when the state university and the communities are ready to act." SUNY responded that it would build a four-year community college in Binghamton if the local group raised $2 million by April 1950.

Tolley was, therefore, stunned in November when Bartle came to Syracuse and told the chancellor that the state was ready to act and wanted to know what Syracuse was willing to "contribute." A subsequent university report on the issue claimed that "this was the first time there had been intimation that Syracuse might be asked to *give* the physical assets to the state. In light of the previous declarations, it was unusual coming as it did from a Dean of the college employed by Syracuse University!" Bartle, who had cast his lot with SUNY while still in the employ of Syracuse University, clearly hoped to persuade Tolley to give its assets to the state.

It did not work. On November 18, 1949, it was announced at a meeting of Syracuse's board of trustees that the university was "desirous of cooperating with the state in the possible transfer of [TCC] to the state, but feels it should receive reasonable compensation for its investment in real estate and personal property in Endicott. The state had not yet indicated its willingness to pay Syracuse for its property." One month later, Tolley took his concern straight to a meeting of the state university trustees, claiming that he was willing to discontinue TCC, but that the university would continue to operate TCC until SUNY bought the school.

Tolley hoped that his threat to completely discontinue operations would force the state to act. It did. Less than a month later, SUNY announced that it was taking over TCC, and that Bartle would be its

first provost. According to a university report, "Syracuse read it in
the newspapers!" Eurich formally contacted Tolley a few weeks later
and told him that Bartle had been put on the state payroll, and he had
been ordered to prepare a new catalogue; Tolley reminded Eurich
that Bartle could not serve two masters.

SUNY blinked first. On June 25, Frederick Greenman, chairman
of the committee on four-year colleges, met with Tolley in Syracuse.
During that meeting, it was agreed that all physical assets of the college, other than bookstore inventory and the library, would be sold
to the state at a total price of $215,000, and that the funds would be
paid in equal installments over three years. It was also agreed that
$91,000 would be paid for the library and that the bookstore inven-
tory would be sold by the state, with the proceeds paid to Syracuse.
According to the above mentioned report, Greenman called Tolley on
June 28, informing him that Eurich had agreed to the deal.

However, on July 6, Eurich called Tolley to tell him that the controller objected to crediting the local community with money paid as
rent. Eurich also wanted the library taken out of the deal. While Tolley agreed to let the state use the facilities without a deal, on July 19
he wired Eurich with a new proposal—Tolley had upped the ante to
$310,000 for the entire facility, including the library. Anxious to get
the project underway and unwilling to let Tolley make any more
money, Eurich wired back the same day with a third proposal—he
accepted Tolley's original offer of $215,000 for the college and of-
fered $21,175 for the bookstore. On August 1, 1950, the sale was
consummated. TCC became known as Harpur College at Endicott,
named after Robert Harpur, early settler of Broome County and
founder of Harpursville.

*   *   *

As noted earlier, the performance of the students in the medical
school during World War II had been one of the university's crowning achievements of the period. And yet, by 1950, Syracuse had sold
its medical school to the state of New York. Facing a period of
immense physical expansion, the poor financial condition of the medical school had become problematic. The historian of the medical
college notes that by comparison to other institutions, the Syracuse

Left: College of Medicine; right: Memorial Hospital

University Medical College had never brought in big donations, and as a result, it had a small endowment. More important, it was not paying for itself. In 1949 Tolley reported that the medical school had accrued an operating deficit of $400,000, not including the debts for the new academic building. Although Tolley denies in his memoirs that money was a factor in his decision to divest the university of its medical school, it is unlikely that this was the case. The moment that an opportunity presented itself, Tolley moved quickly to get rid of the struggling school. In an irony that few people missed at the time, that opportunity came from SUNY.

In 1948 the Young Commission had recommended, and the state had accepted, a proposal to create both an upstate and a downstate medical center as part of the new SUNY. Sensing an opportunity to divest himself of a potentially losing situation, as well as get in on the ground floor of SUNY growth in Syracuse, Tolley offered the Syracuse Medical College to SUNY as an incentive for the state locating its upstate medical center in Syracuse. On January 10, 1949, four months after the creation of SUNY, college dean Herman G. Weiskotten and Tolley testified before the board of trustees of SUNY in New York City. Weiskotten told the board that the college appeared before them "not as opportunists who see a possible way out of financial difficulties. We come before you rather as a group who for more than twenty-five years have been working without any outside support toward the development of a medical and health center." Making his own pitch, Tolley made it clear that "we are willing" to make the resources of Syracuse available to the state of New York. He referred the university's million-volt x-ray machine, its school of nursing, and its central location in the state as but a few reasons to consider locating the college there. Tolley believed it was understood that any sale implied a cooperative program and an intimate relationship between the university and the Upstate Medical Center. Apparently the state did not see it the same way. On May 9, 1949, Weiskotten was dispatched to Albany to meet privately with the committee to discuss such cooperation; he reported that one member of the committee reminded Weiskotten that the state would be well within its rights to fire the entire faculty, including the dean, if they took over.

Shortly after the University of Buffalo had put in its bid, Syracuse University made its formal offer to SUNY chancellor Eurich in a letter dated May 16. In it, Tolley valued the College of Medicine building and its land, contents, and equipment at $2.5 million. As had been done with the College of Forestry, he offered the state the land for free, and offered to lease the state the teaching and clinical facilities of the University Hospital of the Good Shepherd for $1.00 per year, until a new hospital could be erected. Tolley also proposed to donate the income from all funds for medical education now held in trust by the university to the program of the Upstate Medical Center. SUNY was asked to pay the bonded indebtedness of the Medical College Building (a $509,323 mortgage held by First Trust), reimburse the university for the operation of the medical college over the past year, and pay the deficit on University Hospital up to $100,000. The university would continue to operate University Hospital for the state university on a contract basis, and the state would take over responsibility for the Syracuse Free Dispensary—the university's role would be that of landlord. On June 16, the SUNY trustees announced that the Upstate Medical Center would be located in Syracuse. The state assumed financial responsibility for the conduct of the college as of July 1, 1949, and for its full administration as of June 1950. On April 15, 1950, Governor Dewey signed the bill authorizing the transfer of the medical school to the state, and on June 27, 1950, ceremonies marked the transfer of the medical school to the state university. Dewey was the main speaker, and Weiskotten was named Upstate's first dean.

However, the deal went sour even before the signing of the transfer. In October 1949 Tolley learned that SUNY would not be paying the college for support of the medical college program until the transfer was complete. In a scorching letter to Eurich, Tolley railed that "it will be a long time before we see any money," and compared the situation to an impending marriage where the parents of the bride were being told that they should continue to advance housekeeping bills for the couple so that they might continue to cohabitate before the nuptials. Then came a fight that paralleled the fight going on at the same time between the university and SUNY over the College of Forestry—would the Upstate Medical Center, using the free facilities of the old medical school with its students having the privileges of all Syracuse University students, offer a joint degree from SUNY and Syracuse University? In all the correspondence, the degree was to be "worked out" between Eurich and Tolley; the status of students and faculty was to be the same as that at the College of Forestry—a dual relationship. Tolley would later write that he "assumed" that this type of relationship would occur, and that "we had been led by representatives of the State University to believe that there would be a vital continuing relationship between the Upstate Medical Center and Syracuse University. . . . We were unprepared for the proposal by the State University that . . . Upstate . . . would be completely unrelated to Syracuse University." A furious Tolley, citing breaches of an "assurance" that SUNY and Syracuse would cooperate, and that it was now "evident that *separate status without affiliation* is the State University Policy for the State College of Medicine," pulled the plug on many of the privileges of Upstate employees, including remitted tuition, publication of their names in the university directory, and staying in university housing.

A potentially more damaging issue was that of the fight over the jurisdiction of the medical school endowments. In 1954 SUNY brought suit against the university for the immediate transfer of all income from the endowment funds of the medical college still held by Syracuse. One of those endowments was the Manley Research Fund, initiated in 1938 by two brothers, physicians Thomas and George L. Manley, for research in surgery at the Syracuse University Medical College. George Manley made it clear that he did not want SUNY to gain control of this money simply because it had bought the medical school. To try to shield the money from the state, the principal from the endowment was transferred to the athletic fund. However, the state felt that it had the right to this endowment, and to others like it, that had been attached to the medical school before its sale. The university lost the suit, and in January 1955 the parties settled out of court; the university eventually delivered a check for $87,842 (principal plus interest on the endowments) to SUNY.

*   *   *

In 1960 Governor Nelson A. Rockefeller formed a commission (the Commission on Higher Education) headed by Henry T. Heald, former chancellor of New York University, to study the administrative and managerial constrictions placed on SUNY. The Heald Report, finished in November 1960, concluded that SUNY should be "freed of handicapping procedural requirements . . . which now limit its capacity to act decisively and effectively." It also concluded that SUNY should be given greater authority to pursue construction goals, and freed SUNY from the control of the board of regents. The decade-long battle between the state and Syracuse had been won by SUNY.

Jawaharlal Nehru, prime minister of India, with Paul Appleby

CHAPTER 9

The Challenge to Academic Freedom

Red*ucators.*

A common term in the 1950s used by conservatives
to typify college professors.

O NE OF Tolley's most vivid memories of his undergraduate years at Syracuse University was a professor of economics named Frederick Roman. Roman was a taskmaster—each class, there was a one-question quiz, and students either earned a hundred or a zero. But Tolley was most impressed by Roman's adherence to the controversial ideas of Henry George. In his 1879 masterpiece *Progress and Poverty,* George had argued that poverty was at the root of all of America's problems, and that the way to cure poverty was with a single, leveling tax that would bring about an equality of wealth throughout the nation. An optimistic book that argued that poverty could be cured, *Progress and Poverty* had sold over two million copies by 1905. However, the single tax was anathema to traditional economists, and the teaching of George's ideas was considered heretical by many college administrators. Chancellor Day apparently thought so, too, and fired Roman during Tolley's junior year. Tolley remembered that Roman's dismissal "taught me a lesson I did not forget. Professor Roman was not a radical. Like so many professors, he was simply one who thought otherwise. He had his own ideas, and he loved to advocate them. . . . Because he invited tough, intellectual discussions, he was a great teacher. He should have been promoted, not fired."

Plato defined academic freedom as the right and duty of a scholar to follow an argument "withersoever it may lead." It is a privilege that has been linked for centuries with the issue of job security—recognizing the right to research and teach the ideals that one holds, without fear of monetary or employment retribution by the institution. It is, however, an ideal that was not formally protected until the early twentieth century. Scholars were subject to retribution or dismissal at the whim of the political state, boards of trustees, heavy-handed administrators, or financial benefactors. Examples abound of academic freedom's abridgment in the history of American higher education, but scholars became particularly vulnerable targets during the 1890s, particularly those who criticized the preeminence of big business or its philosophies. Many high profile examples illustrate the late–Gilded Age witch hunts: the 1893 dismissal of Richard Ely from the University of Wisconsin for his views on the corporation's abuse of labor; the 1896 dismissal of John R. Commons from Indiana University for the same offense; the pressure put on the eminent sociologist William Graham Sumner to stop using Herbert Spencer's *The Study of Sociology* in his classes at Yale; and the 1900 dismissal of Edward R. Ross from Stanford University—at the insistence of the wife of the institution's founder and chief donor—because of a series of speeches opposing Asian immigration. Indeed, the rash of faculty dismissals in the latter part of the Gilded Age led one Kansas State scholar to lament in 1901 that "with the arrogance equalling that of the slave power, our plutocracy has issued its edict that the colleges and universities must fall into line."

In 1915 the American Association of University Professors (AAUP) was formed, largely as a bastion against any possible infringements of academic freedom during World War I. Many from within and without the academy decried the new institution as a union that was only lightly disguised as a professional organization. Nevertheless, after weathering both the firings for disloyalty during the war and a steamy controversy over the signing of loyalty oaths at the height of the depression, in 1940 the AAUP, in association with the Association of American Colleges (AAC) passed the Statement of Principles of Academic Freedom. This document asserted that "the common good depends on the free search for truth and its free exposition," and that "academic freedom in its teaching aspect is fundamental for the protection of the rights of the teacher in teaching and of the student to freedom in learning." Yet the statement also made it clear that this freedom "carries with it duties correlative with rights," as it warned the teacher not to "introduce into his teaching controversial matter which has no relation to his subject." The instructor was also reminded that "he should at all times . . . exercise appropriate restraint . . . [and] make every effort to indicate that he is not an institutional spokesman." Despite the AAUP's vigilance, several states formed committees in the early 1940s that were charged with ferreting out "subversive" elements on the nation's college campuses. The investigations of one such committee, the Rapp-Coudert Committee of the New York State legislature, led to the dismissal of British philosopher Bertrand Russell from a professorate at the College of the City of New York.

The postwar period brought with it an onslaught of such investigations, most notably those of the House Committee on Un-American Activities (HUAC), formed in 1938 but given a rebirth by the fear that the Soviet Union was working from within our borders, largely in the open air of the universities, which were protected by their claims to "academic freedom." HUAC was particularly noxious to academics, who were dragged before the committee in large numbers to defend everything from their past affiliations to their present teaching of everything from Soviet studies to Jewish culture. Senator Joseph McCarthy of Wisconsin, as part of his crusade to ferret out communist infiltrators from high government offices, increased his exposure by targeting institutions of higher learning as well. He argued that he would be particularly excoriated for this role, as "the more you do that, all hell breaks loose. From coast to coast you hear the screaming of interference with academic freedom," a freedom that he defined as "their right to force you to hire them to teach your children a philosophy in which you do not believe." The AAUP argued that membership in *any* political party or organization was not in and of itself cause for dismissal, but throughout the 1950s it was but a voice in a wilderness of oppression.

Syracuse University in the postwar period was, by any measure, a conservative campus in a conservative city served by a conservative press. In this regard, Syracuse University fit the national norm. Several scholars and observers of the 1950s have noted that the vast majority of universities withdrew into themselves to escape the repression of the early cold war period, taking with them their most thoughtful scholars, who either waited out the witch hunts or resigned, and the students, who had no role models on either the faculty or the administration who would lead them toward questioning either campus or national political structures. Being a conservative campus did not shield Syracuse from attacks by the conservative watchdogs of the period. It is in the stories of these attacks that Syracuse breaks from the norm—its chancellor defended his faculty members.

As noted earlier, Tolley dealt with his faculty members with the sense of noblesse oblige that typified the chief executive officers of the 1950s. Secure in his belief that he knew what was best for his faculty, Tolley kept his finger in every area of faculty hiring, advancement, and development. But despite his proclivity for micromanaging his administrators, Tolley was no corporate martinet. He had long been associated with the development of the issue of academic freedom in American colleges and universities. From 1936 to 1944, he had served as chairman of the Committee on Academic Freedom of the Association of American Colleges. In this role, he was largely responsible for the preparation of the 1940 Statement of Principles of Academic Freedom. Unlike many of his contemporaries, who made sweeping statements about the need to eradicate the communist menace from their campuses, Tolley began the postwar era being more of a progressive on the issue, arguing at one point that a lot of the suspicion between the United States and the Soviet Union might have been avoided if there had been less "fumbling" in American foreign policy. In Tolley, Syracuse had one of the few unvarnished supporters of academic freedom that could be found in higher education during the 1950s. This was not to say that Tolley led a quixotic public crusade against McCarthyism—far from it. He covered his advocacy for several embattled faculty members with committee support and statements of condemnation of the general goals of the communist party. But Tolley was not about to allow conservative excesses to stop his faculty from following an argument "withersoever it may lead."

*   *   *

Critics on the right had long held Maxwell in their sights. They made reference to the "red flag that flew over Maxwell Hall," or referred to it as the "little red schoolhouse" or "Marxwell" for its supposed liberal leanings. In point of fact, the opposite was true during the 1950s. Maxwell repressed its political liberalism during the 1950s, as did most other schools of public affairs. Although there was much internal grumbling over the course of the congressional investigations, little was written or opined by Maxwell's leading professors that took McCarthyism to task. In fact, some of the most widely read material from Maxwell scholars, including historian Warren Walsh and Edward E. ("Bob") Palmer, were impassioned anticommunist works (the introduction to Palmer's book warned that "now more than ever we need bold and imaginative people who might provide the leadership to help us meet the challenge of a world almost half of which has gone mad on the communist lie").

One would not automatically think that Paul Appleby, dean of Maxwell from 1947 to 1956, would become the center of a fight to defend academic freedom. The quiet Appleby was a former newspaperman whose roots in the New Deal and World War II bureaucracy were key to the expansion of Maxwell into Washington. However, it was Appleby's scholarship that ruffled the feathers of HUAC. In 1949 Appleby wrote an article for the *Yale Review* that was a condensation of his book *Big Democracy*. In both the book and the article, Appleby defended the growth of the government bureaucracy—a topic guaranteed to anger conservatives. Maxwell economist Jesse Burkhead later remembered that Appleby told him that Tolley had been "subjected to considerable complaint on the part of prominent alumni and perhaps even members of the Board of Trustees about that article." But Burkhead also remembered that in "brusque notes," Tolley had defended his right to write what he chose. A more public blow-up followed when the Syracuse press reminded its patrons that Alger Hiss, who was at the time being grilled by both HUAC and the courts for his alleged participation in a communist youth group prior to his employment with the State Department, had been the speaker at Appleby's installation as dean of Maxwell. For a week or so, Appleby was subjected to a violent attack from a radio talk show host. In both of these cases, Appleby was exonerated by the Loyalty Board, but only after a full field investigation by the Federal Bureau of Investigation (FBI) had been completed.

However, Appleby continued to be a target of the Washington

thought police. In 1953 he was contacted by the chief counsel for the Internal Security Subcommittee of the Senate Judiciary Committee to explain a letter he had written in 1946, claiming that "a man in the employ of the Government has just as much right to be a member of the Communist Party as he has to be a member of the Democrat or Republican party." An obviously chastened Appleby replied that the statement "was a sentence contained within an intra-departmental memorandum written hastily as a way of treating a gossipy kind of charge of Communist affiliation or leaning in the case of an employee known to me as *not* a Red. . . . Even so, my memo was less idiotic at the time it was written than it would be now." There is no evidence that Tolley knew anything about this incident, but the following year, after serving as the university's commencement speaker, Mutual Security Administrator Harold Stassen wrote Tolley with a concern about the contacts between Appleby and the liberals of the Progressive party. Disgusted, Tolley did not even respond to Stassen, and he did not tell Appleby about the correspondence until many years later. In July 1968, following Appleby's death, his wife wrote Tolley, thanking him for his loyalty. Tolley's response to her: "I had forgotten that I had ever shared with you or Paul the story of my experience with Mr. Stassen. We were black-listed for several years, but it was in the cause of freedom and was an easy decision to make."

Appleby's travails stayed rather private, but the case of two other university faculty members made national headlines. William Martin, who had been the chairman of the Mathematics Department from 1943 to 1946, had been an active member of the Communist party before coming to Syracuse. In his testimony to HUAC, Martin claimed that Abe Gelbart, then an associate professor of mathematics at Syracuse, was also an active party member when he had been a graduate student at Massachusetts Institute of Technology (MIT), and he had been present when other party members had visited Martin's house. Tolley recommended to Gelbart that he invoke his Fifth Amendment rights not to testify against himself. Gelbart took Tolley's advice. On May 28, 1953, Gelbart appeared before an executive session of HUAC in Washington. Under oath, he said that he was not then a member of the Communist party, but invoked the Fifth Amendment when asked if he had ever been a member of the Communist party. In previous private testimony, Gelbart told Robert L. Kunzig, counsel to the committee, that he had never been a communist; but he did not say that under oath because it would directly conflict with the testimony of those from MIT, thus leading to expensive legal battles.

Despite this testimony, Tolley was immediately under great pressure—most notably from the Syracuse press and several members of his board—to fire Gelbart. Incensed at what he perceived to be a simple issue of the protection of academic freedom, the chancellor took the opportunity to educate his bosses on the subject. On May 29, 1953, Tolley read a statement to a meeting of the full board, a statement that was immediately made public. While arguing that "no one should challenge the right of Congress to conduct inquiries and investigations of un-American activities," Tolley warned that even though colleges cooperate with those investigations, "they should . . . distinguish carefully their responsibilities as custodians of academic freedom from the responsibilities of Congress and the responsibilities of the courts." Tolley railed that "there is no room at Syracuse for a member of the Communist Party," but he enjoined that "we have tried, however, to protect members of the faculty from false accusations and have followed the good American practice of assuming innocence until guilt is clearly proven."

Tolley's was a rather singular statement. Few, if any, college presidents were speaking in such a way in 1953. However, Tolley needed to protect many people in this case—Gelbart, the institution, and himself. Therefore, Tolley charged the executive committee of the College of Liberal Arts, chaired by Dean Eric Faigle and joined by the chair of the campus chapter of the AAUP, to offer its recommendation on whether Gelbart should be retained on the faculty. After an investigation that took several months, the university announced that its committee had recommended that Gelbart be retained, a decision that, according to one report, "was strongly supported by Chancellor Tolley before the Board of Trustees." However, what the press was *not* told about the committee's decision was that it had also voted that Gelbart should not have invoked the Fifth Amendment against the advice of private and legal counsel, while at the same time privately and repeatedly proclaiming his innocence of the charge of communism (8–2), and it had unanimously recommended that Gelbart be retained *on probation* (meaning ineligible for promotion or for contract teaching) until such time as the chancellor and the board saw fit to remove that probation.[1]

In Tolley's mind, the committee had decided correctly. Both academic freedom and institutional viability had been protected. In November 1953 he told the trustees that they should understand that "dissent and heresy we must defend or freedom of inquiry would be emptied of meaning. Conspiracy and treason we must oppose if we are to preserve a government which fosters and preserves freedom."

*   *   *

Tolley's private defense of his faculty members was courageous enough, even when augmented by committee support. However, Tolley took the extraordinary step of taking on HUAC in public. In a February 1956 interview with the *Syracuse Post-Standard,* Tolley noted that internal communism was no longer a big issue in America, the way that it was in "backward countries and in many countries that are not backward." Later that year, in an address before the Syracuse Manufacturers Association entitled "New Issues for a New Day," Tolley declared that "without minimizing the danger of the Communist conspiracy, I think it is safe to say that the battle for men's minds in America will not be won by the Communist party. The victory here is clear-cut and final." Once again, the Syracuse newspapers exploded in opposition, arguing that Tolley was selling short the potential danger of the Red Menace.

It was now time for the faculty to support Tolley. Jesse Burkhead remembered that Roscoe Martin, then the chairman of the Political Science Department, lined up a number of faculty members to speak in favor of Tolley's speech before the faculty senate; several of them, including Burkhead, did so. Martin then made a formal motion of support for Tolley, and after a rather spirited debate, the motion carried.

In the eye of the storm that has been pejoratively named McCarthyism, Tolley defended faculty members who were under official

---

1. Gelbart was retained on the faculty, was subsequently promoted to a full professorship, and remained at Syracuse until 1958, when he assumed the directorship of Yeshiva University's new Graduate School of Mathematical Sciences.

scrutiny. This was extraordinary for the time. But in many ways even more extraordinary was the faculty's official statement of support when Tolley came under fire. In 1965 many of them would look back at that moment and shake their heads in amazement.

Ben Schwartzwalder and Lew Andreas

CHAPTER 10

Sports, Part One

In October 1954 Tolley noted that many university supporters were upset that Canada Dry, a sponsor for broadcasts of Orange football, was promoting their products as a drink mixer. Athletic Director Lew Andreas dutifully informed Sports Information Director Arnold Burdick to contact Canada Dry. They changed their ad.

I was right at the beginning of a fine tradition.

—Bill Gabor

THE UNIVERSITY'S first football game was a practice game with Syracuse High School in 1889—the Orange won, 28–0. In their first intercollegiate game on September 25, 1907, Syracuse defeated Hobart—also by the score of 28–0. Attending games in the venerable Archbold Stadium, with its echoes, swirling winds, and biting November cold, was the most endearing collegiate memory for many alumni. As was the case for most large institutions, the fate of the football team was the yardstick by which many alumni measured their continued loyalty to the institution: good teams meant good alumni involvement. Much of the hope of football—and of university sports in general—had long been in the hands of Lew Andreas. A native of Sterling, Illinois, Andreas had served as an ambulance driver in World War I. In 1919 he entered Syracuse University, graduating with his bachelor's degree in 1921. For the next four years, he taught at Norwich High School, resigning to come back to Syracuse as a physical education instructor and head basketball coach in 1924. Andreas coached basketball from 1924 until 1950, compiling a

record of 355–134 and a national championship team in 1925–26. In
1927, he was also named head football coach, a position he held until 1929. In addition to his coaching responsibilities, Andreas served
as athletic director from 1937 to 1963. One former football player
described Andreas as a "man of principle . . . [a] straight arrow . . .
you may not have liked Lou, but you had great respect for him." Tolley trusted no man more with decisions on athletics.

Tolley, however, had inherited a football program that was on the
mend. The 1936 season had resulted in the worst record for a Syracuse team in forty years: 1–7. Coach Vic Hanson resigned and was
replaced in 1937 by Ossie Solem. A gentleman who rarely lost his
temper, Solem brought with him both coaching and intellectual cre-
dentials—he had played end for the University of Minnesota, and after his playing days he had earned a law degree at the Northwestern
Law School at Minneapolis. He had coached for Drake, Luther, and
Grinnell Colleges, and he came to Syracuse from the University of
Iowa, where he had served as both coach and athletic director. Solem
brought with him an extraordinary group of assistants; Charles "Bud"
Wilkinson, Clarence "Biggie" Munn, and William Boelter would all
go on to head coaching positions. Solem immediately opened up
Syracuse's game, as he introduced the Y formation to Archbold. In so
doing, Solem reestablished the program. In the fall of 1938, SU won
its first game with Colgate in thirteen years, a victory that led to a
near riot scene in downtown Syracuse. Solem's 1941 squad went
5–2–1, established a new rushing record, and scored more points
than any SU team in a decade. The Orangemen improved the next
year to 6–3 but dropped contests to Colgate and the North Carolina
Pre-Flight Training Center.

The 1943 season was canceled thanks to the war, but the sport was
reinstated following the June 1944 Normandy invasion (the argument advanced by the university was that D-Day had brought hope
to the war effort, therefore football could be reinstated at Archbold).
However, it is not surprising that the departure of men into the service led to several mediocre seasons. Wartime football at Syracuse, as
elsewhere, was played with teams made up largely of 4F's or men
waiting to be drafted who oftentimes heeded their country's call in
midseason. Syracuse went 2–4–1 in 1944 and 1–6 in 1945, despite

the advent of a new rule designed to speed up play—a team could advance a fumble. The star during those two seasons was halfback Ed Dolan, who made the All-East team in 1944.

It was, however, the rivalry with nearby Colgate University that mattered more to the Orange faithful than did the win-loss record. In 1944 Solem's team beat Colgate 43–13; it was Syracuse's first victory over their rival in five years. However, in 1945 the Red Raiders beat Syracuse 7–6 in the last game of the season. Because of that loss, not the team's dismal one-win season, pressure was put on Solem to resign. He left that winter for Springfield College, from where he retired in 1955.

After the war, the situation on the gridiron mirrored the situation in the classroom. The GI Bill allowed many young men who might not have gotten the opportunity to play college football to try out for the team. Many of those prospective athletes were older; many had been on a team before they left for the war. In 1946, 240 young men tried out for the Orange squad—all of them were veterans. The man chosen to coach this rather eclectic mix of athletes was Clarence "Biggie" Munn. Solem had brought Munn with him in 1937 to coach the line; after one year at Syracuse, Munn left to coach the line at the University of Michigan for eight years. Upon his return, Munn would stay at Syracuse for one season, and his team of veterans—both of the war and of football—went a respectable 4–5. However, Munn could not conform to Tolley's belief—a belief that was rigidly enforced throughout Tolley's tenure, long after it had become fashionable to do so—that college athletes should also be college students. When Munn came to Syracuse, he brought a number of players with him thinking that they would simply ease into the program. At the end of the first semester, many on the freshman squad flunked out because they had not been going to class. Munn was furious, telling his coaches that "this never happened at Michigan, and they didn't expect our kids to go to class." At the end of the 1946 season, Munn left to take over at Michigan State in 1947, taking three of his top assistants with him.

Munn was replaced by Reeves "Ribs" Baysinger, who had been the freshman coach and director of freshman athletics at Syracuse for almost twenty-five years. It was a logical choice for a team that was rebuilding—Baysinger had coached virtually every member of the varsity squad while they were frosh, and his personality was particularly suited for motivating young men. Bernie Custis, who would change the way that the nation looked at college quarterbacks, voiced the opinion of most of the veterans of Baysinger's squads when he remembered that the coach was "very reserved . . . [but I had a] close and warm relationship with him . . . he was like a father figure to me." Baysinger tried to start fresh, by taking the team to a new preseason training center at Paul Smith's College in the Adirondacks. He also changed the passing game that Syracuse had been using with only minimal success over the past decade, centering most of his offense around his tailbacks and fullbacks. The offensive system was the I formation—a single wing, where the quarterback was really a tailback who often received a snap, but not always. It was the beginning of the dependence on a blasting running game that would be the hallmark of Orange football for the next thirty-five years. With such changes, the 1947 season was proclaimed a "rebuilding" season in the press.

But the 1947 season will always be remembered for the beginning of a different type of rebuilding, one that would affect the fortunes of the entire athletic program. Early in the morning of January 12, 1947, fire trucks responded to a call at the Archbold gym. The blaze had started in the bowling alleys (Andreas remembered that as he made a postfire inspection of the wreckage, he found that in the alleys the heat had shriveled bowling balls to the size of baseballs) and spread upward. The subzero temperatures hindered the efforts of the firefighting crew, and when the fire was finally under control it was quickly evident that the entire rear portion of the gym had been destroyed. No lives were lost, but one fireman was injured when he was struck in the abdomen and knocked temporarily unconscious by a burst in the hose line. The largest fire in the university's history, the loss was estimated at $2,000,000.

The firemen had, however, succeeded in salvaging the front portion of the building, which soon reopened to a restricted athletic program. An immediate decision was made to rebuild the rear portion of the gym to meet urgent student needs, but both the 1948 basketball and the football teams felt the pinch of losing the building where they had practiced, and the locker rooms where their gear and training facilities had been housed. Andreas had to look all over Syracuse to find places to play and to practice. Despite such adversity, Baysinger's 1947 squad finished at 3–7, a record that featured a 7–0 defeat of Colgate (thanks to Walter "Slivers" Slovenski's fake kick on third down in the fourth quarter, which he followed with a sixty-five-yard run for a touchdown) after which the fans tore down the goalposts.

The next season was nothing if not dismal. The 1–8 record was only partially brightened by the varsity appearance of the first true football star of the Tolley years. Bernie Custis was the first black on a Syracuse University athletic team since Wilmeth Sidat-Singh played football in the late 1930s; more important, Custis became the nation's first black starting quarterback in the collegiate ranks. From Philadelphia, one of the reasons Custis chose Syracuse was because the starting tailback had graduated the year before. A great runner who could throw the ball better than any quarterback in modern memory—the Syracuse press dubbed him "The Arm"—Custis fit right into Baysinger's I formation. Nevertheless, Custis was virtually the only solid player on that year's squad, and the eight losses led to the university's worst record since 1894, when they had not won a game (their only victory was over Niagara University, which dropped football that year, humiliated by their loss to the lowly Syracuse). Custis, however, was named to the All-East squad, after breaking the Orange record for total offense.

The biggest outcome of that dismal season, however, was a revolt against Baysinger that led to the creation of several committees that would change the face of sports at Syracuse University. Following the end of the season, three Football Fact-Finding Committees—one for the board of trustees, one for the Varsity Club, and one for the student body, each ran three-month investigations. All three committees recommended changes in assistant coaches; the first two recommended a change in the head coach. As a result, Andreas recommended that Baysinger be given a job at either Triple Cities or Utica College.

For his part, Baysinger blamed the situation on both his predecessor and Tolley. In a meeting with Andreas and Finla Crawford (to whom Tolley had delegated the responsibility of negotiating with the coaches), Baysinger charged that Munn had hurt the program by bringing with him players who were academically unqualified. He also advanced an argument that would receive a deaf ear from the chancellor—that Tolley's policy that an athlete must work for his room and board put the Orange at a disadvantage when compared to other schools that gave their players full scholarships. On this point, Tolley would not budge. All athletes were expected to hold down jobs to help pay for their educational expenses (remembering that most of them also received GI Bill benefits). More important, Tolley was not yet ready to give Baysinger, or any other football coach, more than twelve scholarships.

Baysinger was offered a two-year contract and was asked to hire a new staff. He refused on both counts, and on March 1, 1949, he and his entire staff were fired (Roy Simmons, Sr., a backfield coach but also head coach of boxing and lacrosse, was the least affected by the decision because he would retain these posts). But the firing of Baysinger was not the only outcome of the fact-finding committee. Tolley had long wanted a tighter ship at the athletics department, and he used this opportunity to get it. Andreas retired as head basketball coach to concentrate on his role as athletic director. Also the Administrative Board on Athletics, created as an advisory committee in 1931, now took greater administrative control of and responsibility for the various athletic programs.

The failure of Munn and Baysinger had given Syracuse a reputation as a "coaches graveyard." It had also embittered alumni and students, and hardened Tolley in his dealings with his coaches. All that was about to change.

*   *   *

Floyd "Ben" Schwartzwalder was a native of Huntington, West Virginia. Despite his light build—ninety-five pounds—he won the spot as quarterback of his high school's freshman squad. Determined to build himself up, Schwartzwalder ended up lettering in four sports, and at 152 pounds he centered at West Virginia University (where he also wrestled). After his 1933 graduation, he was a high school coach until 1942. During the war, Schwartzwalder served as an officer in the Eighty-Second Airborne, and he jumped three times in combat.

During the D-Day operation, Schwartzwalder's unit landed far behind enemy lines, and he not only succeeded in organizing his scattered command, but one week later his unit brought in several German prisoners. Personally decorated by General Matthew Ridgeway, Schwartzwalder retired with the rank of lieutenant colonel. After the war, Schwartzwalder returned to coaching. At Muhlenberg College (Allentown, Pa.) he compiled a three-year record of 25–5 before coming to Syracuse in 1949.

Schwartzwalder served at Syracuse for twenty-five years. In that quarter century, Syracuse went to seven bowl games, won four Lambert Trophies signifying the best team in the East, had twenty-two straight winning seasons, 153 victories, and one national championship. But the biggest immediate difference was in outlook. Custis remembered that when Schwartzwalder came aboard, "[He] brought a winning attitude . . . we had never known that in the Baysinger regime." It was not done with gentle persuasion; it was done with a paratrooper's toughness. Schwartzwalder would not mince words with his players—Archbold Stadium quickly became his domain, and he expected that his players would exude the same power on game day that he directed toward them during practices. John Mackey, who would play for Schwartzwalder in the early 1960s and become the greatest tight end in the history of Orange football, remembered that Schwartzwalder would start doing push-ups when the players were climbing the ropes, and *continue* doing push-ups until they were *done* climbing the ropes. Yet Mackey was quick to say that this leathery coach "communicated with me."

The university knew what it wanted to sell; the first sentence of the *Alumni News* as it announced the appointment of the new coach: "Schwartzwalder is an offense-minded coach, whose teams in the past have been of the high-scoring variety." But this was not what the Orange faithful had received from Muhlenberg. Schwartzwalder continued and intensified Baysinger's approach to a power game. It was Schwartzwalder who replaced Baysinger's I system with the T system, where the backs lined up behind the quarterback, who had the option of handing off the ball to one of the backs or passing the ball. Schwartzwalder threw the ball even less than had Baysinger (Mackey remembered that under Schwartzwalder, pass patterns were not required of the tight ends; when he entered into the pros, Mackey did not even know *how* to run them). The slogan Three Yards and a Cloud of Dust was made-to-order for Schwartzwalder's teams, but it was not always the stuff that made for entertaining football from the stands. Schwartzwalder's detractors (and, despite the legend that has surrounded his tenure, there were many) whined when he refused to pass, even on obvious passing downs. Those same critics sniped at the rumpled clothes that Schwartzwalder wore to games and his tendency to be openly demonstrative on the sidelines. It mattered not to Schwartzwalder, who approached his job with the confidence of a tenured full professor. Schwartzwalder remembered only one thing that hung around his neck like an albatross: "the one ultimatum they served on me . . . I had to beat Colgate."

The 1949 season ended at 4–5, but there were several hopeful high points. The Orange beat Rutgers for its first road victory since 1946; Custis dazzled the crowd against Holy Cross, with three touchdown passes and one rushing touchdown—and they beat Colgate 35–7. Flush with success, during the off-season the university renovated. Six thousand new seats were added to Archbold in time for the opening kickoff of the 1950 season, along with a forty-yard-long press box that could accommodate 250 people. That season the team improved to 5–5, but Colgate was victorious by six points—the margin of victory was a Custis pass dropped in the end zone. The 1951 season was the end of Schwartzwalder's rebuilding period. The team finished at 5–4, the university's first winning season since 1942, and beat Colgate 9–0. After the final victory of the season, over Boston College, Schwartzwalder was lifted onto the shoulders of his team.

In 1952, for the first time since the national championship team of 1926, everything jelled. The 7–2 Orangemen won the Lambert Trophy, losing only to Bolling Air Force Base (made up of pros and former college stars) and Michigan State (against former Orange coach Biggie Munn). A stunning upset victory over Holy Cross, 20–19, put Syracuse into the bowl picture; a 25–7 defeat of Penn State iced it. When the team was invited to the Orange Bowl—the first bowl invitation in the school's history—the students formed a snake dance and slithered downtown to meet the team at the railroad station.

On January 1, 1953, however, Schwartzwalder and his upstart

Orangemen got a dose of reality at the hands of national powerhouse Alabama. At the end of the first quarter, Alabama led by only 7–6. Then all hell broke loose, as the Orange were annihilated, 61–6, and Alabama broke twelve Orange Bowl records. It was not a total loss, however; the bowl profit of $50,000 was sent to the Fieldhouse Foundation for the building of what would become known as Manley Fieldhouse.

The Orange Bowl was also the university's first opportunity to showcase what had become one of the best college bands in the country. They were billed as "One Hundred Men and a Girl," and the girl—baton twirler Dottie Grover—achieved celebrity status that

Dottie Grover

rivaled that of the football players. Attractive, talented, and innovative, Grover and her first band director at Syracuse, Howard Kelly,
choreographed her twirling to the band's music, one of the first college bands to produce such a show. There *was* a question as to
whether the band would go on the trip, but thanks to Grover's popularity, it was settled in the band's favor. In fact, the team's success led
to a welcome change of clothing—the band had been wearing blue
ski suits, quite inappropriate for Miami, so Syracuse's Learbury
Clothier donated navy blue blazers, gray slacks, and white straw
hats. Grover showcased her twirling talents to an east Florida version
of "Sleigh Ride" and was an instant national hit. Throughout her
time at Syracuse, Grover was busy all through the year with perfor-
mances, honorary chairmanships, and fashion shows. Truly, along
with the famous Saltine Warrior, Grover's presence *meant* Syracuse
University sports during the early 1950s.

The 1953 Orangemen followed their previous year's success with
a respectable 5–3–1 record, highlighted by a 34–18 victory over Colgate. Guard Bob Fleck was named to *Collier*'s All-America Team, and
center Ted Kukowski was named to the Paramount newsreel and
Focus magazine team. However, there was no return bowl bid, and as
soon as the season ended, the grumbling began. For many fans,
Schwartzwalder's style of play was at fault—"If only he'd pass on
third down"—but for Schwartzwalder, the culprits were the same as
they had been for Baysinger: scholarships and Tolley. The previous
year he had been dressed down by Tolley after complaining, in a
speech to alumni in Buffalo, about the lack of scholarships. (Tolley
remembered telling his head coach that "one more speech like that
and you can leave for Mars. You come in and quarrel with me about
scholarships; don't promote an insurrection among alumni.") Learning his lesson for the moment, in December 1953 Schwartzwalder
went through the proper channels. He went to Andreas, continuing
his complaint that the football players were required to work five
hours plus during the 1953 season, and that he had been told that
the hours would be *increased* for the next season. Perhaps thanks to
Schwartzwalder's persistence, perhaps thanks to the team's success,
perhaps thanks to pressure put on him by influential alumni, Tolley
was finally convinced. In 1952 the chancellor increased the number

of scholarships to sixteen, then twenty-one in 1953. By 1963–64, the number had hit twenty-five.[1]

But it wasn't the Orange Bowl, or the increase in scholarships, or even the coaching abilities of Ben Schwartzwalder that yanked the Syracuse University football program into the big time. It was the impact made by two multitalented fullbacks—one a moody bruiser whose brute strength bulldozed over opposing linemen; the other a quiet leader whose skittery running style simply ran him *past* opposing linemen.

*   *   *

James N. Brown was born on St. Simon's Island, off the coast of Georgia. When he was seven, he went to live with his mother in Spinney Hill, a black community near Manhasset, Long Island. He quickly fell in with a gang, the Gaylords. Sports, however, changed his life—he was so popular in his Manhasset high school that he was elected justice of the student court. Brown was rejected by Syracuse University twice, despite a favorable report from his superintendent of schools and principal. Kenneth Molloy, Manhasset lawyer and chairman of the Fieldhouse Project, threatened to resign his post on that fund-raising committee unless Tolley spoke to Dean of Admissions John Hafer and got Brown admitted. Tolley interceded, but during his first year, Brown had no scholarship—Molloy took care of raising the money to send Brown to the school himself.

To Schwartzwalder, the key to Jim Brown was his "indestructibility. Jim never missed a minute of play due to injury in three years of varsity ball. And he was always the fellow the other club was gunning for." Yet Brown was as well known for his volatility as for his ability. He threatened to quit the team many times; several times Molloy, or sometimes Roy Simmons, talked him into staying. Brown often slept at practice and regularly skipped calisthenics. Once, after being berated by Schwartzwalder, Brown walked off the field. Schwartzwalder remembered: "I was tired of him. . . . But I was told by peo-

1. For the sake of comparison: in 1953, the University of Illinois had 155 scholarships, Penn State had 70, Colgate had 44, and, according to Lefty James, Cornell had "as many as [we] need" (Andreas to Tolley, 1953, Tolley Records, box 18, Athletics Folder).

ple that I had to take him back. They didn't care what concessions I had to make. Must have been a thousand people come to see me. So I talked to Jim."

Brown began his Orange football career in 1954 on the second team varsity; he was assigned jersey number 44 primarily because no one had ever used it before. Before the year was up, he had worked up from fifth-string to part-time varsity player. He made the first team for good in his sixth game, when he ran for 151 yards against Cornell. Brown gained 439 yards for the 4–4 Orangemen, a team that defeated Colgate for the fourth straight year, 31–12. Few observers expected that the 1955 squad would do much better—one preseason publication predicted that the team would win only one of its games. However, Brown singlehandedly took Syracuse to a 5–3 record, leading the team to upset wins over Army and nationally ranked West Virginia, and to a 26–19 victory over Colgate. Brown, who had now been dubbed the "Manhasset Mauler" in the press, finished the season with 666 yards, seven touchdowns, and All-East honors.

Brown's senior season not only propelled Syracuse into its second bowl game, but it turned out to be the stuff of legend. The season began with a shocking 26–12 upset win against powerful Maryland. Brown ran for 154 yards—more than the entire Maryland team. Against seven victories, the team's only loss was to Pittsburgh, 14–7. Brown's most stunning performance came during the season closer, a 61–7 blitzing of Colgate during which the back scored 43 points, gained 197 yards, and set a new Syracuse one-season rushing record. The 1956 Orange were easy Lambert Trophy winners; it was Syracuse's best season since 1923, when Roy Simmons quarterbacked the Orange to an 8–1. In January 1957, Schwartzwalder was named the coach of *Sports Illustrated* magazine's silver anniversary All-American roster.

Although they were the best in the East, on paper the 7–1 Orangemen were not a team that could rival other teams of national caliber. They received a bid to the January 1957 Cotton Bowl against Texas Christian University of the Southwest Conference largely because Navy had refused a bid. However, the Orange came close to pulling off the upset of the season, losing 28–27 on an extra-point kick (Brown was kicking) blocked by TCU's Chico Mendoza. Right halfback Jim Ridlon's oft-quoted comment—"We had a lousy football team, and if it weren't for Jimmy Brown we would have had nothing"—was far too exaggerative to explain any one loss; Ridlon himself was a fourth-round draft choice that year by the San Francisco 49ers.

For his part, Brown was a unanimous All-American pick.[2] He finished third in the nation in rushing—986 total yards gained, with an average of about 125 per game—and near the top in total offense and scoring as well. He was also the first-round draft choice of the National Football League's Cleveland Browns. Syracuse's first four-letter man (football, track, basketball, and lacrosse) since Jim Konstanti in 1939, Brown was, by most accounts, the greatest pure athlete in the history of Syracuse University. Even the normally cryptical Schwartzwalder gushed to the press that Brown was "the greatest straight-ahead runner I have ever seen." Nevertheless, Paul Hornung of 2–8 Notre Dame won the 1956 Heisman Trophy. Even the normally staid Syracuse newspapers shouted racism.

The two seasons immediately following Brown's departure for the pros gave the Orange faithful fits. The 1957 team dropped to 5–3–1, despite a major upset against Pitt and another defeat of Colgate. The 1958 team opened the season ranked number ten in the nation, and went 8–1 (their only loss was caused by a new rule that year—the two-point conversion—as Holy Cross beat the Orange with a run into the end zone). However, in the Orange Bowl against Oklahoma, coached by former Orange assistant Bud Wilkinson, Syracuse lost 21–6, with the Sooners getting all their points in the third quarter. After this third straight bowl loss, Schwartzwalder was hammered once again in the Syracuse press for not opening up the game after Oklahoma had jumped to a 21–0 lead. The criticism did not stop even when Schwartzwalder revealed that his all-East quarterback, Chuck Zimmerman, had been knocked groggy in the first quarter. All criticism, however, would stop the following year.

*   *   *

He was a coachable kid from Elmira, New York, who played football, baseball, and basketball at Elmira Free Academy. He almost went to Notre Dame, but Jim Brown talked to the high school senior

2. For a complete list of sports All-Americans between 1942 and 1969, see appendix D.

and convinced him to come to Syracuse; thanks to this discussion, and the influence of Tony DeFilippo, an Elmira attorney and Syracuse alumnus, Ernie Davis came to Syracuse and inherited number 44. Comparisons between Brown and Davis are legion, but their styles were as different as night and day—Brown ran over the opposition; Davis eluded it. Schwartzwalder, who was loathe to place any of his players on a pedestal, would only say that "Ernie might be a little cuter, but maybe Jimmy had a little more power. Their speed is reasonably compatible." While Brown was the university's best athlete, Davis was its most important and most influential. As a sophomore, he would lead the school to its first and, to date, only national championship in football.

Sports Illustrated called it "Orange Hell on Piety Hill." The backfield, dubbed the "Four Furies"—quarterback Dave Sarette, halfbacks Ger Schwedes and Ernie Davis, and fullback Art Baker—got most of the press. However, the difference between the 1959 squad and those that came before was the quality of its defensive line. Known as the "Sizeable Seven," Fred Mautino, Maury Youmans, Bob Yates, Bruce Tarbox, Al Bemiller, Roger Davis, and Gerry Skonieczki opened the holes for Davis and Schwedes, and—most important—made it through the entire season without major injuries.

The 1959 Syracuse University Orangemen rank as one of the best collegiate football teams of all time. Consider the team:

- First in rushing offense, total offense, points scored, rushing defense, and total defense. Tied for the most touchdown passes.
- The *entire* first string made at least Honorable Mention All-East.
- Schwartzwalder was named Coach of the Year.
- Three linemen—Roger Davis, Yates, and Mautino—were named All-Americans.
- Ernie Davis, who broke Jim Brown's records for average yards per carry and for a single game, was also named an All-American.
- Schwedes's sixteen touchdowns set a new Syracuse record, and his one hundred points scored was second in the nation.

Consider also each game of what was to be a perfect season:

- University of Kansas, 31–25. Syracuse outgained the Jayhawks 93–57, even with All-American John Hadl at quarterback.

- Maryland, 29–0. The Terrapins rushed for only eight yards in what was the first big game for Ernie Davis—77 yards and one touchdown.
- Navy, 32–6. The game was played in Norfolk—the first time that blacks had played in that stadium.
- Holy Cross, 42–6. The Crusaders were held to minus-28 yards of rushing.
- West Virginia, 44–0. The Orangemen had 589 yards of total offense.
- Pittsburgh, 35–0. At the end of their blanking of the Panthers, the Orange were ranked third in the nation.
- Penn State, 20–18. The closest call of the season, and, in many minds, the beginning of the great rivalry between the Orange and Nittany Lions. Joe Paterno, Penn State's backfield coach at the time, on Davis: "You can't instruct a boy to tackle a man if he can't catch him." At the end of the game, Syracuse was ranked number one in the country.
- Colgate 71–0. Eight separate Orangemen scored. On November 30, 1959, after stating the obvious—that the rivalry had "lost much of its traditional luster"—Tolley and Colgate president Needham Case announced that at the end of the 1962 season, the schools would no longer meet on the gridiron.
- Boston University 46–0. The Terriers were held to minus-88 yards rushing.
- UCLA, 36–8. The Orange had completed a perfect regular season. UCLA coach Billy Barnes: "They are one of the greatest teams I have ever seen."

The January 1960 Cotton Bowl against the University of Texas, which would decide not only the national championship but also whether the Orange would have a perfect season, was marred by several racial incidents. Syracuse's three black players—Davis, fullback Art Baker, and offensive lineman John Brown—were discriminated against in their housing and were asked ahead of time to leave the awards dinner at a point prior to its conclusion (however, Syracuse made it a condition of its playing that the black players be eligible to participate in all official functions—including that dinner). During the game, Texas players spit on Syracuse's black players. One fight broke out when Brown took a swing at Texas tackle Larry Stephens for calling him a "big black dirty nigger." One Syracuse player remembered it quite simply: "Texas was really dirty. We never met a bunch like that before." Nevertheless, as he had been all season long, Davis was the key to the game. He had pulled a hamstring before the game, and few expected him even to play. But he did, and his performance was superb. He caught an eighty-seven-yard touchdown pass and intercepted a Texas pass in the third quarter that led to a touchdown. Final score: Syracuse 23, Texas 14.

Immediately following the winning of the national championship, Tolley penned a reaction that would be absolutely inconceivable in the present day:

> I assume that if permission was given to students to miss classes following the long Christmas holidays such permission was given by his [Dean Faigle's] office. I think we need some new ground rules for next year. One of the most important questions is whether we should go to a bowl game two years in succession, (or if we are invited next year) three years in succession. If we do go to a bowl game is it possible to keep the members of the football squad hard at work in the

National champions, 1959

classroom until the official beginning of the Christmas vacation? If we do permit our boys to go to a bowl game should we have a spring practice in that particular year or could the spring practice be reduced in length and character so as to protect the academic program? Academic standards are easily eroded and I have the feeling that by making a series of minor concessions we are compromising our position that the athletes are held to precisely the same requirements as all other members of the student body.

*   *   *

In terms of money, attendance, and media attention, all other sports at Syracuse played second fiddle to football in the 1950s. However, 1959 was a championship year in another sport.

In 1851, Yale and Harvard began formal college rowing. Eight years later, Brown and Trinity College joined the two pacesetters. Representatives of Harvard, Brown, Amherst, and Bowdoin formed the Rowing Association of America in 1871. Citing the close proximity to the waters of Onondaga Lake, Syracusans had lobbied for a rowing team virtually since the inception of the school. However, Chancellor Alexander Winchell, an austere and somewhat foreboding scholar, refused to allow the sport to take hold. It was not until Chancellor James Roscoe Day gave his support to the endeavor that the first Syracuse University crew took to the water in 1900.

Suspended from 1942 until 1947, the sport hit an immediate resurgence. In 1947 the freshman crew won all its races, and in an unprecedented move they were designated as the university's official entry in the International Rowing Association (IRA) regatta at Poughkeepsie, where they came in second. However, the next year the team finished ninth at Poughkeepsie when the rigging of stroke Jack Castle snapped off and he was forced to jump overboard rather than weigh down the shell with an unemployed stroke. In 1949 Syracuse finished ninth again, and coach Ned Ten Eyck retired. He was replaced by Gosta "Gus" Eriksen, former freshman coach at Washington.

Crew had been badly hurt by the resurgence of football; Andreas remembered that the rowing teams were often populated with football players, until spring practice became an important event. However, in 1952 a decision was made that would yank the sport back to life. Poughkeepsie had been the site of the IRA regatta since 1895, but the city had become a shell of its former self after the war, with little interest in the regatta. In an attempt to revitalize prewar interest, the IRA first moved its contest to Marietta, Ohio, but spring floods and virtually unnavigable waters for two years in a row ended the IRA's Ohio connection. After considerable lobbying from Syracuse alumni and officials, most notably Andreas and Gordon Hoople, the IRA chose Onondaga Lake for the site of its fiftieth annual regatta, held on June 21, 1952. During the first three years of the regatta on Onondaga Lake, Navy was the dominant squad. The results were the same from 1952 to 1954—Navy was the clear winner, with Syracuse coming in ninth. In 1955 Cornell finally beat its rival from Annapolis, but the Syracuse crew continued to be disappointing.

To counter this trend, in 1955 a group of Syracuse rowing alums formed the Syracuse Alumni Rowing Association (SARA). Hoople served as its first president, and its first act was to engineer the resignation of Eriksen, who returned to his native Sweden to coach the national team. The new coach, Loren Schoel, came to Syracuse from Cornell, and immediately the fortunes of Syracuse rowing began to change. Although the 1956 varsity continued to be weak, the freshman beat out Navy by only a few yards to give the Syracuse frosh their first IRA championship since 1932. The following year, Syracuse placed fifth—its best showing in the regatta so far. Schoel opened the 1958 season with a practice camp in Tampa—it was the farthest that the team had been since a 1947 race in Seattle. That spring, the varsity race at the regatta was so close that the judges waited for a few moments to decide. Cornell beat out the Orange by only a few inches.

As it was in football, the 1959 season was the season of glory for the crew team. Early in the 1959 season, Schoel got his first victory—over Cornell, Navy, and Rutgers at Ithaca. At the IRA regatta, Wisconsin took first, and Syracuse beat out Navy for second place by one and one-tenth of a second. Syracuse then entered the Pan American Game trials, and defeated the Vesper Boat Club of Philadelphia on June 28. As a result, the 1959 crew became the first university team to represent the nation in any international event. The Pan American games were held in Chicago, and the Orange faced teams from Brazil, Canada, and Argentina. In an exciting race, Syracuse beat the Canadian boat by two lengths. The second world championship team in the school's history, the members of the crew were introduced to the crowd at Archbold during the halftime of a football game that October.

*   *   *

From 1924 to 1950, Andreas coached basketball in addition to his duties as athletic director. As was the case with football, the immediate postwar season was a rebuilding one for the Orange cagers. The 1944–45 squad went 7–12, a season that was highlighted by two losses to Colgate for the first time since 1931–32.

However, the sport sprang back with a vengeance in 1945–46, the first season that had returning veterans on the team. The squad featured several former servicemen; Bill Gabor and Larry Crandall, starting forwards, had both served as bombardiers, and Lew Spicer had been with the army. Most of the team had played freshman ball in 1942–43, just before they were drafted, and they had much of their eligibility left—Gabor was a sophomore, Crandall only a frosh. It was a different type of ball practiced by these young adults—more patient, team-oriented, an offense centered on the passing game.

Nevertheless, the team was Gabor's. From Binghamton, New York, Gabor's flashy style of play brought the fans back to Syracuse basketball and earned him the nickname of "The Bullet." One of the best pure shooters to play the college game, Gabor set single-game (36) and single season (382) scoring records in 1945–46, and was named second-team All-American. At 23–3, Andreas's squad won more games in a single season than had any Syracuse basketball team, and had the highest team point total in a single game (106 points vs. Oswego Teachers). Andreas's top-ten team was catapulted into the National Invitational Tournament (NIT), which was then played entirely in New York's Madison Square Garden and led directly to the crowning of the national championship. Little matter—the third-seeded Orangemen were eliminated in the first round by Muhlenberg, 47–41.

One wonders how Gabor would have developed had it not been for the January 1947 fire that destroyed the Archbold gym. At the beginning of the season, the growth in the student body forced Syracuse to move its home games from Archbold gym, which seated approximately eight hundred, to the downtown Syracuse Armory, which

*"Bullet" Billy Gabor
with Colgate player*

seated about half that number. The team began the season 7–5, and
represented the East in a new National Cage Tournament in Los Angeles, staged in conjunction with the Rose Bowl. But the Archbold
gym fire hurt, as Andreas was forced to find places to practice—one
night it was the Armory; another night it was Central High School.
The constant movement took its toll on the team, which would have
earned an NCAA bid had it not been for a two-point loss to City College of New York (CCNY) at the Troy Armory, during which Gabor
was hobbled by a charley horse. Gabor's senior year was a disappointment; perhaps, as Roderick Macdonald, the historian of Syracuse University basketball, has suggested, the pressure from Gabor
being touted as an All-American took its toll. The team went 11–13
in 1947–48, but Gabor ended his career with a total of 1331 points.
Gabor would go on to play with the Syracuse Nationals of the National Basketball League; he was a member of the 1949 Rookie All-
Star team, and the Nats would eventually retire his number.

   In an effort to infuse some life into his program, Andreas began
the 1948–49 season with an innovative move. He scheduled a double-
header—the Orange played, and defeated, the University of Toronto

and Ithaca College in the same evening. That year's 18–7 squad did not see postseason action, but the following year, Andreas's twenty-fifth and last year as coach, it did. Carried by sophomore Ed Miller, the Orange opened with seven straight wins. Then a loss to the nation's number one team, Holy Cross with its talented Bob Cousy, sent them into a short skid. The team rebounded by upsetting CCNY— the team that would eventually win an unprecedented NCAA and an NIT title—at Madison Square Garden. Despite the fact that at 18–9 their record was the poorest of any of the invitees, the Orange won their second bid to the NIT. This time they won their first-round matchup against Long Island University (80–52) before being beaten by Bradley, then the number one team in the nation, 78–66.

The same Fact Finding Committee investigations that led to the resignation of Baysinger as football coach led to the decision to make Andreas the full-time athletic director. He was replaced in the spring of 1950 as basketball coach by Marc Guley, who had been the captain of Syracuse's 1935–36 team, and had worked for Andreas as an assistant. Guley presided over a string of mediocre teams in the 1950s, teams that were hampered by bad luck (in his opening season as coach, his senior playmaker, Tom Jockle, had a severe ankle injury early in the season against Queens and missed a month) and sparked by individual achievement (in 1951, Bill Kiley broke Bill Gabor's all-time university scoring mark of 1,344 points, and between 1954 and 1956, Jim Brown, never really devoting his whole self to the game, nevertheless scored over 560 points). What was missing was the type of team-oriented play that had typified earlier Orange squads. A full half of the teams from the decade were over .500, but only one was strong enough to compete at the national level in postseason tournaments. That was the 1956–57 entry, which went to the NCAA's regional, where they beat Connecticut (82–76) at the Garden and Lafayette (75–71) at the Palestra. The next night they were beaten by eventual national champion North Carolina, 67–58. In the 1959–60 season, the championship season for football and crew, the cagemen went 13–8. As Orange basketball turned the corner into the 1960s, it seemed possible that, like so many other basketball programs of the 1950s, it would be completely eclipsed by the school's gridiron program.

Colgate Weekend at Theta Chi house, 1944

CHAPTER 11

The Campus

"Tip it, Frosh!"

—One of the most common campus greetings of the Tolley era.

T HE STEREOTYPICAL views of college campuses in the late
1940s and early 1950s are legion. Thanks to the popular culture,
they run the gamut from pinning to curfews, proms to goldfish eat-
ing. Syracuse University did, indeed, have vestiges of this type of this
innocent lifestyle. Like the vast majority of campuses in the postwar
period, the students at Syracuse were a rather conservative lot, oftentimes reflecting the provincialism and conservative lifestyle of
their parents. Certainly there was little evidence of the tension that
would soon strike the campus, as both students and faculty often
chose to quietly wait out the 1950s.

However, this is far from the entire story of a school that was radically transformed not by the bobby-soxers but by the return of decorated veterans. When the decision was made by Tolley to accept
every applicant in a uniform, the campus not only got bigger, it got
instant diversity. To members of this student body, many of whom
had seen bloodshed at Normandy and Iwo Jima, collegiate traditions
meant little. They brought with them a sense of the real world that
was both refreshing and unsettling, and, while they stayed, their
sense of reality was passed on to the eighteen-year-olds who shared
their classrooms. A new type of campus life had been born—from it
would come the greatest student upheaval in American history.

*   *   *

Syracuse University had had Greek houses on campus since 1871.[1] Several of them had been forced to close their doors during the war, so as to house the cadets. However, most of those houses reopened in 1945, ready to accommodate the GI Bulge. Then and now, there were many valid reasons to "Go Greek." During Rush Week, pledgemasters emphasized the camaraderie, the sense of social superiority, and the promise of a brotherhood or sisterhood connection with successful alumni. However, the more mundane things often sold a pledge on a house—the prospect of better housing than the dorms, better food, and the high probability of meeting a pledge of the opposite sex who was affiliated with a brother or sister house.

It was Tolley, himself a fraternity man, who defined the role of the Greeks in the first twenty years of his tenure: "A fraternity is a college within the college." Virtually every important social and political activity was controlled by the Greeks. For but a few examples: the football and basketball cheerleaders always included three Phi Gams of the five men on the ten-student squad; members of the Alpha Tau Omega house had fired a cannon in Archbold after every Orange touchdown and winning game since 1922, and the ATO cannon was also used to start pep rallies and fund drives;[2] there seemed to be a beauty contest for *every* group, organization, house, and weekend; every day, with the exception of the war years, when the task was turned over to their sister house, Alpha Phi, the men of Delta Kappa Epsilon (the Dekes) rang the Crouse College chimes. At five o'clock each evening, the alma mater was played from the tower, and a concert followed every home football game in Archbold, ending with the tolling of the score. One of the most venerable of the campus traditions was Step Singing, where each sorority and women's dorm had

1. See appendix E for a complete list of Greek organizations and houses on campus during the Tolley period.

2. At least it was until Oct. 15, 1960, when the cannon blasted during a touchdown during a tense 21–15 victory over Penn State. It fired, but it was followed by a second explosion, which burned several students and sent one flying some twenty feet with flaming clothing (the flames were extinguished by a Syracuse city policeman). Security police ordered the ATO brothers to get the cannon out of the stadium, which they did, and the cannon firing was suspended for the rest of the season. The following season, the Goon Squad unveiled their replacement for the ATO Cannon, the "Goon Gun," which was triggered by a carbon dioxide fire extinguisher and as a result was much safer—and quieter.

The ATO cannon, November 14, 1953; final score: Syracuse 35, Colgate 18

its own chorus, and they competed against one another once per year.[3]

Yet it was the conformity that the Greeks accepted as an established way of life that stood out. It was said by one observer that "you can always tell a Greek; they always dress, look, and act the same, they are so regimented." Again, the examples of this uniformity are legion. Men had to wear ties to dinner—there were fines if they didn't. There were fines for missing a chapter meeting or leaving it early. Perhaps the best known examples of Greek regimentation were the prescribed methods of the Hash system—including the infamous blackballing, whereby new members of Greek houses were either chosen or rejected—that were part of the Greek rituals of

3. One Kappa Alpha Theta sister (1943) remembered that every sister had to compete ("The only way to get out of it was to be a monotone, but even then you had to stand there and move your mouth"), and the competition was intense. The sisters sang popular songs, while standing stiffly, keeping one eye on the judges ("Whatever Happened to 'Rah Rah'?" *Alumni News,* fall, 1974, 16).

membership that any pledge must endure. Stories of the formal parties of the sororities that took a "be-ribboned pledge" to a "pledge-
pinned almost-sister," and the hazing of "Hell Week" and the "line-
ups" that often marked the welcoming of a new pledge to a fraternity
(despite the fact that they had long been banned by the office of the
dean of men) strike the observer as being all the same. This homo-
geneity has long been seen by many as a metaphor for the conformist
1950s; many alumni of the Greek system counter with the belief that
their days in the sorority and fraternity taught them discipline, responsibility, and loyalty.

*   *   *

Nevertheless, such regimentation was not in the plan for those
who had spent the better part of three years in the army. Dick Clark,
enrolling in 1947 as an advertising major, recalled that "practically
everything was taken over by 'the old guys' . . . to a seventeen year
old, they were ancient. . . . In those days, you truly were a child. . . .
I was associating with guys who wouldn't necessarily associate with
us babies . . . and we learned fast." These "old guys" simply had no
intention of abiding by rules set for a seventeen-year-old freshman.
When it came to traditions, veterans simply passed. As one shrewd
observer put it, these veterans did not *want* to "get hazed after being
shot up at the Battle of the Bulge."[4] Randy Christensen of the class
of 1950 was one of the many returning vets who told this author that
veterans simply refused to be subservient to upperclassmen, and ignored such long-standing traditions as tipping a freshman beanie
("Tip it, Frosh") to an upperclassman.

Many veterans had pledged fraternities before their 1943 or 1944
conscriptions. When they returned after three years in a barracks,
tent, or foxhole, they refused to live in one of Tolley's trailers. Thus
they moved back into their old Greek houses, precipitating a crunch
in the frats that paralleled the general housing crunch all across campus. But more important, the veterans changed the demeanor of the

4. The life in sororities was, for the most part, untouched by the influx of veterans,
with one exception—sorority life was simply unimportant for nurses. Only a few
houses would even pledge nurses, because they would only be active for the first two
years, then they were doing their clinical work.

"Tip it, frosh!"

houses. As one veteran, himself pledged to a house before he left for war in 1944, put it: "Grown men . . . women . . . alcohol . . . What were you going to do?"

There has never been a time when drinking was *not* a problem on college campuses, but with the invasion of the veterans it became a campus-wide scourge, particularly in the fraternities. The administration did not ignore the problem, but even the assigning of Vice President Crawford's brother to police the fraternities did not solve the problem. Walter J. "Pat" Mullaney, a student in 1946–47, remembered for a reporter that "Chancellor Tolley used to say that he would have preferred the nearest bar to be in Skaneateles." There was also the issue of having older students in the classroom, with life experiences that had *never* included the inside of a college classroom. These students brought to the classroom a skepticism borne of their wartime adventure. Michael O. Sawyer, then an instructor in the citizenship program, remembered for one writer that "they rattled the bars of the cage." Many faculty members were upset with the new-found independence of mind they were seeing in their classrooms;

others, particularly the younger professors, many of whom had themselves seen combat, took it in stride.

*   *   *

Most traditions survived the flood of veterans quite intact, however. Such is the longevity of well-entrenched customs, particularly when they are perpetuated by groups within the social structure. The Greek system, even though it was being challenged by the newfound realism of the veterans, was one such organization. Winter Weekend was a hugely important event, inspiring floats, dances, and a snow-sculpturing contest that was one of the most awaited events of the school year (when the contest was canceled in 1951 because of a flu epidemic, one house made a large tombstone out of snow with a sign on it reading "Here Lies Winter Carnival. Died, 1951"). The Campus Chest Carnival, started in 1942 as the War Chest Fund, offered students an opportunity to aid wartime charities. In 1954 it evolved into a carnival, during which "slave auctions" sold professors and administrators to the highest bidders, to be used as the students' servants for a day.[5] One of the most revered rituals was Moving Up Day, the traditional changing of the classes that had been a part of Spring Weekend since 1893. In a moving and ornate ceremony, juniors were given the seniors' places in the chapel. Other parts of the weekend included the burning of a freshman beanie, a senior thesis and a senior yearbook, the introduction of new class officers and honorary members, and the Spring Weekend parade, which featured the crowning of the May Queen.

Many of these traditions were both generated and perpetuated by the Traditions Commission. It consisted of some thirty-five juniors and seniors chosen from many applicants, who were charged with the responsibility of orienting the freshmen "to the tradition and morale of the campus." In 1947 the Traditions Commission spawned the Goon Squad, a group of some 200–250 sophomores who served as the enforcement brigade for a host of rituals, most notably the beanie regimen, which, if neglected, could keep a freshman from entering a football game, pep rally, or other social affair. However, the

5. Open houses replaced the Carnival in 1966.

refusal of veterans to "Tip it, Frosh!" led to a gradual disappearance of the custom. By the late 1950s, the Goon Squad was best known for its annual Goon Show, a parody of campus life, and the help that it gave to freshmen and their parents on moving-in day.

There was no tradition or event on campus that came close to the importance—and sheer chaos—of Colgate Weekend. It started in 1891, and continued until the two schools stopped playing football on an annual basis in 1961. It was the biggest weekend of the year for both schools, and the most perilous. "Scalping"—the shaving of C's or S's on the heads of captured students—was the rage throughout the seventy-year rivalry. The physical plant was not immune; statues, buildings, and roads were often painted in the colors of the Orangemen or the Red Raiders. In 1947, because so much damage was done to buildings, and because several students were hurt, Colgate, Cornell, and Syracuse negotiated the "Cazenovia Pact" at the Lincklaen Inn in Cazenovia, New York. The administrators of those schools agreed to ban the use of paint, and damage to property and physical violence were outlawed.

Not surprisingly, it did not work. On November 14, 1949, the Colgate Band arrived at Syracuse's New York Central Station in preparation for the next day's game. Several SU frat men lay in wait. Without telling the drivers of their mission, they had hired two Greyhound buses (for $33.15) to wait behind the depot—their plan was to get the band on the bus and then whisk their prisoners to Thornden Park for a mass shaving. The first step of the plan worked to perfection—the SU students had bribed the train's porters, who put the band men on the bus. But the drivers got wind of the trick and refused to pull out of the station. Several Syracuse students then bodily seized some of the band members, and a major-league fight broke out. One Colgate student and a Syracuse policeman were taken to the hospital. But this did not end the issue. As the bandsmen were packed into genuine Colgate buses, some did not move out of the parking lot fast enough and were commandeered to the SU campus, where their passengers were shaved bald. In 1953 Colgate got even—after breaking into the Alpha Tau Omega house, they stole the ATO cannon, then moved onto the main campus to paint the statue of the Saltine Warrior bright red. In 1958 Orange fans rented a plane and dropped orange dye into Hamilton's Taylor Lake. 'Gate tried to reciprocate by bombing Archbold Stadium, but their red paint fell on the visitors' side and succeeded only in painting many automobiles belonging to Colgate faithful.

By 1960, when the scores of the Colgate-Syracuse games had become embarrassingly lopsided, the intensity of Colgate Weekend had burned out. But that did not keep the hijinks of the weekend from remaining in the minds of alumni of the period as being, in the words of one, "the best damn time I ever had."

*   *   *

The most important social result of the GI Bulge at Syracuse University was not the perpetuation of social traditions on campus, nor the challenges that it brought to those social traditions, but rather the changes that were made in a student body that had changed little since the school's inception in 1875. Prior to 1946, Syracuse drew the majority of its students from upstate New York. It was a student body that was largely Methodist, usually privileged, and predominately undergraduate. Thanks to the GI Bill, the flavor of the student body changed as radically as did its numbers. The percentage of students from Central New York declined, and the percentage of students from downstate, particularly from the New York City area, increased dramatically. Several observers—both contemporary and present—believe that this shift was deliberate on Tolley's part, that Tolley "built a new identity," particularly by tapping into New York City for both recruiting and fund-raising. If so, it was never overt.

This "downstating" of the institution did not instantly mean racial diversification. Only a thimbleful of black students had attended the university before 1942—historian and Syracuse alumnus Harvey Strum has noted that during the 1920s black enrollment averaged a total of twenty-five students per year, and in 1942 only three blacks attended the university. Strum points out that any attempt to protest the situation was met with disdain on the part of the administration, but such protests were few and far between, as the community and campus generally supported the university's policy of limiting black attendance by making financial assistance virtually impossible for a person of color to obtain. For all intents and purposes, the GI Bulge did little to increase the number of blacks on campus. While accurate records are hard to find, administrative interview sources claim that the number of blacks in the 1950s was never more than thirty students.

The campus did become religiously diverse in the 1950s, and this was the most important demographic change of the Tolley years. Hoping to increase the number of students, Chancellor Day had formally changed Syracuse from a Methodist institution to a nonsectarian institution. The actions of Day and his immediate successors reflected the nativism and anti-Semitism of the times, as they tried de facto to keep the institution's Methodist flavor. Religious discrimination was both overt and obvious. Throughout the twenties and thirties, restrictive quotas were set for admissions of Jewish students, and from 1927 to 1931 Jews were housed apart from Christians. Fraternities and sororities openly admitted that they would admit neither Jew nor Catholic—particularly Italian and Polish Catholics. Although there were not admissions quotas for Catholics as there were for Jews, nothing was done to challenge the anti-Catholic passions, particularly among the Greeks. As a result, one historian has estimated that between 1920 and 1942, the combined Jewish-Catholic enrollment was 30–35 percent, with the balance of the students remaining Methodist. However, with the GI Bulge came a stunning increase in the number of both Catholic and Jewish students. During the 1945–46 school year, Jewish enrollment surpassed one thousand students, and by 1950 the number of Methodists on campus had been completely eclipsed by Jewish and Roman Catholic students. In that year, according to the annual census of religious preference taken by Hendricks Chapel, the largest bloc of undergraduates listed Roman Catholicism as their faith—more than all those who listed their faith as either Protestant or Jewish combined. Throughout the 1950s, the enrollment of Jewish students continued to increase. By 1957, the chapel's survey showed that 23.5 percent of the students were Roman Catholic, 21.9 percent Jewish, and 45 percent listed their faith as a Protestant denomination. These numbers would stay just about the same into the early 1960s.

As the number of Jewish students increased, so did the desire by the Syracuse community to attend to the needs of their faith. The Jewish Student Fellowship Foundation was founded in 1948, with

Rabbi William Schwartz, a former military chaplain, as its director. One of his most famous innovations was his "Colgate Eve Brotherhood Service," born of the impossibility of conducting Friday services on Colgate Weekends. Each year, Schwartz brought a well-known Christian minister to speak on the Friday before the game, and the service in Hendricks was packed despite the hoopla. In 1959 Rabbi Louis Neimand was Syracuse's first Hillel Foundation rabbi; he was followed in 1963 by Rabbi Louis Jordan.

*   *   *

However, a more diverse campus did not instantly turn into a more tolerant campus. Tolley's acceptance of Japanese-American students in 1943 was a welcome sign for those looking for more tolerance on Piety Hill. Fundamentally, Tolley was more enlightened on racial and ethnic issues than had been any of his predecessors, and he took several important steps to lessen the amount of discrimination on campus. The university integrated its dormitories and openly opposed racial and religious barriers in honor societies. Tolley was also a driving force behind the drafting of a report on discrimination for the Association of American Colleges that recommended the elimination of discrimination.

Yet Strum's conclusion, that "between 1942 and 1952, Syracuse University had made substantial progress in eliminating discrimination," needs qualification. Both anti-Semitism and anti-Catholicism continued to flourish in the political environment of the 1950s, charged as it was with a distrust of all that could even vaguely be construed as Eastern European. However, there was a difference in its intensity. As one writer has noted, anti-Semitism had "simply become unfashionable and unpopular, and had therefore gone underground." The same can be said of anti-Catholicism, particularly on college campuses. There was, however, nothing opaque about the racial bias that continued to be virulently clear at even the most "enlightened" northern campuses. In such a climate, discrimination did not magically disappear at Syracuse in the postwar period; the university continued through the 1950s to struggle with its own strands of racial and religious prejudices. The evidence is anecdotal—mostly alumni speaking off-the-record in interviews with the author—and the vast majority of these comments centered on the bigoted policies of the Greek system. One alumnus characterized the fraternities as "the most discriminatory body" on campus and remembered that his frat had a "Catholic quota," but that "you didn't have to have a Jewish or black quota—it was zero."

It was, however, the relationship between the now-majority Catholics, and the still-Methodist university administration, that dominated the 1950s. The issue pitted Tolley against the equally strong-willed university advisor to its Catholic students, Rev. Gannon F. Ryan. Ryan, a native Syracusan who had been appointed as the university's first resident priest in 1935, complained quite regularly of anti-Catholic bias on campus, emanating particularly from the Maxwell faculty. He was also publicly outspoken in his belief that Catholics were being persecuted on the Syracuse campus. Again, anecdotal evidence points to the truth of both of Ryan's contentions. Where there can be no debate, however, is that Ryan and Tolley were at odds much of the time. To cite but one example: in 1951, Ryan was outraged when a faculty member accused of leftist beliefs, whom Ryan had refused to allow to speak at an interdenominational dinner, was asked by Charles Noble, dean of Hendricks Chapel, to address a Protestant service instead—presumably with Tolley's approval.

This was a clash between two conservative titans: Tolley, trained as a Methodist minister and missionary, trying to keep Syracuse a Methodist institution long after it had effectively ceased to be one, and Ryan, the anticommunist Catholic prelate, demanding equality for his faith at an institution that only a decade before had openly persecuted its followers. Ryan was helped, both on campus and in the public eye, not just by the rise in Catholic enrollment but by the success of John F. Kennedy, Catholic senator from Massachusetts, in the presidential arena. The Kennedy election gave hope to Catholics everywhere, and strengthened Ryan's cause at Syracuse. By the early 1960s, Ryan had effectively broken with Hendricks, refusing to recognize the administrative function of the chapel, objecting to the university's religious census, and refusing to clear his routine administrative matters with the university.

Tolley tried to strike back. In a 1961 letter to Charles Noble, the chancellor sputtered that "the university made a serious mistake in permitting the Roman Catholics to hold religious services at the hour of the official university services. I am fully conscious of the wide variety of approaches to religious faith and practice among the Protestant denominations. . . . None, however, will be permitted to conduct religious services at the hour of the official university service in Hendricks Chapel." But by 1961, the break was complete. For all intents and purposes, the Catholic church, through Ryan's St. Thomas More House, acted as an independent entity, representing the largest group of students on the Syracuse campus free from administrative control. Ryan died on December 6, 1962, leaving the administration in a quandary as to what to do about its Catholic students. Nevertheless, in an undated memo, Tolley was clear: "Perhaps it is too late to prevent the crumbling of our freedom at Syracuse. The Roman Catholic Church has called the tune increasingly for three years and now speaks in commanding tones. I propose that the University call the tune from now on."

This is not to say, as mentioned above, that steps were not taken by all sides to try to lessen the amount of evident discrimination on campus. The most important one was the Syracuse Discriminatory Clause Board, founded in 1951, which sought to change and regulate the admissions procedures of the Greek houses. A rule was passed requiring all chapters of national Greek societies whose constitutions were known to contain clauses allowing for discrimination in their membership procedures to register such information with the administration. But this was far from the solution to the problem. Between 1952 and 1963, only twelve fraternities had removed discriminatory clauses from their constitutions, and even those that had done so were accused, both at the time and in subsequent interviews, with practicing de facto discrimination long beyond the Tolley years. This discrimination began to erode the position of prominence that the Greek houses held on campus, and placed the independents in a much better political position as the decade turned.

In the long run, a more successful step was taken by the Diocese of Syracuse, when in December 1962 it named Rev. Charles Borgognoni to replace Ryan. Borgognoni was a native of Canastota who had last served as assistant pastor at Our Lady of Pompeii Church in Syracuse. An outgoing, often boisterous man, Borgognoni recognized the need for the More House to reach out to the campus at large, and he used his zealous interest in theater (he said once that he saw "anything that's good" on Broadway) to that end. He instituted a series of coffee receptions at the More House, and the Pompeiian Players, a repertory company that he had taken over in 1950, performed at these receptions. Syracuse students would eventually join the ranks of the Pompeiian Players, often with lead roles. Orange sports fans remember Father Charles as the man at the end of the bench at every football and basketball game, both at home and away, jumping and yelling wildly with every play. But it was his presence as a spiritual leader on campus that helped to slowly heal the wounds of prejudice that had marred the 1950s.

*   *   *

Once again, there have been those who argued that Tolley, a Methodist minister who was well aware of the potential for conflict once the institution diversified its student body, actually welcomed this tension. Jesse Burkhead of the Maxwell School of Citizenship viewed the situation in that light for an interviewer:

> It had always been thought that we were here primarily to perhaps educate the sons and daughters of Methodists from Upstate New York. But the student body changed very greatly. Immediately, or certainly when I got here in 1948, and in the next several years, there were a great many more downstate students. . . . But to be perfectly blunt about it, there was a bit of anti-Semitism around the university, among the old guard faculty particularly. I never detected any of it from Dr. Tolley. Indeed, I think he welcomed this ethnic diversity, religious diversity, and saw it as a way of making this a more lively and interesting institution. Certainly there was no evidence in appointments of faculty or anything of this kind.

Did this influx of veterans, instant diversity, and challenge to the Greek system lead to campus revolt? Hardly. Several of the less defensible social traditions of the day were, indeed, changed. The most public of these was the protest against a thirty-eight-year-old seating regulation that put coeds and men in separate sections of Archbold Stadium during football games; mixed seating began in the fall of 1947. While some of the sensibilities of what would be called the sixties were already being felt in the 1950s, the student body remained essentially staid and conservative, despite—perhaps because of—the influx of more adult students. This was, after all, the campus where, in 1955, coeds voted through their student council representatives to ban the wearing of bermuda shorts in classrooms, in public vehicles, in administration and faculty offices, at university functions, and in downtown Syracuse (the reason, according to the president of Women's Student Government, was that "Syracuse University is a co-educational school and not similar to a women's campus").

A more serious example of this conservatism was the *Daily Orange,* which was far from the "jazzy . . . very independent newspaper" that was described for the author by one of its former editors. Throughout the 1950s, the editorial page of the *DO* could be counted on to reflect the opinion of the administration in virtually every conflict of consequence. This is, in and of itself, an important political statement. With a mixture of veterans and younger students on the staff, one might expect more challenges to administrative authority. Indeed, as the student body changed in the 1950s, the *DO* did not, remaining a rather staid, conservative publication. As the student body became more vocal toward the end of the decade, alternative publications would spring up that were more iconoclastic in nature. Throughout the early years of student awareness of the 1960s, the *DO* would remain a bastion of button-down conservatism.

It was, in point of fact, an era in which serious dissent was muffled by a desire to escape the tumult of the atomic world and revel in the safety of tradition. College campuses were no different in this regard than the rest of society in the 1950s. These traditions were so comfortable—for university inhabitants as well as for the rest of society—that it would take a tremendous body blow to destroy those traditions. It would also take the abandonment of the traditions by those in authority—not the students, but the faculty members. Both things were about to happen.

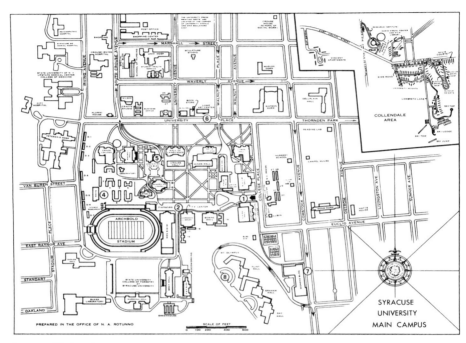

Syracuse University campus, 1962

CHAPTER 12

The Building Bulge, Part Two
The Syracuse Plan

Mr. Newhouse had it and the Chancellor wanted it.

—Dean Wesley Clark of the School of Journalism, when asked how
Syracuse got the money for the Newhouse Center

I had never dreamed that a great library should bear my name.

—Ernest Stevenson Bird

THE SUCCESS of the Building and Development Fund had convinced Tolley—and others—that Syracuse University was
finally capable of raising big dollars. The Building Bulge of the 1950s
had convinced outsiders (Tolley certainly needed no reassurance on
this score) that Syracuse had arrived as a major institution. But Tolley was not yet through. Indeed, as the decade turned, Tolley's first
major action was to ask his trustees to join him in seeking what
seemed at face to be the impossible. On March 25, 1961, after reflecting that Syracuse had been judged by colleagues in other universities
as "on the threshold of greatness," Tolley announced to his board
that the university was committing itself to raising the staggering sum
of $76 million by 1970—the year of the university's one-hundredth
anniversary. Tolley's wish list for the money featured physical plant
needs for the university; the three big ticket items were the new
school of communications, improvements to the research facilities,

and a new university library. Once again, the endowment was not on Tolley's mind—it would receive $5 million of the total raised.[1] Dubbed "The Syracuse Plan," or by some public relations wags, "Seventy-Six for Syracuse," it was Tolley's most ambitious project to date. To make it work, he had to reel in a big gift from one of his most ambitious donors.

*   *   *

The son of a Russian immigrant, Samuel I. Newhouse never got beyond the eighth grade. Nevertheless, by age twenty-six, he had bought his first newspaper, the *Staten Island Advance,* for $98,000. At the time of the 1964 dedication of the communications center at Syracuse University that bore his name, Newhouse owned eighteen newspapers, twelve magazines, and nine radio and television stations, at an estimated worth of close to $250 million.[2] Tolley's first meeting with Newhouse had all the elements of a comic opera. The two men were both guests at a dinner at New York's Waldorf-Astoria, but Newhouse had inadvertently sat in Tolley's place. Tolley found out who he was, and went and sat in Newhouse's seat. During the course of the dinner, Tolley walked over, and introduced himself to the publisher: "Chancellor Tolley, I'm Sam Newhouse, and I've always wanted to meet a real live chancellor!" Newhouse looked down at his placecard and exclaimed, "My God, did I do that?" Tolley remembered that the two men immediately struck up a friendship.

Tolley understood that Newhouse responded to a mixture of blunt bravado and shameless flattery, and the chancellor provided equal amounts of both motivators. He reminded him that the Syracuse newspapers had been the springboard for the Newhouse empire. He gave him an honorary degree in 1955, fawned over the fact that both of Newhouse's sons had attended Syracuse, and saw to his election to the university's board in 1959. When Tolley went to ask Newhouse for a contribution, he was cognizant of how much help the workaholic publisher could be for the university. When Lou Ryan, chair-

1. For the complete Goals and Priorities of the Syracuse Plan, as presented by Tolley to the board of trustees, see appendix F.

2. This included both the Syracuse dailies—the morning *Post-Standard* and the evening *Herald-Journal*—the Sunday *Herald-American,* and the WSYR AM and FM radio and television stations.

man of the fund-raising drive for the new fieldhouse, called Tolley and asked if Newhouse might be convinced to spring for a $50,000 gift they wanted to announce at that evening's dinner, Tolley balked but eventually agreed. He made an appointment to see Newhouse, and, as Tolley remembered it, walked into the publisher's office: "Sam, we have a dinner tonight. I have to have $50 thousand, but I don't care how many years it takes you to pay it. Anytime at all. Sign here." Newhouse did, and Tolley was out of the office in less than three minutes.

The big game that Tolley had in mind for Sam Newhouse was a building to house the School of Journalism, which had been in exile in the old Women's Gymnasium since 1953, when the Yates Castle had been given to the state as part of the transfer of the medical school to the SUNY system. Tolley began discussing the project with Newhouse as early as 1958, and the publisher was willing to consider a major donation—but on his terms. He originally stipulated that "one of the branches" of the donor—in this case, the *Syracuse Herald-Journal*—would give $100,000 to the university each year for ten years, so that Newhouse could write the money off as a business expense. Intrigued, Tolley had Joe Lubin look at the contract; Lubin proclaimed the arrangement a valid business expense. Not quite convinced, Tolley contacted the office of New York's senior senator Jacob Javits. There is no record in Tolley's files of a response, but by December the idea of such a contract had been abandoned, and Newhouse had decided to make an outright gift from his foundation to operate the School of Journalism. The convincing argument, according to insiders, was Tolley's promise "to build within your lifetime." Newhouse promised Tolley $1 million for a new building, to be paid in three equal installments over the next three years, and an additional $700,000 to operate the school. Newhouse did not come cheap, however; as part of the same deal, the university agreed to contract with Newhouse for "research, market surveys, and other services from faculty and students in the School of Journalism in an amount totaling $30,000 a year and continuing for a period of ten years."

Unlike some of Tolley's other donors, Newhouse was as good as his word. By 1962, his pledge for the building had been paid in full. However, Tolley's dreams had expanded in that period. He now saw a two-building complex that would bear Newhouse's name—a complex that would need considerably more money that the $700,000 Newhouse had outstanding on his pledge. To get the publisher to up his ante, Tolley pointed out that a major donation to the university would take the publisher off the hook from the many Jewish organizations that were asking him for money. Within twenty-four hours of that July 1962 pitch, Newhouse had pledged $15 million—the largest single gift in the history of the university to that point—to the building of a new school of journalism.

Planning had begun on the first of the two buildings in 1961. It was built on the University Place site of the Student's Supply Company—better known as the "Corner Store." Despite the initial reluctance of the owner to sell, it was eventually bought by the university for a price of $100,000 (paid for, not surprisingly, by a "donation" of $100,000 to the university from the *Syracuse Herald-Journal*). Originally the architects were to be the King Brothers, but New York architect I. M. Pei, fresh off the worldwide success of his development of the Place Ville Marie in Montreal, had found out about the project through Newhouse. Pei offered his services, and the Kings were agreeable. The partnership produced a building that was imposing. Pei had become known for his innovative use of reinforced concrete, and Newhouse I was his boldest use of that medium to date. The concrete and glass cruciform structure won First Honor in the annual awards bestowed to new construction by the American Institute of Architects in 1965. The judges noted that the building "exemplifies a powerful manipulation of mass and plane to enclose space. Its relation to its environment is superb, its materials simple and logical, its detailing excellent." Newhouse I included two experimental underground classrooms, where the students answered exam questions by pushing buttons while a computer instantly added up their scores, and rooms that were set up as working newspaper city rooms.

Completed in early 1964, Newhouse decided to pull every string he had to make sure that the dedication of the result of his largesse was an inspiring one. In March 1964 he visited the White House and asked President Lyndon Johnson to attend the dedication. Johnson agreed immediately after their meeting. In his memoirs, Tolley relates the story of riding from the airport with the president and Newhouse, and professes his amazement that Johnson made it clear that the only reason he was in Syracuse was to get Newhouse to commit the editorial support of his newspapers to the upcoming Johnson campaign. It worked. Newhouse wrote to Johnson only a week after the dedication that "I want to again assure you that I will 'love' and support you in November, even as enthusiastically as I pledged to do on my happiest of days—August 5, 1964." Less than a month later, in September 1964, the *Herald-Journal* announced its editorial support for Johnson.

As the dedication grew closer, major problems popped up. The Syracuse chapter of the Congress of Racial Equality (CORE) threatened to picket the event, charging that the Johnson administration was not doing enough to locate three civil rights workers who had disappeared earlier that summer while working in the Freedom Summer project in Mississippi.[3] The administration had cause to be concerned about such a threat. Rioting that summer had already occurred in Harlem and Rochester, and there had been violent civil rights protests in Syracuse only a year before—protests that had included university professors and students. Nevertheless, the issue eventually died out. More troublesome to the politically astute president, however, was the fact that a presidential appearance on the same dais as Newhouse would be taken by many labor groups as implicit support of management in what had become a bitter labor dispute between the publisher and several of his papers in the Northwest.

All this, however, was quickly overshadowed by events in Vietnam. On August 1, four days before the scheduled dedication, the destroyer *Maddox* had encountered a North Vietnamese torpedo boat while operating in the Gulf of Tonkin. There was a brief engagement, and Johnson ordered the destroyer *C. Turner Joy* to join it. On August 4, both ships reported that they were under attack. The details were sketchy, but the administration was already poised for an attack. Late that afternoon, Johnson authorized strikes against the torpedo boat as well as bases and oil dumps on the North Vietnamese mainland.

---

3. Earlier that month, three student civil rights workers, Michael Schwerner, Andrew Goodman, and James Chaney, had turned up missing while working in Meridian, Mississippi, establishing "Freedom Schools" and helping blacks register to vote. Six weeks later, their bodies, mangled by bullets, were discovered in an earth dam some miles away.

President Lyndon B. Johnson and Tolley at dedication of Newhouse Communications Center, August 5, 1964

Most observers were surprised that in the midst of this crisis, Johnson kept his word to Newhouse and made the trip to Syracuse the next day. The Syracuse *Alumni News* noted that Johnson was somber throughout the entire dedication ceremony; only a "flicker of a smile crossed his lips" when the crowd of some twenty thousand applauded his receiving an honorary doctorate.[4] Although the president had already spoken to the nation on the crisis, he took the occasion at Syracuse to announce that "in the last twelve hours, air units of the United States Seventh Fleet have sought out the hostile vessels and certain of their supporting facilities. Appropriate armed action has been taken against them." The first step in what later historians would learn was a carefully planned series of events by the Johnson administration to escalate the war in Vietnam was announced to the world from the steps of Sam Newhouse's newest gift.

*   *   *

In the last five years of Tolley's tenure, there was no slowdown in the construction that had been present on Piety Hill since 1945. Next to the Newhouse School, the biggest accomplishment was Manley Fieldhouse, completed in 1962. Tolley's commitment to providing more dormitory space continued with the 1963 dedication of Booth

4. Johnson was the first president to receive an honorary degree from Syracuse University. Governor Franklin D. Roosevelt was voted a Doctor of Civil Laws in 1930, and Senator John F. Kennedy received an honorary Doctor of Laws degree in 1957.

Hall, which held 315 men and was named for Willis H. Booth, the founder of the Booth Ferris foundation and a university trustee. In November 1965 Lawrinson Dorm for men was dedicated in the name of the parents of a New Jersey dairy executive. A singular structure, the twenty-one story Lawrinson was the largest reinforced concrete structure in New York State outside of New York City, and Syracuse's second-tallest skyscraper.

Tolley also kept a promise that he had made to two of the schools that had grown the fastest during the 1950s. Tolley had wanted to add an auditorium to the law school's White Hall at the time of its 1953 construction, but the money had not been there. Now, in 1962, Tolley announced that trustee Arnold Grant, alumnus of the College of Law and member of the board, and Tolley's contact to alumni donors in Hollywood, had donated the money for the auditorium. Grant Auditorium, which seated approximately seven hundred students and included a lounge area, was dedicated on April 28, 1967. Tolley had also promised to build a building that would rescue the physics program from a research lab that had been erected under the steel stands of Archbold Stadium. In October 1962, Ralph Stolkein pledged $1.2 million to the university for a physics building, and ground was broken for the project in 1965. However, in July 1968, Stolkein went bankrupt. Despite the loss of this major pledge, Tolley went ahead with construction. The building was not named the Stolkein building as promised, but when the building was completed in 1967, it did include the Stolkein auditorium.

*   *   *

As was true for any chancellor, problems with funding new projects, of which the Stolkein story is an example, plagued Tolley throughout his tenure. Put most simply, pledges did not always immediately convert to real dollars for the university. Where Tolley differed from many of his contemporaries, however, was that he never let that fact get in his way. The massive amount of construction on campus will always be testimony to Tolley's daring as an administrator. He often went ahead with buildings using a sort of deficit spending—starting construction on the promise of funds to be collected later. When the money did not come in, as was the case with Stolkein, Tolley was most often able to find a donor or a grant that would pick up the slack, even if he had to wait for the money until after the building had been dedicated. As a result, the rather abrupt end to Tolley's chancellorship left his successors with an awkward situation—several buildings had not only been left incomplete at the time of Tolley's May 1969 retirement, but several of them had not yet been fully funded. One example was the School of Engineering Building II, being built adjacent to Hinds Hall. Building had begun in 1968, but despite gifts from Edwin A. Link, the founder and chairman of the board of Link Aviation and Link Aeronautical Corporation, and a matching grant of $607,000 from the National Science Foundation, when Tolley left office in 1969, Link was under construction and close to $4 million short of being fully funded. Much of this must be blamed on serendipity—as will be seen, Tolley expected to be in office at least one year past the time that he actually retired. Some must be blamed on Tolley's deficit spending, and some must also be blamed on the capriciousness of vexing donors. The very best example of this interrelated set of circumstances is the story of the building project that, despite the fact that it was not finished when he retired, continued to lay claim to Tolley's soul.

*   *   *

Library renewal had long been Tolley's pet project.[5] In April 1958, on the first page of a new university publication—the *Syracuse University Library Associates Courier*—Tolley wrote that "it has long been clear that we must have a new building. . . . Only a very ambitious program can assure a library adequate for the standing of this university." During the first decade of Tolley's leadership, this "ambitious program" centered on acquisitions. The holdings of the Carnegie Library had grown from approximately 417,374 volumes in 1955 to 522,549 volumes in 1960, ranking it fifty-second in the country in the size of its total holdings for college libraries. By 1969 its holdings had increased 280 percent from its 1950 level—the fourth highest growth rate in the nation.

        5. This piece, in amended form, has been previously published as John Robert Greene and Karrie A. Baron, " 'I Had Never Dreamed that a Great Library Should Bear My Name': The Planning and Funding of Bird Library," in *Syracuse University Library Associates Courier,* 30 (1995). The author wishes to thank the editor of that journal for permission to include that work in this book.

Carnegie, built in 1907, simply could not hold such a collection and adequately serve its clients. The venerable building shared with Hendricks Chapel, Yates Castle, and the Hall of Languages the distinction of being the most recognizable buildings on campus. However, Carnegie had also long been in a state of serious disrepair, and one 1968 estimate suggested that the building now contained twice the number of books and six times as many staffers as it had been intended to house. A short-term solution to these problems was a troublesome system of branch libraries. After its purchase by the university, older books were stored in the lower three floors of the old Continental Can Company on Erie Boulevard (many a student would go to Carnegie and ask for a book, only to be told "it's in the can" and could not be retrieved for a week or more).[6]

As a result, there was markedly little debate over whether a new library would be built—by 1961, it was an assumed fact. Originally, Tolley's thinking led him to plan for a system of libraries to replace the antiquated Carnegie building. The first of these new libraries would serve the needs of the constituency upon which Tolley had sparked the expansion of the university in the 1950s—upperclassmen and graduate students. Unlike Carnegie, then, which was at that point largely an overstocked general library, the university's new library would be a modern research facility. It would have to be a massive building, and none of the sites proposed to Tolley by his various planning boards suited the size of the building he had in mind.

Tolley began to look beyond the confines of the quad for a location for the library, and as a result he immediately clashed with fraternities and sororities, several of which would have to be relocated to accommodate the site. It was not until February 1967 that Tolley was able to announce the site to the University Senate—the block of Walnut Park between the Lowe Art Center and the Delta Kappa Epsilon fraternity house. However, it was not the site that bid most observers pause, but the size of the projected building and its cost. Tolley boasted that the new building (one of what Tolley originally

6. Along with the approximately 90,000 catalogued volumes, and some 8,000 volumes listed by author only in Carnegie's card catalogue, the Continental Can building also housed all the manuscript collections that could not be accommodated in the Harriman Room at Carnegie, as well as the Order Department, Gift and Exchange Department, and Music Library.

envisioned to be three libraries—this large central library, a smaller undergraduate library, and a separate building for rare books and manuscripts) would consist of a basement, six operational floors, and a penthouse, which would also house the university's Arents Rare Book Room and manuscript collections. According to Tolley's first estimate, all this would cost the university approximately $9,835,000—a price that Tolley was quick to point out was growing with every day that the university delayed the start of construction.

The search for the funding for this new project hardly began in 1967. Ten years earlier, tobacco magnate George Arents, who had funded the Rare Book Reading Room in Carnegie, had bequeathed $2,000,000 to the university "which shall be used toward the cost of constructing and maintaining a new library for the university." By the early sixties, the dividends on Arents's gift had increased it by $1 million, but this was still little more than a good start for a building such as Tolley envisioned, and the chancellor struck out for other contributions, as he made the library one of the lead beneficiaries of the Syracuse Plan. Yet fund-raising monies could not completely be counted upon, and Tolley began to seek a name donor for the new library.

His first quarry seems to have been former New York governor Averell Harriman. In May 1964 Tolley wrote to Harriman, then serving as Lyndon Johnson's undersecretary of state for Political Affairs, asking him to donate both his own personal papers and those of his family to Syracuse University. In return, Tolley suggested the creation of "an Averell Harriman University Library which would house your family papers as a part of our major research center in the field of public and international affairs and the humanities." Tolley noted that while "governmental, industrial, and foundation resources are increasingly available for higher education . . . we must look for help to a few dedicated individuals. . . . We need your help." Although the university would eventually acquire Harriman's gubernatorial papers, he made no promise of a substantial monetary donation. Tolley would have to look elsewhere.

Ernest Stevenson Bird was born in 1894 on a farm near Andover, New Jersey. He graduated from Syracuse University in 1916 with a degree in liberal arts, and he had been a classmate and fraternity brother of Tolley's brother, Harold. Upon graduation, Bird taught high school math and science and coached at Ithaca, New York; Newark, New Jersey; and Wilmington, Delaware. After leaving the world of secondary education, Bird became a salesman for the American Book Publishing Company. On his 1946 retirement from that company, he was vice president in charge of sales.

Bird responded to Tolley's Syracuse Plan appeal for monies for a new library. The original pitch was that if donors gave a certain amount of money, they would get a deferred income from the university based upon the amount donated. This appealed to the seventy-three-year-old Bird, and he asked how much money he and his wife would get for a $10,000 donation. Bird then wrote the university a second time, mentioning a $50,000 donation. Now quite interested, Tolley dispatched P. Lachlan Peck, the director of the Deferred Giving Programs, as the university's representative, to try to get a sizeable donation from Bird. Peck was accompanied by Horace Landry, professor of accounting, who would offer Bird tax advice about a possible donation. Landry remembered that "we began to realize that there was a lot more money in their estate. They didn't have any children or family, so the University was Steve Bird's first

Ernest Stevenson Bird

thought." In October 1967, largely due to the efforts of Peck and Landry, Bird pledged the assets of two of his investment accounts to Syracuse University. At that date, the accounts were expected to be valued at about $2.5 million. A deferred gift, the university was to provide the Birds a yearly sum of $224,000, or 7 percent of the total of the portfolio, over their lifetimes; when they had both died, the university would be able to either spend or invest the principal.

At first Bird made no stipulations on his gift, save for the annuity. Peck was the first to mention a use for the money—a student union building that Tolley had long been promising. But Tolley had other ideas. Five days after being apprised of the gift, Tolley wrote Bird that "your gift . . . will, I think, prove to be the largest ever given by a graduate of the University," and suggested that

> I think both faculty and students, however, would agree that our major building need is a new library. It will probably cost about ten million dollars. We have some three million dollars in hand and we think we can get federal grants for about a third of the cost. We could also, if necessary, borrow from Federal sources as much as three million dollars at low interest. . . . No building will be more important or have a wider influence. . . . I don't think we need to settle this immediately, but I would hope that while you are alive and able to find pleasure in it you would be involved in the planning of the building to bear your name and could have the satisfaction of seeing it while you and Mrs. Bird are still here. Our problem is not so much to have cash in hand for construction as to know that it can and will be financed.

Bird responded in a letter of some warmth:

> When your letter came I read it to my wife but the reading process was interrupted several times by the inability of my eyes to see and of my voice to function properly. Your letter has made me very happy and my wife very proud. . . . I had never dreamed that a great library should bear my name. I am truly overwhelmed. . . . I naturally wish our contribution could have been larger and I am sorry the market chose this particular time to turn bearish.

As the new year opened, the university had a promise of the largest gift ever given by an alumnus, and it seemed that Tolley would soon have his library. However, what had begun as a tremendous example of alumni beneficence soon turned into a frustrating situation for all concerned. Despite his promise, Bird suddenly seemed to be unwilling to transfer his stock portfolio to the university. The January 1968

Tet Offensive in Vietnam had sent the stock market into a nosedive, and it seems that Bird was holding onto his portfolio until the market recovered so that he might deliver the total amount promised to Tolley. Concerned, Peck and Landry traveled back and forth to see Bird, hoping that they could cajole him into transferring the portfolio as soon as possible. Bird would not be rushed, and he was rankled by Tolley's sense of urgency. On January 16, 1968, Bird wrote to Peck claiming that "I fear that you and Dr. Tolley wonder why I have delayed making the transfer and the longer the delay the more concerned I have become. I feel as though I were a pecan between the jaws of a nut cracker. I don't particularly relish this kind of pressure—in fact, I'm not standing up to it too well . . . the market is not doing what I hoped it would. I'm beginning to wonder *if* it will and *when* it will."

Tolley quickly responded to his newest benefactor:

> Lachlan Peck has shared your letters with me. I think I can understand the way you feel as the stock market reflects the bearishness of world and war news. Our concern is not about the value of the portfolio at the present time. I am confident that before the Ernest S. Bird Library is completed the market will be higher that it was six months ago. What bothers me is the possibility of severe shrinkage of the estate by legal and banking fees, possible litigation and taxes by State and Federal authorities if something should happen to you before the transfer of securities is made.

Nevertheless, another month passed by, and the portfolio had yet to be delivered. Clearly frustrated with the situation, Bird wrote Tolley in March, noting that it is "more of a worry giving away this money than it was accumulating it." Bird also acknowledged making a mistake in not turning over the portfolio at the end of 1967, but he had "expected the customary rise in January and that never developed."

Yet the status of Bird's portfolio was not the only problem Tolley was facing as he attempted to bring a new library to reality. Other events were converging on Tolley, many of them reflecting the passion caused on campus by the antiwar and civil rights movements. However, such events, and Tolley's reaction to them, had led many arms of the university to nudge Tolley to retire in this, the twenty-sixth year of his chancellorship. Tolley knew that Bird Library would be his last physical contribution to the campus that he had rebuilt—the pressure was now on to at least have construction begun at the time of his retirement. Landry and Peck stepped up the pace of their negotiations. Landry remembered that "the last time that [we] were out there together we finally persuaded him that now was the time to do it. The market was in good health and rising. . . . He hit it right."

The transfer of Bird's portfolio was finally completed on April 23, 1968. The total of the original gift was $2,903,400.82, which included a $150,000 gift from his wife. However, when Bird found out that the university's press release had announced that he had given $3 million, he sent a gift that would ensure that the amount was raised to that level.[7]

Even Bird's gift did not solve the university's financial woes regarding the embryonic Bird Library. The contract to construct the building was signed on May 16, 1969. The low bidder, Vincent J. Smith, Inc., of Binghamton, budgeted an amount of $11,690,000, some $1,500,000 above Tolley's estimated cost. Yet Tolley would not be slowed. At their June 1968 meeting, he told the board of trustees that "because we felt that any delay would only add to construction costs, we decided to go ahead. The unexpected additional costs will, of course, have an adverse effect on other construction urgently needed." On November 15 he confidently announced to the board that thanks to Title I and II grants, he had all the money necessary to finance the new library, and the building would be completed in July 1971.[8]

---

7. Bird's humility, despite the size of his gift, was quite genuine. He made it quite clear to Peck that he did not want to be mentioned as the name donor in any of the university's press releases, and requested that the building be named the William P. Tolley Library—an honor Tolley declined. Horace Landry also remembers that when the press release announcing the gift identified Bird as the vice president of American Book Publishing Company, Bird protested, claiming that he had been "only a salesman." Horace Landry, interview with Karrie A. Baron, June 29, 1995.

8. The library construction line in the capital budget submitted to the board on that date read:

Estimated cost:	$11,388,000
Cash and Pledges:	$6,675,205

Construction Grants and Loans:

*Title I:	$2,491,264
Title II:	$1,922,931
Total:	$2,023,518 (awarded)

The problem was that Tolley did *not* have all the pledged cash on hand to pay for the building. Although Ernest Bird died in February 1974, his wife lived until 1988, thus tying up the principal of the major gift for the library. Other major gifts to the library drive of the Syracuse Plan had also come unraveled. The gift of Florence Bailey Crouse, who had been a prime mover in getting other trustees to donate to the library, offers but one example of the troubles that Tolley faced. In February 1968, the Internal Revenue Service refused to allow the executors of the Crouse estate to pay the $75,000 she had pledged to the Syracuse Plan in the name of the library. While the IRS recognized that she had indeed *made* the pledge, as it was not in her will it was not an enforceable obligation.

Thus, although construction began on Bird Library in the summer of 1969—several months after Tolley's retirement—it was not entirely clear how the building would be paid for. The final cost to the institution for the Ernest Stevenson Bird Library was in the neighborhood of $14 million. The funding was never completely attained until 1988, the year of Marie Bird's death. Nevertheless, it is hard to disagree with Chancellor Eggers, who contended that "the [Bird] library is Chancellor Tolley's crowning glory. I will forever be grateful for his having gotten that building underway. . . . The cost of that building [is] worth every cent."

*   *   *

Unlike other factors in a university's development, physical growth can be measured by simple statistics. Clearly, as a builder William Tolley had few peers. Between 1946 and 1969, Syracuse University had added close to one thousand acres to its land holdings and had erected forty-seven new buildings, at a total cost of more than $70 million.

---

*Title I award $1,670,923 to date—supplement application to be submitted after construction starts. Title II proposal increased from $1,281,954 to $1,922,931 with change of federal participation from ⅓ to ½ eligible costs.

Balance to Finance: _____

Remarks: Working drawings 70 percent complete; Bid 2/69; completion due 7/71.

Ernie Davis

CHAPTER 13

Sports, Part Two

Just write that Ernie [Davis] was a nice guy.

—An alum to the author

The best freshman basketball player I have ever seen at Syracuse.

—Lew Andreas on Dave Bing

As soon as the 1959 season was over, offers and proposals began to pour into Lew Andreas's office. Ben Schwartzwalder was offered the head coaching position of the AFL Boston Patriots—at double his salary. He refused. In mid-1960, a proposal was made by a business group to have the university contract to play its football games in a proposed stadium at the Fairgrounds. The university responded in the negative. But one proposal, long in the making, was finally completed thanks to the championship season.

*   *   *

Immediately after the destruction of the Archbold Gym in May 1947, Andreas promised the alumni that "Syracuse not only will have a new modern gymnasium to replace Archbold, but we also will have a new fieldhouse, seating upward of 10,000." Two years later, in March 1949, Tolley announced that a fieldhouse was tops on his list of badly needed projects. The student body responded favorably to this announcement, and from this was born the Fieldhouse Foundation, an organization dedicated to the raising of student pledges for the fieldhouse. Rumors began circulating that a fieldhouse would be started as early as 1950; but they were followed by rumors that Tolley had shelved the project until the construction of the Onondaga County War Memorial was finished. In any case, there was little movement on the fieldhouse project throughout the 1950s. But the 1959 season yanked the fieldhouse idea back onto the front burner. Andreas remembered for an interviewer: "It seemed to us after the national championship was a natural time to put the pressure on to get the fieldhouse. . . . It was to be paid for by all the alumni and not interfere with [the Syracuse Plan]. We raised about $2 million, but I don't think we would have got it if we didn't win the national championship."

The largest single donation in that $2 million came from Dr. George Leroy ("Jake") Manley. An alumnus of the Syracuse University Medical School (1920) and a fellow in the American College of Surgeons, in 1960 Manley was chief-of-staff of Chenango Memorial Hospital. In 1951 Manley gave the university $25,000 to set up the George L. Manley Scholarship Fund, and stipulated that students from Mercersburg High School (his alma mater) who were both good students and good athletes had the first crack at it. Soon Manley tried to impose restrictions on the scholarship, asking Tolley to promise that the university match his contribution in perpetuity—a condition that Tolley was not willing to accept. In June 1957, Tolley wrote Manley with a different suggestion for his largesse:

> While the endowment of scholarships is perhaps our greatest single need, I have had the feeling a good many times that you would get greater personal satisfaction from having your name on the new fieldhouse. Costs have skyrocketed so that it is dangerous to try to put a price tag on the fieldhouse. Perhaps we ought to get some preliminary estimates on the cost of this new type of fieldhouse made of aluminum. Costs ought to be cut by the use of lighter materials.

Tolley may have helped seal the deal with Manley's 1958 election as a trustee-at-large, but Manley had always been keenly interested in university athletics and was definitely interested in the fieldhouse project. In mid-1960, the principal and the interest of the Manley Scholarship fund—$127,961.96—was transferred to the Fieldhouse Foundation. Manley also gave a contribution of $250,000, one that was not publicly announced at his request.

On March 14, 1960, the Syracuse Common Council voted to sell the university the eight acres of the old Morningside Park. The George L. Manley Fieldhouse was built on that site, and dedicated on December 15, 1962 (the Orange basketball team beat Army that evening, 59 to 51). The $2 million circular fieldhouse (novel for its day, when most fieldhouses were rectangular, with either a gabled or a vaulted roof), with a central arena of 1.6 acres, was covered by a dome 302 feet in diameter and 75 feet off the floor. The fieldhouse included a public wing facing Comstock Avenue that housed the athletic department offices, ticket offices, a public lobby and trophy room, a press room, and a lounge, and a second wing facing East Colvin Street that housed the locker rooms, a squad meeting room, coaches offices, and a medical/training facility. Normal seating capacity for basketball was fifty-eight hundred, but when the basketball floor was removed, some twelve thousand could be seated for a commencement or other kinds of programs. One problem was that when the basketball floor was removed, what one originally found was a tan bark and dirt floor. Dust quickly became a real problem, even when the floor was down for basketball games. In late 1963, the decision to put down a permanent floor was made.

Manley was a new home for practice for football and competition for basketball, two programs that had achieved national prominence in the 1950s. In the 1960s, Syracuse sports reached the height of both popularity and money-making potential. However, before the end of the Tolley era, both sports were in decline.

*   *   *

Expectations were high for Orange football as the team prepared for the 1960 season. Despite the departure of Ger Schwedes, twenty-three lettermen returned from the championship season, and the rest of the championship backfield was still there—including Ernie Davis. However, two losses came on successive weekends, first to Pitt, and then to Army. The Orange finished at 7–2, and did not win a second consecutive bowl invitation. (In terms of the bowl fortunes of the Orangemen, it should be kept in mind that not only were there fewer bowl games to go to—two losses pretty much kept you out of a bowl—but there were even fewer slots for an independent team like

Syracuse, as the vast majority of bowl invitations were tied to a specific league championship.)

The 1961 season produced what was perhaps the most controversial moment in Syracuse football, and unquestionably its finest individual achievement. The team finished at 7–3 but was supplanted as the number one team in the east by Penn State, who beat the Orange that fall 14–0. In the final game of the seventy-five-year rivalry with Colgate, Syracuse once again demolished the Red Raiders, 51–8. But it was the November game at Notre Dame that would return to haunt Orange fans for decades. Trailing 14–0 in the third period, Syracuse rallied to take the lead, 15–14. As time ran out, the Notre Dame kicker missed a field goal. But Syracuse was called for roughing the kicker, and Notre Dame got another chance, fifteen yards closer to the goalposts. Final score: Notre Dame 17, Syracuse 15. A fuming Schwartzwalder demanded a review, and the review concluded that there had been no infraction and that Syracuse should win, 15–14, a judgment with which the referees, conceding that they had made an error, agreed. But Notre Dame refused to concede defeat, and as a result, the loss stayed on Syracuse's record. Thanks to this game and the national attention it received, the next year the NCAA introduced a new rule—a game could no longer end on a penalty.

In what would have been the grudge match of the century, Notre Dame was invited to play Syracuse in Philadelphia's Liberty Bowl. The Irish declined, citing its long-standing policy against playing in bowl games. Instead, Syracuse played Miami (Florida) in the 1962 Liberty Bowl game, winning by a score of 15–14. Davis singlehandedly won the game for them—carried thirty times for 140 yards.

Yet it was Ernie Davis's winning of the Heisman Trophy—the first African-American player to win the honor, and, to date, the only Syracuse player to win—that made the season singular for Syracuse fans. The trophy was well earned. Over his career, Davis had surpassed Jim Brown's records in total yardage, rushing yardage, and points scored. He had led his school to two bowl games, and had been the driving force in both those bowl victories—one for a national championship. He performed these feats of athletic skill with a gracious demeanor that was remembered by every person he ever met at Syracuse. John Mackey, Davis's roommate at Syracuse and the consensus pick for the greatest tight end to play the professional game, remembered that Davis was "a star when he came on campus — [and he was] only a bigger star when he left." Sylvia Cole Mackey echoed her husband's sentiments and added that Davis was "the most giving person I knew." In the words of another alum: "Just write that Ernie was a nice guy. That says it all." Davis was drafted by the Cleveland Browns, and National Football League fans drooled at the prospect of having Davis and Jim Brown in the same backfield. However, Davis never played a game as a Brown. On May 18, 1963, he died of an advanced case of leukemia.

Clearly, any season that followed the loss of a Heisman winner would be labeled a "rebuilding year." In 1962 the Orangemen went 5–5; the big game was a 34–6 upset of Navy, in which Mackey — who had been moved from tight end to fullback to make sure that he touched the ball more often — scored two touchdowns. The next season was a stronger campaign, as the 8–2 Orangemen scored an average of twenty-three points per game and got even for their controversial 1961 loss at Notre Dame by beating the Irish 14–7. But it was the 1964 team that would once again bring bowl glory to the hill, thanks to a new number 44 — the back that the press would soon dub the "Connecticut Comet."

*   *   *

A shy child from New Haven, Connecticut, whose father died of cancer when he was eight years old, Floyd Little had decided upon attending Syracuse after meeting Ernie Davis. However, Little was a weak student who had to spend several terms at the Bordentown Military Institute to raise his grades before being admitted. In fact, Little almost did not get into Syracuse. After seeing his grades, Piskor turned down his application; however, after an influential alumnus called to complain, Tolley reversed Piskor's decision. Little was twenty-one years old when he entered Syracuse, and perhaps it was this maturity that made him the team leader neither Brown nor Davis had become. Little himself called team meetings and lectured the team at halftime during a game. His comparatively small size (5-foot-11, 190 pounds) kept him from becoming a power running back like Brown. But Little had incredible balance and an uncanny ability to change direction.

Even Schwartzwalder allowed himself to gush a bit: "I even get excited when he has the ball."

Once again the Orange had a quality running game, as Little was joined in the backfield by senior Jim "Bo" Nance, a heavy power runner from Indiana, Pennsylvania, who doubled as a two-time national collegiate heavyweight wrestling champion. After an opening loss against Boston College, the Orange had their home opener against Kansas. The Jayhawks were favored, thanks to the presence of halfback Gale Sayers. But it was Little's five touchdowns and 159 yards that led Kansas coach Jack Mitchell to marvel: "That was the greatest performance by a back that I have ever seen." (Schwartzwalder's comment to the press: "Not bad for a rookie.") The Orange rolled on, including a 39–0 upset victory over UCLA in which Nance gained 148 yards, tripped up only by a season-ending loss to West Virginia. Little and Nance accounted for 1,779 yards and twenty-five touchdowns in 1964; together they averaged 251 yards a game.

The ninth-ranked Orangemen met the seventh-ranked Louisiana State University Tigers in the January 1965 Sugar Bowl. The game featured the most combined losses for two Sugar Bowl opponents since 1945, and Syracuse had not played a Southeastern Conference (SEC) team since the 1953 shellacking by Alabama. Perhaps as a result, the game was weakly billed in the national press, and the crowd of sixty-five thousand was the smallest since 1939. The game, however, boiled down to two simple statistics: Little was held to forty yards; Nance was held to seventy yards. LSU won, 13–10.

The 1965 season began with several early losses, and Schwartzwalder decided to make a quick move to shore up his backfield, hurt by the graduation of Nance (who had gone on to the Boston Patriots of the American Football League), and he moved rookie Larry Csonka from linebacker to fullback. It was a gutsy, and a successful, move. From Stow, Ohio, Csonka had played as an offensive lineman in high school—he had not even tried the fullback slot until his senior year. In his first game against Maryland, he rushed for only 26 yards. But in his second game, a loss to UCLA, Csonka rumbled for 162 yards— just a yard short of Jim Nance's best day (163 against West Virginia in 1964). Later that season, Csonka carried for 216 yards against West Virginia, a new school record. He finished the season with 795 yards. Together, Little and Csonka ran for 1,860 yards in 1965, and Little became the first Syracuse player to rush for more than 1,000 yards in a single season (1,065). Little also tied the record for the most pass receptions in one season at twenty-one, and had a repeat season as All-American.[1] His assessment of the season: "I achieved the goal that I set back in September. I finished the season in one piece."

In 1966, after two heartbreaking losses to Baylor and UCLA, the Orangemen never looked back. Csonka ran for 1,012 yards, and Little, now in his senior year, surpassed Ernie Davis's career rushing record with 2,704 yards. Little's personal accomplishments were astounding: in 1966 he set a record for the most total yardage in his career (4,947) and the most touchdowns (46); he held new Syracuse single-season marks for rushing (1,065), touchdowns (19), points (114), and punt-return yardage (423); and he tied the single-season mark for pass receptions (21). Not only did Little lead the team in yardage, he was a leader of the team. He played hurt, gave impassioned locker-room speeches, and was the deciding factor in the Orangemen being invited to Jacksonville for the January 1967 Gator Bowl versus Tennessee. The first half of the game was all Volunteers; the second half was all Little, who gained 216 yards. It was, however, not enough: Tennessee 18, Syracuse 12. Grumbling alumni pointed to Schwartzwalder's decision—fourth and two, on the Tennessee four-yard line—to pitch the ball not to Little or Csonka, but to halfback Oley Allen, who was thrown for a loss.

With the graduation of Little, all eyes were on Csonka for the 1967 season. When asked his game plan for that season's game against Penn State, he replied: "Just run over 'em." This he did all season, rushing for 1,217 yards. But the team had other strengths. One of the best quarterbacks in Syracuse history, Rich Cassata, broke the record in 1967 for most passes completed in a season (92), and in the Orangemen's 32–14 upset victory over UCLA Cassata broke a twenty-year-old record for total offense in a single game. Halfback Tom Coughlin caught passes for 257 yards and rushed for 256 more.

1. For a complete list of sports championships and All-Americans from 1942 to 1969, see appendix D.

But it was Csonka's team. By the time of his graduation, The "Stow Steamroller" had eclipsed many of the records of Brown, Davis, Nance, and Little—as a fullback. He was a unanimous All-American, finished fourth in the Heisman balloting, and the team was twelfth in the nation. Their 8–2 record came too late, however—the major bowls had all been filled up.

The graduation of Cassata and Csonka led to the first of what were to be several rebuilding years for Schwartzwalder. In 1968 the team started the season with an impressive—and surprising—5–0 record, only to experience athletic meltdown following a 43–0 loss to California, finishing the season at 6–4. The 1969 season—the centennial of Syracuse University football—was a 5–5 disappointment, despite the success of the team's true personality, soccer-style place-kicker George Jakowenko. Schwartzwalder would endure three more disappointing seasons before retiring. When he left the hill at the end of the 1972 season, his record at Syracuse stood at 153–91–3.

*   *   *

As the football team continued to prosper in the sixties, it seemed that the basketball team was headed toward oblivion. Their performance early in the decade was horrendous—the 1960–61 team was 4–19, and the 1961–62 squad went 2–22—before Marc Guley retired. He was replaced by Fred Lewis, who had played with the Sheboygan Redskins and the Baltimore Bullets in the old National Basketball League, then coached both high school ball and college at Mississippi Southern before coming to Syracuse. In the 1962–63 season, Lewis struggled through, helped by the fact that it was also the first season for the Manley Fieldhouse (the first game in Manley was on December 1, 1962, a 36–35 victory over Kent State). But all eyes were on the 13–4 *freshman* team. The Tangerines were led by one of Lewis's first recruits, an athlete Lew Andreas would call "the best freshman basketball player I have ever seen at Syracuse."

Dave Bing, a 6-foot-2 sophomore from Washington, D.C., single-handedly resurrected the Syracuse University basketball program from the dead in 1963–64. In his first year on the varsity, Bing scored 556 points, averaged 22.2 per game, and led the squad in scoring and assists. With the help of center Chuck Richards, who had transferred from Army (and who was instrumental in holding Bill Bradley to

Dave Bing, 1966

seventeen points in a victory over Princeton), as well as Bing's room-mate Jim Boeheim, the rejuvenated Orangemen received an invitation to the NIT, where they were defeated in the first round by New York University, 77–68. But Bing and Richards had established new scor-ing records for a sophomore and a junior, and had become just the second and third players to go over 500 points in a season. The fol-lowing season, the Orange went 13–10, but Bing scored 533 points, averaged 23.2 per game, and established an all-time SU record for points scored by a junior (45 points against Colgate.)

Lewis's 1965–66 squad finally jelled. They hit the hundred-point mark an incredible fourteen times, and finished the season at 22–6— the best record since Syracuse's national championship year of 1925–26. Senior Jim Boeheim (who won the Varsity Club's MVP Award for the Cornell game) and junior Rick Dean contributed to a balanced attack, which earned the Orangemen an invitation to the NCAA tournament. Syracuse drew a first-round bye, then beat

Davidson in the second round, 94–78. Their loss to Duke in the Eastern regionals, 91–81, was a bitter disappointment for Orange fans.

Four players averaged in double figures that season, but it was Dave Bing's team. The senior made the first team of every All-American squad chosen, Syracuse's first basketball All-American since Vic Hanson, some thirty-nine years earlier. When his career was completed, Bing had 794 points, which made him the all-time scorer in SU history. He had averaged 28.4 points per season, and was a key rebounder and assist leader.

The Orangemen did not immediately enter into a post-Bing slide. The 1966–67 team went 20–6, went to the NIT, but lost in the first round to New Mexico, 66–64. The slide began in 1967; in the next two seasons the Orangemen went 11–14 and 9–16.

*   *   *

To discuss every sport played at the university during these years would take another book. But two deserve our attention, not just for their tradition at the university, but also for a peek into the future. While not a major sport during the Tolley years, baseball was certainly the most venerable sport at the institution. The first athletic contest at Syracuse University was a baseball game, an 1873 loss to Hamilton College. Lew Carr, who had been coaching since 1910, retired after the 1942–43 season. Following the war, Forest Evashevski led the team for one season, and he was replaced in 1946 by Ted Kleinhans. Kleinhans had had fifteen years experience in organized baseball. He had played with the Cleveland Indians, Chicago Cubs, Philadelphia Nationals, and Cincinnati Reds; pitched for the 1936 world champion New York Yankees; and, in a final stop, he had played with the Syracuse Chiefs. He would coach the team for the next twenty-one years, and until 1962 he would experience only one losing season. The 1960 and 1961 teams were outstanding, featuring future major-league pitchers Dave Guisti and Billy Connors. In 1961 Syracuse went 18–3 and was invited to the College World Series. In Omaha, the Orange went 2–2, beating Colorado State and Western Michigan and losing twice to Oklahoma State.

But from 1961 to 1967, the team began a slide that culminated in the 1966 retirement of Kleinhans. Andy Mogish, who had mostly coached freshman sports on the hill, took over the team. In that same year, the university took all baseball scholarships away. This makes the 15–5 record of the 1968 Orange entry so surprising. However, the team was snubbed by the NCAA tournament. The sport would be phased out in 1972.

The future of the sport that the native Americans called *bagataway* was much brighter. In 1916 the College of Forestry put together the university's first lacrosse team (they lost to Hobart in their first game, 8–1). In 1921 Syracuse won the world championship, as they beat Oxford-Cambridge 4–3 in Archbold. Ten years later, Roy Simmons, Sr., took over the team. A tailback in high school who was recruited by Amos Alonzo Stagg to play football for the University of Chicago, "Simmie" earned the nickname "the hobo quarterback" after he played in a game for his old high school while enrolled at Chicago. Expelled for this action, Simmons came east to Syracuse. Simmons would skipper the team until 1971. Between 1931 and 1965, Simmons would coach only one losing team, while also serving as a coach of the football team.

The story of Syracuse lacrosse between 1945 and 1956 was good seasons played before small crowds. Then Jim Brown picked up a lacrosse stick. An All-American high school lacrosse player as well as a football star, one observer looked at Brown and observed: "[He] weighs 220 pounds and runs like the wind, and what do they do with him? They give him a stick to hit you with." In 1957 Brown led Syracuse to an undefeated season, but not the nation's number one ranking—that went to also-undefeated Johns Hopkins. Injuries plagued the lax teams of the late 1950s, and the 1959 squad was Simmons's first losing season in twenty-seven years. The mediocre performance extended into the 1960s, interrupted only by Simmons's 1965 induction into the Lacrosse Hall of Fame. In 1967 Simmons lost six of his top freshmen, declared academically ineligible. However, by the turn of the decade the team had begun to right itself, going 9–4 in 1968 and 9–1 in 1969. Lacrosse was but a few years short of establishing itself as the third major intercollegiate sport at Syracuse.

*   *   *

Before the 1903 arrival at Syracuse of Katherine Sibley as the first instructor of women's physical education and athletics, women's sports was limited to an activity called "Physical Culture for Young

Ladies," a program largely confined to calisthenics. In 1905 Sibley
founded the Women's Athletic Association (WAA), the governing
board that regulated all Women's Athletics at Syracuse, and served as
its first president. In 1908, through Sibley's efforts, WAA won the
right to use the campus gymnasium, previously for men only, three
afternoons a week. Throughout the Tolley period, as it had been for
the previous four decades, WAA was one of, if not the major organization for women on the campus. During the 1940s, WAA conducted
the balloting that led to the establishment of the women's cheerlead-
ing team, and in the 1950s it sponsored the annual blazer sale that
was one of the biggest fund-raisers of the academic year. In the sixties, WAA was spearheaded by Doris Soladay, professor of health and
physical education. It sponsored a Sports Convocation, two intercollegiate sports days every year, a blood drive in the fall and the spring,
and a spring banquet that drew more coeds than any other social
event.

WAA planned women's athletics during the period with virtually
no funding,[2] and with an innovative system that put the burden of
women's athletics solely on the shoulders of the coeds themselves.
WAA organized athletic clubs that were, in themselves, responsible

2. The total amount budgeted for Women's Athletics during the Tolley years, with
some earlier figures for comparison:

1924–25	$3132.65	
1927–28	$2021.00	
1928–29	$2182.70	
1950–51	$200.00	
1954–55	$917.71	
1955–56	$1000.00	
1956–57	$1000.00	
1957–58	$1037.00	
1958–59	$600.00	(total budgeted for home and away sports: $285.00)
1960–61	$1039.00	
1962–63	$1125.00	
1963–64	$1125.00	
1964–65	$1125.00	
1966–67	$1199.00	
1967–68	$1534.00	
1968–69	$1749.00	(Basketball budgeted for $40.00)
1969–70	$3500.00	

See Women's Athletics Records (RG 12), Syracuse University Archives, box 2, doc-
uments folder, and box 4, minutes folders.

for scheduling their extramural matches with other schools, and the student managers were responsible for getting their teams to the places on time. These clubs were open to almost any woman student who was interested, although in some instances absolute beginners were discouraged from attending the WAA activity and encouraged to take a physical education class. Every club had a student manager and a faculty advisor, and each club met twice a week. All Syracuse women were associate members of WAA, and they became active members upon 50 percent participation in an activity, or with membership on the WAA Board or Dormitory Council.

There was, then, intercollegiate athletics for women during the Tolley years. However, it was on a club level—when an SU team went to play at another school, it was listed, for example, as the "Syracuse University WAA Hockey Team." Starting in 1961, WAA sponsored a "Sportsday," when women from area campuses came to Syracuse to compete in basketball, fencing, swimming, and volleyball. There would not be any steps taken toward parity between men and women in the university's athletic department until 1972, when Title XI prohibited federal aid to institutions that discriminated on the basis of sex. Even then, there would not be a full intercollegiate athletic program for women until 1975.

*   *   *

Despite the proclivity of armchair quarterbacks to moan about the behemoth nature of college sports and how it has become a corporate enterprise in and of itself, it must be argued that no student activity—football, chorus, or drama—exists in a vacuum, cut off from the university or the world at large. The changes in the nation between 1960 and 1963 were astounding, and none captured the public imagination more than the civil rights movement. Syracuse University found itself in an interesting position in December 1963, when the Syracuse University Committee on Equality requested of the athletic board that the university drop segregated schools from its schedule. Black athletes representing the former Methodist school on Piety Hill had been the victims of the worst kind of prejudice throughout the university's history—the treatment of Wilmeth Singh and the treatment of the four black football players at the 1960 Cotton Bowl are the best known, but far from the only examples of this treatment. For example, Bernie Custis remembered that at the end of the 1951 season, he was asked to play in the East-West Shrine game in San Francisco. When the Sports Information office sent out a picture of him, and the bowl selection committee found out he was black, it rescinded its invitation.

And yet by 1963, Syracuse University football—not a conference member whose champion was locked into a bowl berth, but an independent who had to make do with the few bowl invitations that would be given to independents—was trying to play a truly national schedule that would get the attention of the New Year's bowl committees. In February 1964 the United Press International released a story blazing that "Syracuse University today refused to drop segregated colleges and universities from its sports schedules. . . . Acknowledging that it was 'unsportsmanlike' to discriminate against an athlete because of race, the board said it was also unsportsmanlike to refuse to compete against a worthy opponent." The Syracuse chapter of the AAUP went on record calling for the university to not participate in athletic contests with any school that had segregated admissions policies.

In theory, at least, Tolley supported the stance of the AAUP. But he also noted the hypocrisy of the alumni who were arguing that the school should not play Virginia Military Institute (VMI) that fall (the football contest that had precipitated the controversy), but quietly looked the other way when bowl bids came in the mail. In an angry letter to one alum who was pressing Tolley to drop VMI from the schedule, the chancellor shot back that "it is interesting to note that no one suggested we should not play segregated Texas in the Cotton Bowl when we had John Mackey, John Brown and Ernie Davis. Nor has anyone suggested that we should withdraw from Olympic competition because we must compete with Russia."

This was far from the end of the matter. On March 13, the university senate went on record as opposing the playing of segregated schools, and eighteen black athletes, including Jim Nance and Dave Bing, issued a statement supporting the senate's stand on antisegregation play. On May 10, protesters picketed the Spring Weekend game, carrying signs that read "Football Victories should be Moral

Victories." Early the next week, Tolley announced that the board of athletics said that it would consider, as a factor in scheduling, "the concerns with regard to playing segregated schools." Tolley said that this policy statement "clearly indicates a decision not to schedule segregationist institutions."

*   *   *

A well-versed wag once said that sports imitates life. Such a protest as the one that surrounded the decision to keep VMI on the schedule could never have happened before 1964. The parts necessary for the conflict—a bubbling civil rights movement, a rejuvenated university senate, and a student body willing to be activated for a cause, were not present on the campus even five years earlier. Syracuse University was about to embark on a decade of challenge unlike any that it had ever seen. By the time it was over, the traditional power structure of the university had changed, and Tolley was gone.

George Wiley

The Challenge of Civil Rights

I ask that you offer to the political arena, and to the critical problems of our society which are decided therein, the benefits of the talents which society has helped to develop in you. I ask you to decide, as Goethe put it, whether you will be an anvil — or a hammer. . . . The duty of the scholar — particularly in a republic such as ours — is to contribute his objective views and his sense of liberty to the affairs of state and the nation.

—Senator John F. Kennedy, Commencement Address,
Syracuse University, May 1957

[The] most significant change in the university during the last four years, difficult as it is, for these years have been extraordinary ones, I would have to point to the increased strength of the faculty.

—Tolley in the *Daily Orange*, May 14, 1965

THE GROWTH experienced by Syracuse University between 1942 and 1962—William Tolley's twentieth year as chancellor—was little short of phenomenal. In 1942 Syracuse University had 5,705 students. In 1962 it had 19,048, including 5,200 in off-campus centers. Eighty percent of the faculty in 1962 had joined the staff *after* Tolley became chancellor. In 1962 there were 249 sponsored research programs at SU, amounting to some $9 million. By 1962 the amount of spending on new constructs had risen to $42 million. In 1942 the operating budget of the university was $5 million; in 1962 it was $38.5 million.

The same thing was going on in California. In his 1963 *The Uses of*

a University, University of California president Clark Kerr looked at
his own institution and found that it had changed profoundly since
the war. He noted that this evolution, which had created an organization that operated at a budget of half a billion dollars with a total
personnel of forty thousand people, "brought departments into universities, and still new departments; institutes and ever more institutes; created vast research libraries; [and] turned the philosopher on
his log into a researcher in his laboratory or the library stacks." He
noted the creation of university presses, research centers, and graduate schools, and he singled out the development of extension programs. His university was now, to use Kerr's term, the "multiversity."
He compared it to a small state or city, with "fractionalized power"
that must be governed. But, Kerr warned, there was no longer a consensus as to who would govern this conglomeration. He observed
that the faculty and students were now lobbying for a role in the gov-
ernance of the multiversity along with the president, and suggested
that to properly walk the institution through the landmines to come,
the president of the multiversity must not be a "giant" as of old, ruling autocratically from on high, but a "mediator" whose job was to
find "peace within the student body, the faculty, the trustees; and
peace between them and among them."

Like California, Syracuse had become a multiversity. And it was
precisely this growth that made Tolley's institution—and Kerr's California, Grayson Kirk's Columbia, and dozens of other universities
that had modernized and diversified in the 1950s—such perfect
targets for the faculty and student uprisings of the 1960s. A newly
engaged student and faculty body, freed from the shackles of Mc-
Carthyism and spurred on by the call of the New Frontier, grew to
see the multiversity as an impersonal machine that had lost touch
with its humanistic roots. They demanded that it become proactive
in questions of human rights and political issues.

Clashes were inevitable, and arbitrators were, as Kerr predicted,
quite necessary in the chancellor's office. But neither Kerr nor Tolley
were "mediators." Kerr would lose his university before Tolley did,
as he faced the complex demands of the Free Speech Movement. Kerr
was a technocrat; a cold type who fit the profile of banker-chancellor
that the New Left perpetuated. Tolley was no less authoritarian than

Kerr in his managerial style, and just as successful. But as we have seen, Tolley had an air of noblesse oblige about him. At heart a philosopher and a theologian, Tolley was authoritarian because he was convinced that he was acting in the best interest of what he constantly referred to as his Syracuse University "family." Tolley applied the doctrine of *in loco parentis* to both his students and his faculty. In the 1950s, Tolley had protected the academic freedom of his faculty, but he had broached no significant dissent; he alone, for all intents and purposes, controlled the finances of the institution, but it was also largely Tolley who was responsible for its stunning growth; students were not treated as chattel, but neither were they peers to be negotiated with. He not only defended the unwritten "rule number one" of all administrators—that attendance at a university was not a right, but a privilege—he *believed* in it. He was, as Kerr put it, a "giant," a man who ran his university, but would not *deal* with it. A man such as William Tolley could not be expected to compromise with the New Left—and he never did.

The 1960s, then, were a time of battles of epochal proportion between chancellors who were "giants" and their newly proactive multiversities. Large portions of campus communities, galvanized by the events surrounding them in the nation, wanted not just to play a part but to take a leading role. This mood came in direct conflict with administrations that were determined to protect the multiversity from itself as long as possible. Syracuse University was one such campus, and the clash between the proactive university and its protective chancellor would first be seen when Syracuse, and the nation, collided with the speeding train of civil rights.

*   *   *

The Congress of Racial Equality (CORE) was founded at Chicago Theological Seminary during World War II, largely through the efforts of James Farmer and Bayard Rustin. Their original focus was a protest against conscription; in so doing, CORE adopted the ideals of Mahatma Gandhi and pioneered the tactic of nonviolent demonstration that would later be embraced by Martin Luther King, Jr. In 1948 CORE organized one of the first campus sit-ins at the University of Kansas (done during a football game, CORE members had to be carried from the playing field, where they were protesting the school's segregated athletic teams). CORE also supported two large marches on Washington in 1957 and 1958, named the Youth Marches for Integrated Schools, and they actively supported the boycott that followed the February 1, 1960, sit-in of four college students from the all-black North Carolina Agricultural and Technical College at a Woolworth's lunch counter in Greensboro. The sit-ins, boycotts, and the June 1961 Freedom Rides, which took CORE passengers on dangerous bus rides into the heart of the South so as to show the inequity of segregated travel, brought CORE national attention and northern liberal support.

CORE's Syracuse story is inextricably linked to Syracuse University. In November 1961 eleven Syracuse graduate students and chemistry professor George Wiley met. Before their meeting was over, they had formed the Syracuse chapter of CORE and picked Wiley as their chairman. On the surface, Wiley did not seem to be a logical choice to chair a radical organization. He had grown up middle class in a suburb of Providence, Rhode Island, the son of the publisher of one of New England's most influential black newspapers. Shielded from much of the racism of the times, young Wiley had white playmates as a child; Wiley later told friends that he had grown up considering himself white. He developed into a scholar of some note, winning a scholarship to Rhode Island State College in 1949 and taking his Ph.D. from Cornell in 1957. While at Cornell, Wiley rejected the ideas of CORE as too radical. Coming to Syracuse in 1960, Wiley was one of two black faculty members, and a promising young star in the field of organic chemistry. However, both the times and Wiley changed quickly, and the earnest young conservative was converted to activism by the successes and the setbacks of the early civil rights movement in the South.

Syracuse CORE's first real test came in the summer of 1962, when it demanded that the city of Syracuse desegregate its schools. Arguing, in effect, that the problem did not exist, the board refused. This set the scene for several tense meetings between Wiley and David Jaquith, the chairman of the school board. Wiley persuaded Jaquith to back down, and Syracuse CORE sprang to life. In April 1963 CORE reached into the campus with the creation of the Committee on Equality at Syracuse University, which included members of Syracuse CORE and university professors and staff members who wanted "to continue to make known areas where civil rights of individuals are violated."

The events of the next few months galvanized both Syracuse CORE and the nation. In May the nation saw Birmingham police chief Eugene "Bull" Connor unleash his dogs not only on black protestors but also on their children. The Birmingham riot energized the young Syracuse CORE, which picketed the Hotel Syracuse in August until that establishment agreed to hire black waiters and bellmen—thus giving them access to jobs that had higher tips. The Hotel Syracuse confrontation was largely ignored in the Syracuse press, but all eyes were on Syracuse CORE following its participation in the August 28 March on Washington for Jobs and Freedom. Some three hundred Syracusans marched, including Wiley, who had since relinquished the chair of Syracuse CORE, and Bruce Thomas, who had succeeded Wiley.

While momentarily tolerant of Wiley, Tolley clearly did not agree with his tactics. In an April 28, 1963, interview for the *Syracuse Herald-Journal,* Tolley scolded professors in general for "undercutting attempts by the administration and the trustees" to curb student protests. He went on: "I believe with all my heart in academic freedom. The issue is the place of violence. . . . We talk about permissive parents . . . but we ought to begin to talk about permissive faculty people who really encourage disruptive activities." Tolley's definition of academic freedom was an intellectual one, not an activist one. He had defended his teachers' right to think and teach as they pleased; he would never defend their right to *do* as they pleased. But there was not yet any move on the part of Tolley to sanction Wiley or any of the other professors involved.

*   *   *

Syracuse's Fifteenth Ward, also called the "Washington Water-Strip," held 90 percent of the city's black population. It was a dilapidated slum area where rents had been inflated 20–40 percent. The city, as part of its commitment to urban renewal, was planning to tear down the Fifteenth Ward's slum, and replace it with new public housing and a stretch of the Interstate Highway System (what would become Route 81). In the early fall of 1963, the bulldozers moved in. Wiley assessed the situation as the perfect showcase for the problem of black housing—despite the new housing, the city's actions would eventually displace some two thousand families who were unlikely to find a new home in predominately white neighborhoods. As his biographers also note, Wiley hoped that tilting at the housing windmill "would engage more university liberals, who supported the national civil rights movement with rhetoric but did nothing at home."

Joined by the Syracuse chapter of the National Association for the Advancement of Colored People (NAACP) and the Civil Rights Committee of the International Union of Electrical Workers from General Electric, Wiley presented Syracuse mayor William Walsh, a conservative republican, with a nine-point action program. Walsh refused to negotiate. On September 13, several hundred pickets showed up at the construction site on Harrison Street between State and McBride Streets. They padlocked themselves to heavy construction equipment and climbed onto roofs of apartments that were about to be smashed by wrecking balls. Walsh ordered the immediate arrest of fourteen of the demonstrators; most notable was the fact that eight Syracuse University students were among those arrested. Three days later, after themselves meeting with Walsh, nine university students, four of them graduate assistants, were arrested at the Harrison Street site during a Syracuse CORE–sponsored sit-in and picket. The arrests electrified the Syracuse campus. On September 17, a rally of about 250 sympathizers was held on the steps of Hendricks Chapel. During the rally, several faculty members spoke; one argued that "we may violate literal laws, but spiritual laws are more important."

Tolley responded quickly. The same day as the rally, the university released a statement of policy with respect to "recent demonstrations regarding SU personnel":

> No one is above the law. For those whose conscience dictates a deliberate violation of law and order, the university may have compassion, but it cannot stand between them and the civil authorities or offer them institutional aid. Civil disobedience is a grave act fraught with serious consequences. . . . Those who feel or reason their way to this position must be willing to accept the penalties and consequences for themselves.

The proclamation was for naught. On September 17, the same day as the rally and Tolley's proclamation, CORE sponsored its largest protest yet. At the construction site, Wiley circled behind the policemen and then ran into the center of the construction zone, shouting "Remember Birmingham!" Several university students climbed to the top of a seventy-foot boom crane. In the end, eight more students and two faculty members—Wiley and sociology professor Byron Fox— were arrested and taken to the Willow Street jail. The soft-spoken, very religious Fox had joined the faculty in 1947 and had served as the national president of the Society for the Study of Social Problems in 1957–58. For his part, after his arrest Wiley yelled, "They can handcuff my hands, but they can't take away my freedom."

The next day, the *Syracuse Herald-Journal* reported that several key donors had refused to contribute to the Syracuse Plan unless the institution did something about the protestors. The institution did. That day, Eric Faigle, dean of the College of Liberal Arts, announced that any students arrested would be immediately placed on "disciplinary probation." Tolley also requested that Charles Noble, dean of Hendricks Chapel, cancel an all-campus meeting that had been scheduled by Syracuse chaplains to discuss the urban renewal situation as it affected the university. Noble concurred, telling the press that Tolley had asked for a postponement "in order to line up the right speakers for the meeting." Tolley was more candid with his friend Gordon Hoople, then chairman of the board of trustees, when he wrote that he had canceled the meeting "to slow things down a bit and give everybody a chance to think things through."

Nothing slowed down. On September 19, fourteen more students and two professors—Irwin Deutscher, associate professor of sociology and director of the Youth Development Center, and Warren Haagstrom, assistant professor of social work—were arrested. The next day, five more professors—Seymour Miller (sociology), Walso Whitney and Philip Morris (assistant professors of social work), Hans Levy (chemistry), and A. Dale Tussing (economics)—and thirteen students were arrested. By September 20, the incarceration tally stood at fifty-one students and nine faculty members.

Urban renewal was not halted by Syracuse CORE that fall. Twenty-seven blocks of the Fifteenth Ward were razed. Even after the addition of new public housing, approximately 75 percent of the city's black population, four of the five predominantly black churches, and a vast majority of black-owned businesses no longer had homes. But the protests were about to mortally wound *in loco parentis,* as Tolley decided what to do with his prodigal protestors.

*   *   *

Tolley's September 18 decision to automatically place any arrested student on probation raised an immediate hue and cry that he had violated the students' right to due process—they were assumed to be guilty without even the pretense of a hearing. The campus chapter of the AAUP was the first to lodge a protest. The day Tolley announced his policy, Jesse Burkhead, then the chapter president of AAUP, wrote to the chancellor: "We urge that, particularly in these cases, the Administration observe the same standards of due process for students that are now followed for faculty, to further strengthen academic freedom on this campus." But Tolley simply did not believe that the doctrine of academic freedom absolved the institution from its responsibilities under *in loco parentis.* On September 23, the university put out a "clarification" of the disciplinary probation announcement: there would be no change in the policy.

But Tolley was learning that the administration could no longer declare a unilateral end to such issues. The American Civil Liberties Union (ACLU) issued a statement asking the university to reconsider its policy on the disciplinary probation. The AAUP countered Tolley's rebuff to Burkhead with a warning of its own, published in the *Daily Orange:* "Institutional authorities are reminded that not every conviction under law represents an offense with which an educational institution must concern itself." And, perhaps most important, the campus activists refused to quit. On October 1 seven students and two faculty members—Barbara Jackson of home economics, and Roy Doi of bacteriology and botany—were arrested during a sit-in outside Walsh's office. The next day, Professor Joseph Masling and graduate assistant Edwin Day were arrested. The total number of university students and faculty who had been arrested had now reached one hundred.

Perhaps it was the fact that the actions of the activists had been front-page news for over a month; perhaps it was, as several have suggested, the intervention of the ACLU; perhaps it was the student demonstration to support the protestors held outside the administration building on October 3. Whatever the reason, the administration blinked first. On October 4, Frank Piskor announced the creation of the Committee on Graduate Welfare to adjudicate the fate of the arrested students. In his announcement Piskor argued, all evidence to the contrary, that "graduate students are adults, that the university has never acted *in loco parentis* to them and that it has no predisposition to do so now."

As the committee deliberated, attention turned to the arrested faculty, who were claiming that academic freedom protected them from institutional retribution. For his part, Tolley refused to accept that the doctrine gave his faculty the right to break the law. The showdown came in a rather unexpected place—the university senate. Up to this point, the senate had been either moribund or a rubber-stamp for the administration. Jesse Burkhead remembered serving on the senate's Agenda Committee in the 1950s: "That was not a particularly pleasant experience . . . the general attitude, I fear, of both Dr. Crawford and Dr. Tolley, [was] somewhat authoritarian. The agenda was to be controlled by Dr. Crawford, although the Senate by-laws provided for the election by the Agenda Committee of its chairman. Somehow or other, Dr. Crawford was always elected as long as he was Vice Chancellor." Tolley tacitly agreed with Burkhead's assessment in his memoirs, when he remembered that whenever the senate decided an issue by a close vote, he would adjourn the body, have it rethink its position, and return to a second meeting to try to achieve consensus.

Had this been 1959, it is quite likely that the senate would not have even heard the plea of the faculty—or Tolley would have had Piskor, who usually chaired the senate in his absence, gavel down the complaint. But it was a new day, and the faculty was rebelling against *in loco parentis* as it applied to *them*. On October 4, the Agenda Committee's Subcommittee on Academic Freedom, Tenure, and Professional Ethics approved a statement saying that if a faculty member is "convicted of committing an offense in connection with a civil demonstration, this committee will investigate to determine whether

the circumstances of the offense and conviction are a necessary concern of the University, and if so, whether in its opinion the faculty
member has acted in consonance with high standards of professional
responsibility." This was a direct challenge to the authority of the administration to act in such cases, a challenge that was followed three
days later by a stunning memorandum to Tolley, signed by ninety-five
faculty members, entitled "University Leadership in Crisis." The
memo noted the faculty's concern for the lack of "basic democratic
ideals" on campus, specifically noting the decision to place all arrested students on disciplinary probation, and asked for "a statement
of a principle that procedural guarantees will be established, in the
spirit of equity, to protect the rights of *all* members of the Syracuse
community—faculty, graduate students, and undergraduate students
alike." Everyone waited for the response from the administration
building.

Even the faculty was stunned when they learned that Tolley had
given in. On October 8, the day after receiving the faculty's memorandum, the university publicly rescinded its directive for probation
for any student arrested in connection with the civil rights demonstrations. Dean Eric Faigle explained to the press that the order was
rescinded because "The period of immediate danger is over." Two
weeks later, Tolley announced that "No one has or will suffer punitive action by the University because of participation in the recent
civil rights demonstrations in Syracuse. We needed a cooling off period of a few days to head off the danger of violence and personal
injury."

*   *   *

It was early afternoon, November 22, 1963. Freshman David
Tomkinson was in a zoology class in Lyman Hall. A student came in
and whispered the news. The professor closed his book and said:
"President Kennedy is dead. There is no reason to go on." Tomkinson remembered: "There was a pall. No one knew where to go."

*   *   *

The assassination of John F. Kennedy was not, as some popular
writers have argued, the first shot of the revolts of the 1960s. Both

Eisenhower's and Kennedy's administrations had been plagued by civil rights upheavals, upheavals that neither administration was capable of solving or truly willing to try to solve. As a result, Lyndon Johnson inherited a nation that had, for almost a decade, faced the issue of civil rights head-on but had been able to solve little. Kennedy's assassination was a factor in the quick passage of the Civil Rights Act of 1964, which made certain forms of discrimination illegal but by no means adequately protected the whole of the nation's black population from discrimination or segregation. A sizeable cross-section of black youth had become disenchanted with the moderate tactics of national CORE, the NAACP, and Dr. King. Many of them joined the Student Non-Violent Coordinating Committee (SNCC) and were calling for a more immediate solution to the problem. All in all, 1965 promised to be a year of bloody confrontation on the civil rights front.

Syracuse had become one of the hotbeds of that civil rights agitation. Despite Wiley's move from the Salt City to Washington in March 1964 to assume a post on the National Action Council of CORE, Syracuse CORE continued its challenge to the Walsh administration, and university professors and students continued their involvement in the struggle. However, as it did throughout the nation, the March 7 bloodshed at Selma, Alabama, galvanized Syracuse CORE. Since the beginning of the month, it had been protesting against what it claimed to be the unfair hiring practices of Niagara Mohawk, a public power utility centered in Syracuse. Selma lit a fire under the Niagara Mohawk protest. On March 25, five people, including university graduate student David Hutchinson, were arrested while picketing outside the Niagara Mohawk office building. Two weeks later, on April 7, four protestors chained themselves to rental cars so that Niagara Mohawk workers could not get to work. The next day, Professors Fox and Deutscher and several others were arrested outside the office building. Deutscher, a former marine, stood up in court and gave an impassioned speech in front of the judge about how he had fought in World War II, and how the reaction of the police to the protestors was wrong. The *Herald-Journal* sniffed that the protestors were "racial showoffs."

The issue stayed alive into the late spring. In early May, twenty-one blacks from Selma came to Syracuse to join the picket lines (one participant remembered that many in the movement began to refer to the city as "Selmacuse"), and on May 5 CORE head James Farmer spoke at a rally at Clinton Square. Warning of a long, hot summer in Syracuse, a city that he predicted would become a "major testing ground for human rights," Farmer shouted that "Before I would be a slave, I would go to my grave." Before the end of the summer, Niagara Mohawk capitulated and resolved to follow a nondiscriminatory employment policy and to upgrade the skills of nonwhites. However, the community continued to talk about what had been widely reported as the radicalization of Syracuse University, and waited for the next explosion.

It came on August 11, 1965. Before the rioting in South-Central Los Angeles—the Watts district—had subsided five days later, thirty-four people were dead, four thousand had been arrested, and Watts had been annihilated. Both Los Angeles mayor Sam Yorty and Chief of Police William A. Parker blamed the riot on the presence of civil rights workers in the city.

Stuart Gerry Brown

CHAPTER 15

Challenged Curricula

[It will] cause serious trouble.

—Charles Walker, head of the Syracuse Housing Administration,
on the Community Action Training Center

A S WAS THE CASE in the 1950s, Syracuse University in the 1960s
continued to be innovative in the development of its curricula
and programs. However, the fight against *in loco parentis* soon spilled
out into curricular matters. All-college requirements were questioned, or, in many cases, discarded, and college courses were used as
an active part of the civil rights and the antiwar movements. Those
who would argue that faculty members could not proclaim their politics as they pleased soon found themselves objecting to what those
faculty members taught, and the way they taught it.

*   *   *

Under the leadership of Paul Appleby and Harlan Cleveland, the
Maxwell School had expanded in both the national and international
arenas. But in its desire to expand its influence, the school began to
reassess a required offering that had been George Maxwell's pet project and one of the conditions he placed upon his largesse—the citizenship requirement. Disappointed with the youth of the 1920s,
Maxwell's original plan called for the teaching of citizenship to every
student at Syracuse. This unique course, begun by Dean William
Mosher, was originally entitled "The Introduction to Responsible
Citizenship," and utilized a text edited by Mosher and his Maxwell

associates.[1] According to the instructors, the major objectives of the course were "the development of a personal appreciation on the part of the student of what it means to live with others in this complex society of ours, and secondly, the development of critical insight into social situations." The course was, as Maxwell mandated, a requirement for all students in arts and sciences. But, as happens with any required course after a number of years, lectures became stale and the faculty fatigued. Mosher's death in 1945 took from the course its chief defender, and many on campus began to argue that it had become a general "introduction to social science" course and thus had lost its citizenship focus. By 1947 the course was taking on a hail of sniper fire from all quarters.

Responding to this criticism, Appleby hired Stuart Gerry Brown from Grinnell College and charged him with rejuvenating the course. Brown, who would go on to become the first biographer of Adlai Stevenson, had served as the director of the Army Specialized Training Program during World War II and had taught English and philosophy at Grinnell. From his perch as chair of Maxwell's American Studies program and director of the Citizenship course, Brown went to work. He renamed the course: first it was "Responsible Citizenship" and then "American Issues." He also instituted a case-study approach, whereby students would discuss a specific topic throughout the semester, earning one credit. Brown also pulled a half-dozen Maxwell professors together, and in 1951 they released *Great Issues,* which replaced Mosher's text as the required text for the course. But it was the general quality of the course instruction that markedly improved under Brown's aegis. Citizenship drew some of Maxwell's most prominent professors—Fenton Gage, Robert Engler, T. V. Smith, and senior political scientist Phillips Bradley served as four of its most dynamic teachers. Even Tolley was listed as a faculty member in citizenship. However, it was the graduate students, many of whom were working for the D.S.S., who did most of the teaching. Many of them would go far in their chosen career of teaching; two of them—Edward E. (Bob) Palmer, and Michael O. Sawyer—would

1. William E. Mosher, ed., *Introduction to Responsible Citizenship* (New York: Henry Holt, 1941), with chapters by Herman C. Beyle, Marguerite J. Fisher, W. Freeman Galpin, Douglas G. Haring, Ralph V. Harlow, and James A. Ross, Jr.

not only become full-time faculty members, but also in their turns become directors of the Citizenship course.

However, by 1960 the fundamental premise of the course—that it should be required of all social science and liberal arts students— came under fire in the university's Curriculum Committee. Led by mathematician Otway Pardee and seconded by virtually the entire philosophy department, a motion came forth to strip the course of its status as a requirement. Many of its opponents opined that the course was a holdover from the cold war period, where little was done in it save flag-waving and polemicizing that the government of the United States was the best in the world. There were other subtexts to the dispute: departmental jealousy over the amount of attention and faculty funding that Maxwell was receiving as a result of the requirement, and the enmity that the often haughty Brown had earned for himself among many of his colleagues. But at its core, Citizenship was under attack because it was an all-college *requirement*. And by 1960 other colleges and departments refused to acquiesce to such academic regimentation.

Brown, who had several years earlier given up the directorship of the course to Palmer, was incensed, and he vented his frustrations to Tolley and Cleveland. It was to no avail. For the 1961–62 academic year, the Citizenship course ceased to be a requirement; it would later be entirely disestablished from the Maxwell curriculum. Embittered, Brown moved to Florida and then on to the University of Hawaii.

Stephen Kemp Bailey succeeded Cleveland as dean in September 1961. A writer of books on Congress and a former mayor of Middletown, Connecticut, Bailey had joined the Maxwell political science faculty in 1959. It was Bailey's skill as a fund-raiser that yanked Maxwell out of the shadow of the Citizenship fight. In December 1962 the school received a $1 million grant from the Ford Foundation. The grant, which was counted as Maxwell's share of the Syracuse Plan fund-raising drive, was used for the expansion of the school's facilities and personnel. The Southeast Asia and East African programs were expanded; a new master's degree in International Public Administration was introduced, and a five-year program on research into the United Nations and other international organizations, to be carried on in connection with the College of Law, was established. Bailey was also instrumental in winning for Maxwell in 1967 the Albert Schweitzer endowed chair from the state of New York, which came with $100,000, about half of which was paid in salaries and expenses to a distinguished scholar. The first recipient of the chair was Dwight Waldo, director of the Institute of Governmental Studies at UCLA Berkeley. In 1969 Bailey left Maxwell to become a regent for the state of New York. He was succeeded by Alan K. "Scotty" Campbell, who would remain Maxwell's dean until June 1975.

By 1960 all-college requirements were being challenged by the faculty of most multiversities. But there was another, even more troublesome side of the curricular coin in the 1960s. Many activist faculty members tied their research, grant monies, and even their classes to their social agendas. The result was often a bitter clash between town and gown over which institution—local government or the university—was better equipped to improve the lot of the citizenry. There is no better example of this quandary that the story of Warren Haagstrom's Community Action Training Center (CATC).

*   *   *

Lyndon Johnson inherited two wars from the Kennedy administration. One, the war in Vietnam, had an explosive effect on college campuses. The other, the "War on Poverty," was described by Johnson as a "milestone in our 180-year search for a better life for our people." In August 1964 Congress passed the Economic Opportunity Act, which created the Office of Economic Opportunity (OEO), and charged that agency with developing programs to aid in the eradication of poverty in the nation. The sums appropriated for this war—the OEO received $10 billion between 1964 and 1970—were staggering by peacetime standards. Along with many other academicians, Warren Haagstrom of the university's School of Social Work saw in the OEO an opportunity to get funding for a project he had been planning for several years. Originally from Fergus Falls, Minnesota, Haagstrom entered the marines in 1942, fresh out of high school. He earned his B.A. and M.A. from the University of Minnesota, and his Ph.D. from the University of Michigan. Haagstrom came to Syracuse in 1962 as a field instructor and assistant professor in the field of social work and soon after became a member of Syracuse CORE. Described by a CORE colleague as being "cerebral," Haagstrom was one of those who had been arrested in the 1963 protest in the Fifteenth Ward.

Haagstrom had accepted the ideals of community organizers such as Saul Alinsky, who argued that for the War on Poverty to work, intellectuals must help to organize the poor to look out for themselves. Accordingly, Haagstrom put together a proposal for a center that would train lower-income people in self-determination. His idea was to train professional social workers in effective methods of working with low-income neighborhoods, where they would form organizations and neighborhood councils so that low-income families could help themselves. In January 1965 the OEO, described by one author as "eager to show some results of the 'war' as quickly as possible," approved Haagstrom's proposal for a two-year demonstration grant of $314,329 to fund what Haagstrom called the Community Action Training Center (CATC), which was under the auspices of University College, as was its parent school of social work.

Given the state of race relations in the city of Syracuse, Haagstrom's plan was a volatile one from the start. Student interns made up the lion's share of CATC's workers. Once trained, they went out into the black community to try to convince its inhabitants to join together in order to improve their economic lot. The CATC workers had soon formed nine neighborhood organizations, with a total membership of approximately nine thousand people from low-income areas. It did not take long for several factions to converge on CATC, branding it a troublemaker. Only a month after CATC opened in February 1965, several *Herald-Journal* articles and cartoons labeled CATC workers as "soldiers" of the war on poverty—a characterization that brought a quick and angry response from Haagstrom.

But it was the Syracuse Housing Authority (SHA), charged with running the urban renewal housing developments that, as we have seen, sparked the CORE protests of the early part of the decade, that was particularly angered by CATC's tactics. SHA's concern was brought about in equal parts by a genuine fear that CATC would empower minorities to the point where they would rise up and violently strike out at city hall and a fear that CATC was replacing them as the agency of caring in the housing projects. A confrontation between CATC and SHA was inevitable, and it began in April 1965 when Charles Walker, a commissioner of the SHA, wrote directly to President Johnson, claiming that CATC would "cause serious trouble" and requested an investigation of the program and a withdrawal of its grant monies. Walker based his charge on several claims, most notably that the tenants of low-income housing developments had been visited by "organizers" from the university program, representing themselves as being from the federal government, who were soliciting membership in "action committees" that would help the tenants levy their grievances before SHA. Such activity, according to Walker, "create[d] friction along racial lines." Walker's letter, which was "leaked" to the Syracuse press, was quickly followed by a memo from William L. McGarry, also of SHA, to other members of the authority, charging that CATC was using "the old Marxist technique of placing the Authority in a position where it must take the offensive and be the bad guy."

Taking his cue from SHA's characterization of CATC, Mayor William Walsh began to put pressure on the OEO to rescind the grant. In June, Walsh and Haagstrom flew to Washington to lobby their positions. Upon their return, Walsh once again took the offensive, accusing Haagstrom of "complete and total enchantment with . . . guerilla warfare among classes." Concerned that CATC would fuel the fires of an already tenuous civil rights situation in Syracuse, the OEO agreed. Before the end of June, the OEO responded to local political pressure and established a new entity, the Syracuse Community Development Association (SCDA), a nonprofit corporation of local citizens that oversaw the community action program. Although the funding for the teaching and research portion of CATC was kept under the control of the university, the social action (recruitment) function of the program was transferred from CATC to SCDA. Accordingly, the university transferred $46,457 to the association, covering the period from July 1 to September 30, 1965. That December, Sargent Shriver announced that within three months CATC would cease to receive its financing directly from the OEO and would have to apply for funding through Syracuse's official antipoverty agency, the Crusade for Opportunity. Despite a trip to Washington to protest, the final grant, which came in March 1966, was used to phase out the program.

It was the social action side of CATC that dismayed Tolley. Although he continued to support Haagstrom's right to propose and gain a federal grant for any academic project that he wished, Tolley could not reconcile himself to his belief that one of his professors was taking his students—for academic credit and, in some cases, for internship monies—out into the community to stir up trouble. The school of social work was also beginning to get a national reputation as a haven for rabblerousers. An exasperated Tolley wrote to Clifford Winters, then the dean of University College and, nominally at least, Haagstrom's boss, that

> an examination of the materials dreamed up by Professor Haagstrom and his employees in their apparent declaration of war on the Syracuse Housing Authority makes it abundantly clear that the sooner we can get out of social action the better. Once more it arouses my suspicion that scholars deeply involved in social action are not likely to keep their objectivity as scholars in the matter of training and research. Professor Haagstrom's performance to date suggests that when we do unload the social action part of the present contract we probably should look around for a more objective scholar to take over the training and research parts of the program.

CATC, then, was not only an excellent example of the socialization of the curriculum at Syracuse University, but also serves as a further example of the diverging paths that Tolley and his faculty had taken on the issue of academic freedom. Again, Tolley was clear—his faculty could not stir up trouble and expect to be protected by the doctrine of academic freedom. Tolley wrote to Ahlberg that "at the end of the current semester if not earlier," Haagstrom was to be "relieved of all administrative duties and return to full time teaching and research," a decision he called "final." By the end of 1966, Haagstrom had left the university.

DAILY ORANGE

Syracuse University's Daily   Newspaper Since 1903

Vol. 61, No. 106   Syracuse, N.Y., Wednesday, May 13, 1964   10 Cents

Chancellor Tolley 'Canes' Picketer

Eyewitnesses Retell Swatting On the Quad

Three Syracuse University students claimed to be eyewitnesses when Chancellor William P. Tolley struck a picketer in the Army and Air Force ROTC review on the quad Tuesday at the annual Chancellor's review day.

Gordon Jozeloff, Michael Krassner, and Joel Simon said they saw the Chancellor hurry from the reviewing stand and stop the picketers as they were crossing the quad.

Jozeloff, a freshman enrolled in the College of Liberal Arts and a stringer (reporter) for the United Press International, "took a step back, swung his cane and swatted the picketer."

The picketer was identified as James Overgaard, an employee of the Mass Library and an SU student.

Jozeloff said the Chancellor had looked annoyed and irritated but that he smiled after he hit Overgaard.

Simon, a junior in the College of Liberal Arts, said the Chancellor "jumped off the stand and hurried as best he could to the middle of the quad, waving his cane at the picketers to get off the grass."

When the picketers kept on marching, Simon noted, Chancellor Tolley "pulled back his arm with the cane and hit one picketer (Overgaard) on the left arm."

Krassner said he was unable
(See Eyewitness, page 5)

DO STAFF TO MEET

All members of the Daily Orange editorial and news staff will meet 4:45 p.m. today in Prefab 7C, the Hell-box.

All regular staff members as well as anyone interested in working on the DO next year are asked to attend.

The Swing

CHANCELLOR WILLIAM P. TOLLEY (left) in the act of striking JAMES OVERGAARD with his cane during Tuesday's ROTC review.

Overgaard received a bruise on his arm. Looking on is KENNETH LEWIS, another picketer. (United Press International photo)

Demonstrations Disturb Annual ROTC Review

Chancellor William P. Tolley struck one picketer demonstrating against the annual Chancellor's review of Army and Air Force ROTC troops Tuesday afternoon.

The incident occurred about 3:45 p.m. just after the ceremonies had ended. The picketer involved was James Overgaard, a former student and a university library employee.

See editorials, page 2; related stories, pages 4 and 5

Picketers protesting college military training and atomic bombs had entered the center of the quad and followed the withdrawing troops past the reviewing stand where the Chancellor was standing. Overgaard was marching at the rear of the line.

As he passed by Tolley, Overgaard said the Chancellor left the platform and told him to get off the grass. When he refused after two requests, Overgaard said Tolley hit him on his left arm with his cane.

The Chancellor declined to comment immediately after the incident, but an official university spokesman issued the following statement several hours later:

"In permitting peaceful and orderly picketing the university does not sanction interference with official convocations. This was an occasion of military honors.

"Instead of remaining on the sidewalk at the end of the quad as they had been requested, the pickets left the sidewalk and approached any guests at the review before normal observation of courtesy could be allowed. They were twice asked to leave the field."

Bystanders said Overgaard may have made a remark to Tolley as the administrator approached him. This was denied by Overgaard.

The group of picketers changed that Tolley had said "Get off the field, you bums."

The Chancellor later denied making this statement and said
(See Demonstrations, page 5)

At Ceremonies

14 Cadets Receive Medals

Fourteen awards were presented to outstanding Army and Air Force cadets at the annual Chancellor's review Tuesday on the quad.

The American Legion Post 41 award, a medal given to cadets outstanding in academic and leadership achievement was presented to Army Cadet Lt. Col. Edward P. Hoppe and Air Force Cadet A1C Alan Knop.

For outstanding military scholarship, the Daughters of the American Revolution Military Merit Award was presented to Army Cadet Frederick Cook and Air Force Cadet A3C Peter Herman.

Army Cadet Col. Joseph O'Neill and Air Force Cadet Col. Alvin Davis received the Harvey S. Smith Award from Chancellor William P. Tolley. The award consisted of a cup and a $25 stipend to the outstanding senior in both organizations.

The Kiwanis Club presented to the junior cadet demonstrating outstanding drill proficiency, was received by Army Cadet SFC Rostyslav Snyk.

Military merit medals presented by the Onondaga Veterans Council to cadets superior in leadership and discipline were received by Army Cadet
(See Awards, page 4)

Athletic Board Quiet... 'Til Today?

By ANDY PORTE
Editor-in-Chief

The results of the university athletic board's decision on athletic competition with segregated schools will remain secret until the results are presented to the Chancellor.

The board, which met in a four-hour session at Manley Field House Tuesday, decided not to release its decision until the Chancellor had been given an opportunity to hear the board's views.

An official statement, issued by Dean Eric H. Faigle, chairman of the board, read:

"The administrative board on athletics today listened to views of a number of groups and individuals as they affect the matter of athletic scheduling."

"The board discussed the matter at great lengths. It will make its views known when they are reported to the Chancellor."

Representatives from various campus groups appeared before the board. Those who on athletics today listened to approved represented Joint Student Legislature, the Syracuse University Committee on Equality (SUCE) and the graduate students.

Also appearing before the board as individuals were Stephen E. Bailey, dean of the Maxwell School of Citizenship and Public Affairs; James Richard, president of the freshman class, and Negro athletes Sam Penceal and Ted Halunas.

JSL representatives Robert Stern, Marshall Swirnoff and Kathleen Kupsel said they presented the JSL bill opposing athletic competition with segregated schools to the board. Three then added they explained the reasoning behind the bill.

Miss Kupsel said she explained the context of the students in both financial and moral areas. She added that they explained the moral commitment in the bill, pointing out the appearing if any

action taken by the board does not apply to bowl games and post-season tournaments, as well as regularly scheduled games.

The bill requested the university not to schedule any athletic contests with segregated schools, applying to post-season tournaments and bowl games, but not applying to existing contracts.

Penny Haines, representing the all-graduate students who signed a petition requesting an end to athletic competition with segregated schools, said he "tried to talk about morality, but the questions of the board did not pertain to morality."

Halunas said he was told the university does not have any games currently scheduled with segregated schools, but Miss Kupsel said she had been told by a university dean she declined to mention that the university had such a contract signed.

One of the questions asked Halunas, he said, was "Do you remember the time of this Kirkwood game?" After replying sincerity and being more specific he was asked the next question at a World War II.

Dean Bailey said he recommended that the board not
(See Athletic, page 7)

CHAPTER 16

Vietnam

The Students also want to be treated as distinct individuals.

—Clark Kerr, *The Uses of the University* (1964)

I ain't going to Vietnam.

—Sign held by a middle-aged man, whose photo was
prominently displayed in the 1966 *Onondagan*

O N MAY 12, 1964, the *Daily Orange* announced that a demonstration "by an informal group of students who have in common the belief that there are alternatives to compulsory conscription,
and that military training is not compatible with the pursuit of knowledge in a free society" would take place that day during the university's annual review of its Reserve Officer Training Corps (ROTC)
troops. As the review began, protestors waved signs saying "Don't
Teach War at College," "Will Your Children Be Active or Radioac-
tive?" and "The Study of War Is Not a Liberal Art." Campus Security had told the protesters to remain on the north side of the quad,
off the reviewing field, during the ceremonies. The *Daily Orange* reported that despite such warnings, picketers had entered the center of
the quad and followed the withdrawing troops past the reviewing
stand where the chancellor was standing. James Overgaard, an employee of the library and a former Syracuse student, was marching at
the rear of that line. As he passed Tolley, the chancellor rushed down
from the reviewing stand and yelled at Overgaard to get off the grass
—one report had Tolley shouting, "Get off the field, you bums."

After Overgaard refused to budge, Tolley struck him with his cane.[1] Overgaard was treated at Crouse-Irving Hospital for a bruise, but did not press charges. In fact, he was quoted as saying that "I would like to make it clear that I harbor no personal animosity towards the chancellor. There were strong feelings on both sides—only the methods were different."

The caning incident was the first act in a drama that was beginning to unfold on college campuses all over the nation. Colleges in the 1950s reconverted the veteran to civilian life. In the 1960s, many students saw the colleges as a part of the process that moved them into war. And yet in the spring of 1964, the campus was far from united on the subject. The day after the attack on Overgaard, the *Daily Orange* ran an editorial entitled "A Victory for Humanity," which completely excused Tolley for losing his temper and blamed the picketers for ignoring security's warning and Tolley's requests to get off the grass. According to the *DO:* "Regardless of whether the authority is used in a proper fashion, we have the obligation to respect the authority as we see fit. This violation of authority, by persons present as a guest of the university, are [*sic*] as appalling as any swing of the chancellor's cane."

*   *   *

The nation's campuses were hardly aflame in the spring of 1964. Tom Hayden's prediction, eloquently stated in his 1962 *Port Huron Statement,* that the university was a "potential base and agency in a movement of social change," had yet to come to fruition. There was a grumbling about the impersonalization of the multiversity, as well as the inadequacy of society's responses to the call for civil rights, but there had yet been no massive retaliation. The growth of Hayden's Students for a Democratic Society (SDS), the initial participation of students in the activities of CORE, and the call to arms of leaders like John Kennedy and Martin Luther King had energized students but had failed to adequately organize them. As one faculty member remembered, "students had to be encouraged to think about things"

1. Earlier that year, while walking on University Place, Tolley had been hit by a car and had suffered a broken leg.

like civil rights. Even the Free Speech Movement at the University of California at Berkeley, which lasted throughout that fall term, was only a harbinger of things to come. At the time, few recognized the importance of the victory of student activists who, beginning with demands to have their banned literature tables reinstated, ended with a student uprising that forced the university to drop charges against an arrested campus activist. Despite the eloquence of Clark Kerr's prediction of the fate of a multiversity that had no "mediator," most observers felt that ultimately his resignation was simply a result of hubris, mismanagement, or both.

Although the movement against the university in general was smoldering in the fall of 1964, the antiwar movement had been, for all intents and purposes, suspended. Republican presidential candidate Barry Goldwater, who had argued for an escalation of the war, was seen to be the enemy, and most of those who would typify themselves as "liberals" worked for the Johnson campaign, which painted Goldwater as a button-pushing madman, and argued that its candidate would seek a responsible and honorable end to the war. However, as soon as he had disposed of Goldwater, Johnson looked for an opportunity to escalate the war. That opportunity presented itself on February 6, 1965, when the Viet Cong attacked a marine barracks at Pleiku, killing nine Americans. Five days later, Johnson announced that he was initiating a bombing of the North—Operation Rolling Thunder—and one month later, on March 8, 1965, twenty-five thousand ground troops—the first troops since President Kennedy's commitment of nine thousand "advisors" in 1962—were sent to Vietnam. The fact that this first step in the escalation of the war in Vietnam came only one day after the bloodshed at Selma only heightened the stress on college campuses that had already experienced high tension over the civil rights movement, and, with Berkeley as their role model, seemed to be waiting for a reason to detonate. Lyndon Johnson, through his new and expanded Vietnam war, handed discontented faculty and students around the nation a lighted match.

*   *   *

The first group to strike out against the war was the faculty. Few in the academy truly liked Johnson. When on a high plane, it was argued that the proposed reforms of the Great Society were rehashed New Deal ideas that had already cost too much money. But at its core, academia did not like Johnson's style—they despised him because he was not Kennedy, who had made it a point to include them in the highest echelons of administration decision making and had energized intellectuals as no president had done before or has done since.

Johnson's escalation of the war prompted faculty members in all parts of the country to consider the novel idea of calling off classes for a day to discuss the problem of the war in Vietnam. Most textbooks date the beginning of what would be called the "teach-in" movement—defined by one Syracuse University professor as "a convocation of students and scholars who have rediscovered responsibilities to each other"—to the March 24, 1965, teach-in at Ann Arbor that attracted nationally known educators, politicians, and entertainers. However, Syracuse University's teach-in, held on March 12, only four days after the announcement of ground troops, was one of, if not the first teach-in held in the nation. David Bennett, assistant professor of citizenship and American studies, moderated the meeting, which was held in Gifford Auditorium. He was joined by Byron Fox (sociology and anthropology), Stanley Diamond (sociology and anthropology), Robert Shafer (history), and Norman Balabanian (engineering), all of whom spent the evening debating Johnson's recent decisions before a spirited audience.

One month later, a second teach-in was held at Hendricks Chapel. Sponsored by the new Syracuse University Ad Hoc Committee to Stop the War in Vietnam and organized by first-year professor Diamond, the teach-in was attended by some eight hundred students. Dr. Marguerite J. Fisher of political science, who had visited Vietnam in 1954 and 1962, was the first speaker. She was followed by Oliver Clubb, who warned that "we are still not out of the quagmire," and Michael Sawyer, director of the Citizenship Program, who argued against unilateral withdrawal ("Chinese Communism must be contained somewhere"). Other speakers included Paul Meadows, chairman of the Sociology and Anthropology Department ("Here, it's *not* all the way with LBJ"), George Moutafakis, who gave a historical outline of colonialism in the area, and Balabanian, who described his view of the logic behind the American presence in the area. Musa Shamuyarira, an African graduate student, led the group in African dancing and singing, and the teach-in was followed by an all-night vigil for peace.

The April 15 teach-in was a major step in the socialization of Syracuse University. The first month of the teach-in movement at Syracuse University had galvanized students as never before. On the same day as the teach-in, a group of students announced that they would leave within the week for Washington to join an SDS sponsored protest against the war. However, with these giant steps toward the university as social advocate came a rather real reminder that *in loco parentis* still ruled in 1965 — the Dean of Women's office only allowed girls to attend the teach-in if they signed out for a city overnight on their green cards, listing Hendricks Chapel as their "destination."

The teach-ins were merely tolerated by university officials, who throughout 1965 seem to have been waiting for what they perceived to be, in the words of one administrator, "the newest fad" to go away. But combined as they were with reports of death from the jungles of Vietnam, the teach-ins dug in. Throughout the nation, on campuses large and small, in the second half of the year 1965 there were first small teach-ins, and then national teach-ins, like the May gathering in Washington, D.C. (attended by Syracuse professors Diamond, Bennett, Balabanian, and Clubb), where instructors from around the nation faced off against national security advisor McGeorge Bundy while telephone broadcast hookups brought the debate back to forty-nine different campuses. Established groups like the SDS struggled to gain control of the movement, but it was developing too quickly for any one organization or institution to claim ownership. Campuses began to organize groups of concerned faculty and students against the war. It was from these groups that the movement known generically as the "antiwar movement" sprang.

At Syracuse, that organization was the Syracuse University Committee to End the War in Vietnam, formed in September 1965. Early in the fall term, the members of the committee met in Thornden Park and attended a teach-in in Toronto. On October 15, about twenty students, all members of the committee, kept an all-night vigil at Syracuse's Clinton Square in conjunction with the International Days of Protest Against the War. It was a difficult vigil—the protestors were heckled, spat at from passing cars, jeered, and, in several instances, violently attacked.

Along with the efforts of the Committee to End the War in Vietnam, conservative political beliefs were well heard on campus in 1965. Both the Young Democrats and Young Republicans voiced their support for the Johnson administration's effort "to seek a just peace [in Vietnam] through unconditional discussion if possible and force if necessary." On November 4, the *Daily Orange,* still the official outlet for conservative opinion on campus, ran an editorial asking students to "Support U.S. Policy in Viet Nam." On the same day, WAER, in what the *Daily Orange* termed a "tradition-breaking editorial," urged students to join the station and the *DO* in signing a petition supporting the war in Vietnam to be sent to the White House.[2] Within two weeks, they had some two thousand signatures, and by the time the petition was presented in Washington to U. Alexis Johnson, deputy undersecretary of state for political affairs, it had over three thousand signatures on it, including that of Tolley and Stephen K. Bailey, dean of Maxwell. Their stand was reported the *New York Times,* and the reaction of the *Syracuse Post-Standard* was predictable: "Bravo! It is about time that the sensible majority of college students made themselves heard over the student propaganda of the tiny but noisy minorities. . . . But of course the answer of the majority to the beatniks, pacifists, Red sympathizers and others will not be heard in the foreign press as is the clamor of the anti-U.S. showoffs." Later that month, the student senate passed a resolution supporting the Johnson administration's stand against the war; three days later, Jeffrey Moebus, the president of the freshman class, left the university to enlist for Vietnam duty, observing that "I found it difficult to sit and watch and do nothing but talk about Viet Nam."

Any attempts to claim which group—the protestors or the traditional voices—represented the majority of students at Syracuse University during this period is foolish. The vast majority of students continued to be apolitical or simply declined to let their politics be

2. WAER was quickly informed by the Federal Communications Commission that it was most likely the first educational station to editorialize—another first for telecommunications at Syracuse—and it had to say clearly that its views were not necessarily the views of the campus at large.

known, one way or another. But it must be noted that, despite the literature that discusses "the movement" on a national basis, it is difficult, in retrospect, to see any real organizational unity to the antiwar movement at Syracuse University prior to 1968. Other colleges were both more radicalized and more organized. At Syracuse, the early phase of the movement seems to have been more a series of isolated incidents and protests, none of which were started by any one group, but when taken together they show a bubbling of discontent within a large portion of the university community. Some examples of the actions during this period include: student and faculty participation in Norman Balabanian's unsuccessful fall 1966 candidacy for Congress as a candidate of the Citizen's Peace and Liberal Parties; the March 26, 1967, letter to Johnson signed by ninety-two members of the faculty of Syracuse University and Upstate Medical Center, protesting the bombing of the North; the April 28, 1967, protest against the intended visit of Vice President Hubert Humphrey to campus (Humphrey never came, but the protest went on as planned); and the organization of the Syracuse Vietnam Summer Office in the summer of 1967, which sponsored a series of seminars, including a debate between Professor Oliver Clubb and State Department official William Starman.

*　　*　　*

The nation was transformed in 1968; so, too, was the antiwar movement at Syracuse University. Unlike 1964, the war was *the* issue in that year's presidential campaign. The Tet Offensive made it clear that America, despite the rosy pronouncements of her generals, was losing the war; and despite Johnson's desire to get peace talks going in Paris as quickly as possible, there were no longer very many supporters who believed Johnson to be sincere. The hunt for a successor was on. Alan "Scotty" Campbell of Maxwell served as an advisor to the Robert Kennedy campaign; Oliver Clubb was a McCarthy delegate in the local primary. But it was not the election so much as it was two decisions—one made by the government and one made by Tolley—that galvanized the antiwar movement on campus, and led to the largest student demonstration to that point in time in the university's history.

Until November 1967 the draft had been debated on college campuses as a theoretical construct. Some students protested the legal right of the government to take them against their will, others debated the ethics of even having a Selective Service, since its selectivity seemed to have created an army in Vietnam made up largely of blacks and poor whites who could not afford to go to college to get a student deferment. Most debated the point from the safety of a myriad of student deferments. But that November 1967, the issue of the draft became more real than abstract. Lt. Gen. Lewis B. Hershey, the director of the Selective Service, issued a statement that said that student deferrals "are only given when they serve the national interest," and that students who violate the Military Selective Service Act "should be denied deferment in the national interest." Furthermore, Hershey declared that when a local draft board received information of a person's violating the act, it "may reopen the classification of the registrant [and] classify him anew." In February 1968 Hershey announced that graduate students would now be drafted.

The graduate student deferment had led to increased graduate school enrollments in the mid-1960s at most colleges and universities, including Syracuse. When Tolley blasted Hershey's decision, noting that he would not have any objection to a draft if the country was in "grave danger" but until that was proven he saw no need for it, many cynics concluded that he was simply trying to protect enrollment. But from the point of view of the student body, the Hershey letter broke down the last wall of deferment protection for college students. Now virtually no one on a college campus was safe from the draft, and the protest took a new, more desperate turn—students now joined the antiwar movement because they were afraid that the draft would get them killed.

The release of the Hershey letter was followed closely by a second, somewhat related, crisis. Throughout the second half of 1967, universities all over the country had been under pressure to keep off campus recruiters who represented companies that did business with the Pentagon. One of the largest such firms, Dow Chemical, had recruited at Syracuse University for several years, and the administration saw no need to restrict its activities. However, the Committee to End the War in Vietnam and other antiwar groups objected to the fact that Dow was the chief manufacturer of napalm, a thickener made of aluminum soaps that when mixed with gasoline created an

Student protest against recruiting by Dow Chemical, 1968

incendiary bomb that stuck to human flesh. A February 26 protest at the Placement Center, during which two hundred students, joined by Dr. Timothy Leary, attempted to disrupt the recruitment process, was quickly dispersed, but the matter was far from over.

The issues of the draft and campus recruitment quickly meshed together, creating a militant climate on campus. On March 12, 1968, a group of some seventy-five student protestors stormed the Administration Building and locked in forty-five secretaries and administrators for four and one-half hours. While their chief complaint was with Dow, other companies who recruited at the university were also named on the protestor's handouts, including North American Aviation, General Electric, Boeing Company, Hughes Aircraft, Philco-Ford, Naval Underwater Weapons and Naval Oceanographic Institute, Newport News Shipping and Dry Dock, and Caterpillar Tractor. The students' demand was clear-cut: "Let them meet and recruit in a hotel suite—not at our university."

Tolley was in Albany at the time of the lock-in, working for the passage of the Bundy Bill (which would send a large amount of state aid to private colleges and universities), leaving Frank Piskor to meet with two of the protestors for about an hour. Piskor was later joined by economics professor Melvin Eggers, then serving as the faculty representative to the University Senate. Piskor and Eggers convinced the students to leave the building, promising future talks. At 5:30 P.M. the lock-in was ended, and the secretaries and administrators were allowed to leave. The next day, the University Senate also appointed a subcommittee to meet with the students, and then to report to the full senate.

Once again, as it had done in 1965, the senate entered the fray. The day after the lock-in, the Faculty Senate passed a resolution requesting a temporary suspension of campus recruitment by the military services. The full University Senate debated the measure, and, in a novel step, four students were allowed to address that body. Tolley's response was that the senate was merely an advisory body, and that the proposed resolution "implies a formal change in University Administrative policy. Such change in policy cannot be decided upon by the administration or the Board of Trustees without the benefit of a serious study." The problem was that this was no longer absolutely so. The senate had, de facto, taken over much of the agenda-setting for the campus, and since 1965 it had become much more than an "advisory body." Yet it did not as yet control that agenda. Hoping to stall for time until after the committee on recruitment could report, Tolley suspended recruiting by the military services "until this matter has been studied." However, the ban was pro forma, to say the least. Visits already scheduled to the Placement Center would not be canceled, and the ban also affected only military organizations, not "military-connected" organizations—therefore, it did not affect Dow, the organization that had sparked the protest.

The committee set up by the senate to investigate on-campus recruitment was co-chaired by professors Michael Sawyer and Donald Meiklejohn. It found itself "virtually unanimous" in accepting recruitment via the Placement Center as a normal and useful university procedure, but a majority (10–7) believed that the university should suspend military recruitment while the Hershey letter remained in effect. Their report to Tolley quoted from an American Civil Liberties

Union (ACLU) resolution: "We also believe that free speech and academic freedom require that protests on campus relating to recruitment by any segment of the academic community should also be fully protected." An accompanying minority report urged that the college undertake "a complete review of *all* decision making bodies within the University to determine whether students [could] fulfill meaningful roles as members of them." The board of trustees, however, sided with Tolley. On April 5, the executive committee of the board of trustees discussed the recruitment policy. "After extended discussion, the Executive Committee voted unanimously to reaffirm the University's policy of open speaking and open recruiting on the Syracuse campus." But it was a costly victory. It was now clear that Tolley could not control his faculty—a point that several members of the board, who otherwise supported Tolley's stand on the issue, did not miss.

Tolley's response to the student demonstrators was largely the same as his response toward those who had been arrested while demonstrating with Syracuse CORE. When Tolley returned from Albany the day after the barricading of the administration building, he demanded the names of the students involved, so that they could be immediately expelled. This was directly contrary to the spirit of the Eggers/Piskor meeting with the students, which had promised the students a fair hearing. Tolley also seems to have forgotten that during the last fight with students over due process, he had created a panel on Graduate Student Welfare, to which he now had to send the cases.[3] Tolley sputtered, writing one correspondent that "in the case of the graduate students, we have to deal with a graduate appeals board but I can assure you that none of the graduate students who took part in the activities will be here next year." This was a threat that in the climate of 1968 would be difficult to keep. After learning of the scheduling of a hearing from the graduate students, seventeen members of the Physics Department wrote to Tolley expressing their concern for the process, and the severity of the punitive measure of expulsion (three of those charged were graduate students in physics).

3. The panel consisted of: Robert Miller (dean of the College of Law, chair); Virgil D. Clover (professor of transportation); Richard E. Gildersleeve (electrical engineering); Antje B. Lemke (library science); Robert S. Pickett (home economics); and Fritz Rohrlich (physics).

This extraordinary letter made it clear that a significant portion of the faculty had come to believe that not only was the faculty protected by academic freedom, but so were the *students:* "Demonstrations are not news to a university campus. They are in fact sanctioned by the firm belief of the academic community in freedom of speech and in academic freedom. . . . Of course, when such demonstrations exceed permissible bounds as those in question have done, the situation changes. But it would be unwise for any leading university administrator to over-react to juvenile and immature behavior." On April 18, the panel held its first hearing—the affected students had been given only ten days to prepare. On May 3, the university announced the unanimous findings of the hearing: that a suspended sentence be imposed on each of the seven graduate students of one month for each hour the Administration Building was under student control, and that such suspension was conditioned upon the good conduct of the student during the time each was in attendance at the university.

The case of the undergraduate students was even more troublesome. The university catalogue declared, and it was so stated in the charges against the students, that the university had the right to "require the withdrawal of any student at any time for any reason deemed sufficient to it, and no reason for requiring withdrawal need be given." Nevertheless, by 1968 this would simply not be tolerated. An ad hoc Faculty Committee on Disciplinary Proceedings Against Students wrote that "In no other sector of our democratic society— whether in the armed forces or private employment, civil or criminal jurisdictions—are individuals thus subjected to arbitrary authority." Again, Tolley allowed the students only the appearance of due process. Six undergraduate students who had participated in the lock-in were told by their respective deans that they were to appear before an administrative disciplinary body.[4] Their hearing was scheduled for April 18; they were informed of the meeting on April 17. During that meeting, two responded immediately to the charges; the remaining four chose to wait to speak until an April 25 meeting. The students were told that they could bring a friend, but that they could bring no

4. That body consisted of: Jim Carleton (dean of Student Services); Alfred Cope (assistant dean of the College of Liberal Arts); Marjorie C. Smith (dean of women); Frederic Kramer (associate dean of the College of Liberal Arts); and David Tatham (dean of men).

counsel; a request by a defendant to call a witness was questioned on the grounds that it served no purpose. Although they intended to read statements and answer questions on the twenty-fifth, they changed their minds when they heard of a special senate meeting called for April 30 to discuss their plight. As a result, they decided to issue a demurral in their own proceedings to wait for the senate's deliberations. On May 6 the decision of the hearing was announced: all defendants were placed on disciplinary probation for "an indefinite period." And "receipt of a degree or registration for any term subsequent to the current semester shall be dependent upon your good conduct and must be certified by this committee."

*   *   *

In loco parentis was not destroyed by the lock-in at the Administration Building. It did, however, receive a blow from which it never recovered. All subsequent student and faculty actions on campus grew from this moment. It was, in retrospect, the moment when Syracuse University chose a path of social activism that would make it possible for the uprisings of 1970 to occur.

To the end of his tenure, Tolley was firm in his conviction that he knew the root cause of the troubles in the nation's universities—ungrateful professors who misunderstood the concept of academic freedom. As he wrote to a Newhouse professor some three weeks after the lock-in: "What is so thoroughly disillusioning about experiences of the past three weeks is the number of faculty members who really do not believe in academic freedom. The new left is very much like the old right." But it was a public comment from Tolley, published in the *Daily Orange* that April, that raised more than a few eyebrows: "I think if the universities are ever destroyed . . . it will be from inside. . . . It will be by professors who ought to know better, professors who ought to be dedicated to intellectual inquiry, to the patient and persistent pursuit of knowledge and who ought to stand for disciplined thought, who ought to stand for dialogue, and be opposed to violence." Less than two weeks later, Tolley told the board of trustees that he was resigning, effective September 1969.

Ruth and William Tolley with Chancellor John Corbally

CHAPTER 17
New Leadership, Redux

If I did it again, I would be a professor, not a college president.
Professors have the best of both worlds — they can do what they want
and they don't have to do what they don't want.

—Tolley, quoted in *Time*, Sept. 27, 1968

S EVERAL TIMES since 1960, Tolley had publicly and privately
stated that he was ready to retire, if only the board would let him.
But the year 1965 — and Tolley's sixty-fifth birthday — came and went
with no serious discussion of the chancellor's retirement. Many on
the faculty were upset at this decision, not just because they opposed
the policies and attitudes of the chancellor, but because they opposed
Tolley's resolve to stay at his post beyond the age at which many university officials had been forced to retire. Many now suggest that
Tolley had wanted to stay on as chancellor until 1970, the year of the
institution's one hundredth anniversary. The board was more than
willing to accommodate Tolley — the Syracuse Plan had been an over-
whelming success, several new buildings had been begun as late as
1967, and Tolley was about to begin construction on the library.

However, the lock-in at the administration building, and the succeeding fight over due process for the students involved, changed
many minds. Eggers remembered that "the key [was] losing control
of the institution" and described the reaction in different quarters of
the campus to Tolley's threat to dismiss the students: "If that's going
to happen, then we can't live together." For the first time, several
trustees, without openly siding with the student body, grumbled that

Tolley had stayed past his time. As Eggers remembered the situation: "The end had come. . . . His [Tolley's] type of activity was not acceptable to the new faculty and students. . . . [Tolley] used methods that couldn't possibly have been used any longer."

Sensing this, the University Senate grasped the opportunity and elected a special ad hoc Committee on Long Range Planning. The committee consisted of faculty representatives Melvin Eggers, John Prucha, Donald Kibby, Eric Lawson, and Kin Tong, and trustees J. Robert Tomlinson, Royal O'Dea, and Chairman Emeritus Gordon Hoople, who had visited Tolley in Allegheny in 1942 to offer him the chancellorship at Syracuse. The committee also included three administrators: Tolley, Ahlberg, and Piskor. It had no real set charter— Prucha remembered that its broad function was "to determine the direction that the University would take through the next ten years." Such a discussion could be open-ended, and perhaps salve a lot of wounds; Piskor and Ahlberg agreed to the creation of the committee, and Tolley tolerated it.

The group first met in late April at the Minnowbrook Conference Center. Some members of the committee remember that there was a productive discussion of campus issues; others remember that speeches were made that pointedly told Tolley that his time was up. No stenographer's notes of the session exists, but it is likely that both things happened. Upon their return to Syracuse, Eggers reported back to the senate that a number of constructive things had happened at the meeting, not the least of which was an agreement to give the senate more autonomy. Faculty members spoke up with what Eggers termed "legitimate skepticism." In a later interview, Eggers used the term "double-cross" to describe what came next. He remembered that while Tolley "gave the impression that he was willing to let some things be decided by the Senate process," in reality, he was not. The board had had enough. One source claims that it was Hoople who told his old friend that his time was up; another says that Tomlinson, considered by most faculty to be a moderate, met with Tolley and suggested that he resign. A more likely scenario is that after talking to members of the board, who gave only their "best advice" to their friend, Tolley himself decided that it was time to resign.

*   *   *

The board immediately began a search for Tolley's successor. The trustees named a committee of six members; the faculty insisted on the same number, and so did the students, through a group called the Student Committee on the Selection of a Chancellor (SCSC). Soon there was a committee of eighteen members, chaired by Fritz Kramer, dean of the College of Liberal Arts. Frank Piskor led the list of five internal candidates for the job.[1] All concerned with the process agree that Piskor wanted the job. However, he had little support on the search committee, which soon announced that it would consider no internal candidates for the job. St. Lawrence University had long been trying to get Piskor to join them; he became their president that September. The students lobbied for John Dixon, the president of Antioch College, which was then a campus in a state of chaos worse that Syracuse could ever have envisioned. The board members vetoed the students' choice, angering the students to the point where they went public with their belief that the process was rigged against them.

After several weeks of deliberation, it was clear that John Corbally of Ohio State was the front-runner with the trustee members of the committee. Corbally had undergraduate degrees from the University of Washington and a Ph.D. in educational administration and finance from the University of California at Berkeley. He had been a high school principal in Stanwood, Washington, and a consultant for UCLA Berkeley's School of Education before joining Ohio State University as an assistant professor of education in 1955. He served as that school's director of the personnel budget and executive assistant to the president until being named vice president for administration

1. Internal candidates who applied or were nominated for the chancellor's position included Clark Ahlberg, Stephen Bailey, then dean of Maxwell; Alan ("Scotty") Campbell, then the director of the Metropolitan Studies Program at Maxwell; John H. McCombe, then dean of Hendricks Chapel; and Piskor. Former Syracuse University officials considered were: Harlan Cleveland, former dean of Maxwell, then serving as the U.S. Ambassador to NATO; John F. Olson, former vice president and executive assistant to Tolley, then president of Oklahoma State University; and Robert Fisher Oxnam, former assistant to Tolley and dean of the School of Speech and Dramatic Arts, then president of Drew University. There were twenty-seven external nominees or candidates for the position. (Brief Bios of Candidates in Tolley Records, RG1, box 115, Chancellor: Selection of folder.)

in 1964. In 1966, he was named vice president for Academic Affairs and Provost.

*   *   *

The impending search for a new chancellor did nothing to brighten the mood of campus as the 1968–69 school year began. The summer of 1968 had been highlighted by the riot at the Democratic National Convention where many of those who had gone to Chicago to affect the political system were met instead with mace, billy clubs, and the disappointment of a crumbled McCarthy campaign. The nomination of Vice President Hubert Humphrey—seen by disaffected McCarthy supporters to be little more than a clone of Johnson—to face off against Republican Richard Nixon and Independent George Wallace, perceived by most liberals to be unrepentant hawks, led many to believe that there was no hope for a political solution to the war. Nixon's promise of a plan to end the war that he could not yet divulge to the public did little to convince anyone.

On the evening of October 15, 1968, as part of the fall events of the National Mobilization Against the War, between six and ten thousand marchers from the university area marched by candlelight from the hill to Central Tech High School for a peaceful rally. It concluded a day of moratorium activities that included the petitioning of area residents for an end to the war and a counter-moratorium rally at LeMoyne, attended by about five hundred people. Three days later, Bob Tompososky of the Syracuse University chapter of SDS announced that the organization was considering taking over the administration building again, saying about the administration: "They don't give a damn about free speech. . . . [Tolley] gave us a lot of ridiculous rhetoric and told us to come back any time for discussion." No such takeover occurred during that school year, and the May 1969 student protest during the chancellor's annual ROTC review was a weakly organized affair that left little impression.

Tolley's last months also included the first major outbreak on campus of a phenomenon known as Black Power. As noted earlier, the number of students who participated with George Wiley in his CORE crusades was dedicated, but small. The same words might describe the black students at Syracuse University in general. The diversification of the 1950s had brought more black students to campus, but hardly in the numbers that were at larger institutions—in 1966, there were eighty-five black students enrolled. However, the civil rights movements of the early 1960s had not left the black student body at Syracuse untouched. CORE had excited them, even if they did not participate in Wiley's protests. They had met with the Cornell and Oswego leadership of the Student Non-Violent Coordinating Committee and had heard SNCC chairman Stokely Carmichael speak on campus. They were engaged by Selma and the passage of the Voting Rights Act, and enraged by the carnage in Watts. By 1969 the situation had changed in favor of black activism at Syracuse University. The successes of the CORE protest and the antiwar movement certainly spurred black unity. Tolley's status as lame duck may well have played a role. So, too, did the organization that blacks had been able to achieve during the decade. Five black student groups had already formed by the spring of 1969.[2] Perhaps the most important development as the campus moved toward the volatile 1969–70 school year was the election of Charles Hicks, a black student, as the head of the student body.

On March 10, 1969, a memo signed "Black Students" was sent to Tolley and Piskor, asking them to join them for a meeting at Beebe Cottage on March 12. Tolley once again was out of town, and despite counsel to the contrary, Piskor agreed to meet with the students. At what instantly became a very tense meeting, the students said that without Tolley being there, the discussion could not move forward. They requested that Tolley and Piskor meet with them the next day, despite the fact, according to Piskor, that they knew that Piskor had an appointment in Washington. Later that day (March 12), Piskor wrote to them, saying that he would meet with them anytime on Friday or Saturday. The students' reply was immediate: "You have failed to realize the importance and urgency of Black Student Problems. Irregardless of your other official University Business, we feel that the black issues here should take first priority on your agenda. With this in mind, the Black students, standing united demand the presence of

2. The Freshman Action Committee; Omega Psi Phi, a black fraternity and the second largest fraternity in the United States; the House of Lords, an off-campus organization; The Student Afro-American Society; and the United Society.

both William P. Tolley and yourself *only* at a meeting" on March 13. There was no such meeting held.

On March 14, about 150 black students carrying black two-by-fours and a black banner demonstrated briefly outside the Administration Building. They called themselves the United Black Students, representing the major black groups on campus, and in their press release they noted that they were there to demand a meeting with Piskor and Tolley. They took pains to define their sense of solidarity to the press. They explained that the black garb worn by the demonstrators represented unity; the black sticks carried by the men represented black force; and the flag represented the universal black cause. Piskor came down to meet with the group, who listed the demands— a house for Omega Psi Phi, a predominately black fraternity; a black student directory; and an increase in the budgetary allotment for the Student Afro-American Society (from $1500 to $3800). Piskor led the group to believe that he was sympathetic toward their demands and agreed to meet with the group again on March 24. The group then dispersed. Piskor did meet with them on March 24, where he agreed to the creation of the Afro-American Cultural center and the thousand-volume Martin Luther King Memorial Collection. In terms of the Omega house, Piskor remarked, no doubt with tongue in cheek, that racially segregated housing was illegal. Nevertheless, in the fall of 1969, the first black studies program was offered at Syracuse University. The university also committed itself to admitting 10 percent of its freshman class in the fall of 1969 as black students, and to increasing the number of black admissions officers.

Tolley's final student predicament occurred in late April. It was neither a Black Power protest, nor strictly an antiwar protest. On its face, the one-day boycott of classes on April 23, organized by a group called the Students for a Better University (SBU), was to gain "dormitory autonomy," including the possession and consumption of alcoholic beverages in the dorms, a request that was granted by Piskor immediately. Defiant to the end, Tolley nixed Piskor's decision, telling the *Daily Orange* that "the university stands for certain moral and spiritual concepts, including decency and temperance." However, the SBU's demands went to the heart of what had been changing at Syracuse over the past eight years. The group demanded the revocation of rule number one, in which the university stated that attendance at the university was a privilege and not a right. The best that the university could say was that they would take this demand under advisement.

*   *   *

On March 25, 1969, Chancellor-elect John Corbally was introduced to the faculty in a packed Maxwell auditorium. At that meeting, in a note that would prove during his administration to be greatly ironic, Corbally declared that "a university should remain an open institution so no one has to tear the place apart to be heard."

Bill Tolley, 1969

CHAPTER 18
Some Conclusions

I see in my mind's eye a great university on the Hill. I see a dozen colleges.
Instead of several buildings, I see a score of buildings. Instead of a student body
of 800, I see a student body of 8,000, and the University as the center of the
educational system of the State of New York.

—Chancellor James Roscoe Day, ca. 1895

I N T H E L A S T Y E A R S of his tenure as chancellor, perhaps as a
release from the tensions of the period, William Tolley penned an
interesting and revealing book about his views of the role of higher
education. Entitled *The Adventure of Learning*,[1] the book bemoans the
abandonment of classical education and argues that the enlightened
individual must make up for this dearth by undertaking a rigorous
self-education program, based upon a daily regimen of reading in the
classics. The following quote is quite useful for gauging Tolley's view
of higher education:

> What is true in the life of the spirit is true in the life of the mind.
> Regardless of the state of American culture, with its emphasis on
> things we can see and handle, education must continue to be
> concerned with the intangibles, the questions, the values, the deeper
> longings, and the unseen world of the spirit. Education is preemi-
> nently concerned with a man's inner life, man's development as a
> man, and what we mean by the dignity of man. Education goes off
> the track whenever it assumes, even subconsciously, that the great
> purpose of man's life is the happiness made possible by material and

1. Syracuse: Syracuse Univ. Press, 1967.

technological advance—with all its importance. If we remain
insensitive to all but external values, the essential meaning of education will have escaped us.

This was William Tolley the philosopher at his most succinct and
thoughtful. It was clearly the type of education that he felt to be the
most valuable to the human spirit. Nevertheless, this is not the type
of educational system that William Tolley created during his chancellorship. Instead, he sparked the transformation of Syracuse University from a small liberal arts school to a research university. In this
new configuration, which for many resembled less a college than a
corporate entity, the liberal arts were still taught, but the institution's
success now hinged on its research contracts and its hard science programs. As a result, Tolley helped to set into motion the creation of an
institution that could easily stand in the way of the type of liberal
learning that he praised in *The Adventure of Learning.*

This is but one part of a paradox that emerged in higher education
between World War II and Vietnam; an incongruity that was the
major theme of the development of Syracuse University during that
period. As thoughtful scholars and skilled academic executives like
Tolley took over the reins of power at the nation's universities during
and immediately following World War II, they re-created higher education with bold strokes. Enrollment skyrocketed, thanks not only to
the GI Bill, but to the willingness of schools to accept *any* veteran.
Physical plants grew exponentially to accommodate not only the GI
Bulge, but the government and private research that had now become
the backbone of growing universities.

In so doing, the postwar executives of higher education created institutions that by 1960 would reject their leadership. Accepting anyone in a uniform led to an instant diversity on campus. This newly
eclectic population would become the core of the student movement
of the 1960s. While the Building Bulge expanded the size of Syracuse
University, it was fueled by deficit spending and, in many cases, a
lapse in the growth of the institution's endowment that would plague
succeeding administrations. As the new university grew, it also became more impersonal—a fact that further alienated a thoughtful
student body, as well as faculty members who clearly expected something more from academe as the nation entered the 1960s. As had

happened all over the country to a host of institutions of differing sizes and scope, Syracuse University had, during the Tolley era, become a multiversity. William Tolley was both its creator and its chief victim.

One wonders if there was anything that Tolley, Clark Kerr, Grayson Kirk, and their colleagues might have done differently to avoid being swept up by the upheavals of the 1960s. Doubtful. These men firmly believed in *in loco parentis* as a fundamental tool of administration, and to the end of their tenure they refused to accept the defeat of their belief that attendance at a university was a privilege, rather than a right. In one of his last official pieces of correspondence as chancellor, written to J. Leonard Gorman, the publisher of the *Syracuse Post-Standard,* Tolley reiterated: "We won't change Rule #1. It is liberal enough now." Also, neither Tolley nor any of his colleagues were delegators. As we have noted, Tolley kept political power—the ability to affect the direction of an institution—to himself. This would prove ultimately fatal to the relationship between chancellor and faculty, when it became clear that the faculty believed that the decisions of Tolley's deans and other administrators—on everything from salary to other personnel matters—were being reversed by the chancellor. It is also inconceivable that these men, trained in the closed academic societies of the 1920s, would ever come to view students as anything other than passive players in their own educational experience. As Melvin Eggers remembered, "there was no experience in resiliency" among college presidents of the postwar period, only a hard-line opposition to the demands of students. It was the ultimate irony—those strong men who had created the multiversity were, by virtue of their training, character, and vision of higher education, destined to come to blows with the institutions they had created.

*   *   *

The summer of 1969 is a particularly inauspicious moment to have to end the story of this paradox in higher education as it applies to Syracuse University. So much had yet to be decided. The growth of the university would continue for the next three decades, no mean tribute to the foundation left by Tolley and his colleagues between 1942 and 1969. Yet there were difficult tests ahead, many of them directly caused by the clash over *in loco parentis* that had plagued Tolley, many more caused by the social growing pains that Tolley had long argued would never affect Syracuse. Indeed, within a year of Tolley's departure, the Syracuse University community would tear at itself again, as racial problems within the athletic program and the community's reaction to Richard Nixon's strategy to end the war in Vietnam almost led to bloodshed. Both crises played a key role in the premature departure of Tolley's successor, and both led to the naming of a former faculty leader as the university's new chancellor.

The legacy of William Tolley, then, cuts a wide swath in the history of both Syracuse University and the community. He was one of several "giants" (to borrow once again Clark Kerr's phrase) who made significant changes to the landscape of higher education. Such men will be revered by many and reviled by others. This was the nature of their leadership—it affected everyone at their institution in an all-consuming way. Tolley was not an anonymous bureaucrat—he *was* Syracuse University for almost three decades. Central New York will bear his mark for generations to come.

APPENDIXES

A NOTE ON SOURCES

INDEX

APPENDIX A

William Pearson Tolley
A Bibliography

BOOKS

Tolley, William Pearson. *At the Fountain of Youth: Memoirs of a College President.* Syracuse: Syracuse Univ. Press, 1989.

———. *The Adventure of Learning.* Syracuse: Syracuse Univ. Press, 1977.

———. *The Idea of God in the Philosophy of St. Augustine.* New York: R. R. Smith, 1930.

EDITED TEXTS

Hocking, William Ernest, Brand Blanshard, Charles William Hendel, John Herman Randall, and William P. Tolley, eds. *Preface to Philosophy: Textbook.* New York: Macmillan, 1947.

Hooper, Ross Earle, Raymond Frank Piper, and William P. Tolley, eds. *Preface to Philosophy: Book of Readings.* New York: Macmillan, 1947.

JOURNAL ARTICLES, BOOK CHAPTERS,
AND ACADEMIC REVIEWS

1941. "Report of the Commission on Academic Freedom and Academic Tenure." *Association of American Colleges Bulletin* 27 (Mar.), 122–29.

1942. "A Counterfeit Bachelor's Degree." *Educational Record,* July, 593–601.

1944. "Planning in the Large University." In *Proceedings of the Institute for Administrative Officers of Higher Institutions,* vol. 16, *Higher Education in the Postwar Period,* edited by John Dale Russel, 44–52.

1947. "Report of the Commission on Academic Freedom and Academic Tenure." *Association of American Colleges Bulletin* 33 (Mar.), 225–26.

1948. "Report of the Committee on Minority Groups." *Association of American Colleges Bulletin* 34 (Mar.), 150–55.

1948. "Some Observations on the Report of the President's Commission on Higher Education." *Educational Record,* Oct., 371–80.

1948. "The Doctor of Social Science Program at Syracuse University." *Journal of General Education* 3 (Oct.), 1–4.

1953. "The Junior College in American Education." *Junior College Journal,* Apr.

1959. Review of *Memo to a College Trustee,* by Beardsley Ruml and Donald H. Morrison. In *President's Bulletin Board,* Dec.

1960. "The Nature of a University." *The Methodist Story,* Mar., 5.

1984. "Ivan Mestrovic Comes to Syracuse University," *Syracuse University Library Associates Courier* (Fall), 3–5.

MAGAZINE AND NEWSLETTER ARTICLES

1943. "Education for Tomorrow." *Think,* Nov.

1945. "The News That Moved a Nation to Prayer." *Think,* May, 11.

1969. "Disruption, Coercion, and Academic Freedom," *Trustee,* Sept., 1–2.

SPEECHES

1936. "Higher Education and the New Tax Laws." Lafayette College, Apr.

1937. "New Wines and New Wine Skins." Allegheny College, June 6.

1938. "The Instruments of Freedom." Allegheny College, July.

1938. "The Continuing Adventure." The Brothers College, Oct.

1940. "The Summing Up." Allegheny College, Aug.

1941. "The Faith That Is in You." Allegheny College, June 8.

1942. "A Bachelor's Degree for Sophomores." Allegheny College, Aug.

1942. "The Contribution of the University to the Winning of the War and the Peace." Syracuse University, Inaugural, Nov. 14.

1943. "The American College in an Age of Crisis." Villanova University, Centennial Convocation, May 3.

1943. "A River Clear as Crystal." Syracuse University, May 9.

1944. "Education for Tomorrow." Syracuse University, May. Reprinted in *Think,* Nov. 1944.

1944. "Unfinished Business." Syracuse University, June.

1944. "Once More the Wilderness and the New World." Colgate University, Sept. 21.

1944. "Prerequisites of Progress." IBM, Department of Education, Oct. 13.

1945. "Seventy-Fifth Anniversary." Syracuse University, Apr. 26.

1946. "The Atom and World Peace." Hobart College, Commencement, Feb. 2.

1946. "The Dreams of Youth." Hood College, June 6.

1947. "The Greeks Had No Word for It." Syracuse, N.Y., Jan.

1947. "The Truth Shall Make Us Free." Syracuse University Commencement, Jan. 30.

1947. "Syracuse University and its Communities." Formal Opening of University College, Apr. 16.

1948. "American Education and the Testing Movement." Jan.

1948. "Forestry in Human Welfare." Syracuse University. Reprinted in *Proceedings: Society of American Foresters,* 1948, 368–73.

1948. "Education for our Common Life." Northeastern University.

1948. "Unfinished Business in Higher Education." Syracuse University, Feb. 2.

1948. "Some Observations on the Report of the President's Commission on Higher Education." American Council on Education, Oct.

1949. "Progress Through Ethical Standards." Eleventh Annual Conference on Health, Physical Education, and Recreation, Syracuse, N.Y., Jan. 27.

1949. "The Present Time." Bennett College, Commencement, May 13.

1950. "Educational Tensions and Religion." Boston University, Commencement, May 13.

1950. "College as Opportunity." Syracuse University, Sept. 15.

1951. "Smith-Corona Typewriters and H. W. Smith." To Newcomen Society, Syracuse, N.Y., Apr. 11.

1951. "The City and the University." Oklahoma City University, Oct. 5.

1951. "The Mission of the American College." Alfred University, Nov. 1.

1953. "Academic Freedom and Tenure." To the board of trustees, Syracuse University, May 29.

1953. "Foreign Education." To foreign teachers, Syracuse University, Dec. 16.

1954. "The Aims of American Education." Syracuse University, June 4.

1954. "Great Expectations." Address to freshmen, Syracuse University, Sept. 20.

1956. "New Issues for a New Day." Forty-sixth annual meeting of the Manufacturer's Association, Feb. 8.

1958. "The Future of American Education." Syracuse University, Mar. 28.

1958. "The Transcendent Aim." Address to freshmen, Syracuse University, Sept. 22.

1958. "New Sources of Power." Buffalo Regional Technical Meeting of Iron and Steel Institute, Dec. 4.

1959. "Looking Ahead for Adult Education." University of Texas, Oct. 12.

1960. "Possibilities Unlimited." Address to freshmen, Syracuse University, Sept. 26.

1961. "Accent on Quality." Syracuse University, College of Forestry, Apr.

1961. "The Hope of the Future." Syracuse University, Sept.

1961. "The Inauguration of Robert Fisher Oxnam." Drew College, Oct. 12.

1961. "Burstone Campus Dedication." Utica College, Convocation, Oct. 19.

1962. "The Education of a Prince." Syracuse University, Commencement, June 2.

1962. "Shared Loyalties, Responsibilities, and Beliefs." Address to freshmen, Syracuse University, Sept. 16.

1963. "Imagination and Experience." Seventy-fifth Anniversary Convocation, University of Puget Sound, Mar. 17.

1963. "Education for Freedom." Pace College, Commencement, June 9.

1963. "What Makes a College Great?" Allegheny College, June 15.

1963. "Learning to See." Address to freshmen, Syracuse University, Sept. 8.

1963. "Eulogy for George B. Cressey." Hendricks Chapel, Syracuse University, Oct. 24.

1964. "Higher Education—1964." University Festival, University of Houston, Apr. 24.

1964. "The Promethean Faith." Syracuse University, Sept. 12.

1964. "Eulogy for Charles Wesley Flint." Binghamton, N.Y., Dec. 15.

1965. "The Spirit of Youth and the Spirit of Learning." Syracuse University, Sept. 11.

1965. "The Kipling Exhibition." Carnegie Library, Syracuse University, Nov. 19.

1965. "The Contribution of the University to the Great Society." Hotel Pierre, New York, Jan. 26.

1966. Untitled. Chamber of Commerce, Syracuse, N.Y., Apr. 20.

1966. "American Universities in Transition and the New Role of Adult Education." Fourth Marsbridge Lecture, Leeds University, England, June 16.

1966. "The Quest for the Golden Fleece." Syracuse University, Sept. 10.

1966. "Centennial Address." Syracuse University, Dec. 6.

1968. "Eta Pi Upsilon." Syracuse University, May 4.

1968. "The End for Which the University is Governed." Syracuse University, May 31.

1969. "Some Personal Observations." Syracuse University, Feb. 22.

1969. "Power Without Responsibility." Onondaga County Bar Association, Mar.

1969. "Zeta Beta Tau." Syracuse University, Apr. 30.

1969. "On the Duties of the University Towards the Nation." Syracuse University, Fall.

1969. Untitled. Skidmore College, Oct. 29.

1970. "The Spirit of Youth/The Spirit of Learning." Elmira College, June 1.

1972. "What is a University?" Syracuse University, June 3.

1978. "The End of a Golden String: An Adventure in Excellence." Drew University, Sept. 30.

A representative selection of Tolley's speeches can be found in Frank P. Piskor, ed., *The Transcendental Aim: Selected Addresses.* Syracuse: Syracuse Univ. Press, 1967.

BIOGRAPHICAL SKETCHES OF TOLLEY

Allen, James E., Jr. *An Uncommon Man: The Story of Dr. William Pearson Tolley and Syracuse University.* New York: Newcomen Society in North America, 1963.

National Cyclopedia of American Biography, 1964, "Tolley, William P." 332–33.

* Officer Changes

1943–1945

> Chancellor: William P. Tolley
> Vice Chancellor: Finla G. Crawford
> Registrar: Keith J. Kennedy
> Treasurer: George E. VanDyke
> Admissions: Frank Newton Bryant

1945–1949

> Chancellor: William P. Tolley
> Vice Chancellor: Finla G. Crawford
> Registrar: Keith J. Kennedy
> Treasurer: George E. VanDyke
> Admissions: Frank Newton Bryant
> Business Manager: Hugh C. Gregg*

1949–1950

> Chancellor: William P. Tolley
> Vice Chancellor: Finla G. Crawford
> Registrar: Keith J. Kennedy
> Business Manager and Treasurer: Hugh C. Gregg
> Admissions: Frank Newton Bryant

From Reference Binder, Rare Book and Manuscript Reading Room, Syracuse University.

1950–1953

> Chancellor: William P. Tolley
> Vice Chancellor: Finla G. Crawford
> Registrar: Keith J. Kennedy
> Business Manager and Treasurer: Hugh C. Gregg
> Admissions: John S. Hafer*

1953–1958

> (** changes to Vice President, 1956–1957)

> Chancellor: William P. Tolley
> Vice Chancellor: Finla G. Crawford
> Vice President and Executive Secretary: F. Gordon Smith**
> Vice President and Dean of Public Relations:
>   Kenneth G. Bartlett**
> Vice President and Treasurer: Hugh C. Gregg
> Vice President and Dean of Student Services: Frank P. Piskor
> Registrar: Keith J. Kennedy
> Admissions: John S. Hafer
> Comptroller: Francis Wingate

1958–1959

> Chancellor: William P. Tolley
> Vice Chancellor: Finla G. Crawford
> Vice President: F. Gordon Smith
> Vice President and Dean of Public Affairs: Kenneth G. Bartlett
> Vice President and Treasurer: Hugh C. Gregg
> Vice President and Dean of Student Services: Frank P. Piskor
> Vice President in Charge of Research: W. R. G. Baker
> Vice President in Charge of Development: Newell W. Rossman
> Registrar: Keith J. Kennedy
> Admissions: John S. Hafer
> Comptroller: Francis Wingate

1959–1960

> Chancellor: William P. Tolley
> Vice Chancellor: Finla G. Crawford
> Vice President: F. Gordon Smith
> Vice President and Dean of Public Affairs: Kenneth G. Bartlett
> Vice President and Treasurer: Hugh C. Gregg

Vice President for Academic Affairs and Dean of Faculties:
    Frank P. Piskor
Vice President for Administration and Research:
    Clark D. Ahlberg
Vice President in Charge of Research: W. R. G. Baker
Vice President for Development: Newell W. Rossman
Registrar: Keith J. Kennedy
Admissions: John S. Hafer
Comptroller: Francis Wingate

1960–1961

Chancellor: William P. Tolley
Vice President and Executive Assistant to the Chancellor:
    John F. Olson
Vice President: F. Gordon Smith
Vice President and Dean of Public Affairs: Kenneth G. Bartlett
Vice President and Treasurer: Hugh C. Gregg
Vice President for Academic Affairs and Dean of Faculties:
    Frank P. Piskor
Vice President for Administration and Research:
    Clark D. Ahlberg
Vice President for Development: Newell W. Rossman
Vice President and Dean of Liberal Arts: Eric H. Faigle
Registrar: Edward D. Smith
Admissions: Lester H. Dye
Treasurer and Comptroller: Francis Wingate

N.B.: Baker out as VP for Research, but stays on as Director for Industrial Research.

1961–1962

Chancellor: William P. Tolley
Vice President and Executive Assistant to the Chancellor:
    John F. Olson
Vice President: F. Gordon Smith
Vice President and Dean of Public Affairs: Kenneth G. Bartlett
Vice President and Treasurer: Hugh C. Gregg
Vice President for Academic Affairs and Dean of Faculties:
    Frank P. Piskor
Vice President for Administration and Research:
    Clark D. Ahlberg
Vice President in Charge of Research: W. R. G. Baker
Vice President for Development: Newell W. Rossman

Vice President and Treasurer: Francis Wingate
Vice President and Dean of Liberal Arts: Eric H. Faigle
Registrar: Edward D. Smith
Admissions: Lester H. Dye
Comptroller: Victor J. Colway

1962–1965

(** omit Executive Assistant in 1964–1965; † begins 1964–1965)
Chancellor: William P. Tolley
Vice President and Executive Assistant to the Chancellor:
    John F. Olson**
Vice President: F. Gordon Smith
Vice President and Dean of Public Affairs: Kenneth G. Bartlett
Vice President and Treasurer: Francis Wingate
Vice President for Academic Affairs and Dean of Faculties:
    Frank P. Piskor
Vice President for Administration and Research:
    Clark D. Ahlberg
Vice President for Development: Newell W. Rossman
Vice President and Dean of Liberal Arts: Eric H. Faigle
Vice President for Continuing Education and Special Programs:
    Alexander M. Charters†
Registrar: Edward D. Smith
Admissions: Lester H. Dye
Comptroller: Victor J. Colway

1965–1969

Chancellor: William P. Tolley
Vice President and Dean of Public Affairs: Kenneth G. Bartlett
Vice President and Treasurer: Francis Wingate
Vice President for Academic Affairs and Dean of Faculties:
    Frank P. Piskor
Vice President for Administration and Research:
    Clark D. Ahlberg
Vice President for Development: Newell W. Rossman
Vice President and Dean of Liberal Arts: Eric H. Faigle
Vice President for Continuing Education: Alexander M. Charters
Registrar: Edward D. Smith
Admissions: Lester H. Dye
Comptroller: Victor J. Colway

APPENDIX C

Syracuse University Construction and Real Estate Acquisition, 1942–1969

Year Occupied or Dedicated	Year Construction Began	Building	Cost
1947	Purchased by univ.	Thompson Road Facility (College of Applied Science)	$669,368
1948	1948	Sims Dining Hall	——
1949	1949	Ainsley Drive Warehouse	——
1951	1949	Archbold Gymnasium (Remodeled after fire)	$2,000,000†
1952	Aug. 1951	Lowe Art Center	$294,000
1952	1950	New Steam Plant	$1,800,000
1952	1950	Shaw Dormitory	$1,500,000
1953	Mar. 1952	Gordon Hoople Special Ed. Bldg.	$440,000
1953	Nov. 1950	Women's Building	$2,900,000
1954	June 1953	Ernest White College of Law	$922,000
1954	Nov. 1952	Watson and Marion Halls	$2,893,000
1955	Dec. 1953	Hinds Hall	$940,000
1955	Apr. 1955	Morris Haft Dorm (Haft Co-Op)	$170,000
1956	Feb. 1955	Flint Hall Dorm	$2,200,000
1956	Refurbished Sigma Chi House	Lubin Hall	——
1956	Donated to univ.	Crouse House	——
1958	University purchased Beta Theta Phi House	Chapel House (to be Faculty Club in 1963)	$150,000

—— refers to information not available or not applicable.

Year Occupied or Dedicated	Year Construction Began	Building	Cost
1958	Refurbished Medical School Building	John M. Reid Hall (University College)	——
1958	Purchased by univ.	University Regent Theatre	Sale price not disclosed; assessed at $58,000
1958	Mar. 1957	Day Hall Dormitory	$3,400,000
1959	——	S.U. Good Shepherd Rehab. Center	$601,862
1960	July 1958	Sadler Hall	$3,434,364
1961	Purchased by univ.	Ambassador and Roosevelt Apts.	$400,000
1961	Fall 1959	DellPlain Dorm	$3,184,000
1962	Sept. 1960	Huntington B. Crouse Classroom Building (HBC)	$1,622,000
1962	——	Claude Kimmel Hall	——
1962	1960	George Leroy Manley Fieldhouse	$2,100,000
1962	1961	Biological Research Labs	$1,050,923
1963	1961	Willis Booth Hall	$2,000,000
1964	1962	Newhouse Comm. Ctr.	$3,900,000
1965	Purchased by univ.	Lubin House (NYC)	——
1965	May 1964	Lawrinson Dorm.	$4,000,000
1967	1964	Arnold Grant Auditorium (in White Hall)	$1,400,000
1966	1965	Toomey-Abbott Towers	
1967	1965	Physics Building	$4,000,000
1966	1963	Forestry College Biological Sciences and Library Bldg	$5,750,000
1968	Purchased by univ.	Drumlins	$2,400,000

BUILDINGS STILL UNDER CONSTRUCTION
AT TOLLEY'S RETIREMENT

1970	1968	Link Hall	$6,000,000
1972	1967	Heroy Geology Lab	$5,500,000
1972	1968	Bird Library	$14,000,000
1972	1967	Health Center and Hospital of the Good Shepherd	$1,300,000

The Orange Sports Honor Roll: 1942–1969

WORLD CHAMPIONSHIP

Crew

    1959: Pan American games winners

NATIONAL CHAMPIONSHIPS

Cross Country

    1949: Amateur Athletic Union national champions

    1951: NCAA champions

Football

    1959: AP and UPI national champions

ALL-AMERICANS

43 men, 0 women. Named a total of 57 times in 10 sports.

Baseball

    1949: Walter Slovenski

Basketball

    1966: Dave Bing

Boxing

    1942: Salvatore Mirabito

    1947: Jerry Auclair

    1949: Marty Crandall

    1954, 1955: John Granger

Cross Country

    1947, 1948, 1949: Neil Pratt

    1947: Raymond Trigoney

    1948, 1949: Richard Church

1951: William Irland

1951, 1952, 1953: Raymond Osterhaut

1954: Stephen Armstrong

1954: Lester Verbig

1957: Benjamin Johns

1957: Thomas A. Coulter

Football

1953: Robert A. Fleck (guard)

1956: Jim Brown (halfback)

1958: Ron Luciano (tackle)

1959: Roger Davis (guard)

1959: Fred J. Mautino (end)

1959: Robert E. Yates (tackle)

1960, 1961: Ernie Davis (halfback)

1964, 1965, 1966: Floyd Little (halfback)

1964, 1965: Patrick Killorin (center)

1965: Charley Brown (defensive halfback)

1966: Gary Bugenhagen (tackle)

1967: Larry Csonka (fullback)

1968: Tony Kyasky (defensive halfback)

Golf

1959: Warren Simmons

Gymnastics

1950, 1951: Leo Minotti

1950: Gene Rabbitt

1953: James Sebbo

1964: Sid Oglesby

Lacrosse

1949, 1950: William Fuller

1954: Bruce Yancey

1956: Stewart Lindsay

1957: Jim Brown

1962: Richard Finley

Swimming (Men)

1957, 1958: Warren Frischmann

1957: John McGill

Wrestling

1959: Arthur Baker

1963, 1965: James Nance

1967: Tom Schlendorf

Greek Letter Organizations at Syracuse University, 1943–1969

SOCIAL FRATERNITIES
(followed by date of establishment at Syracuse, if known)

Acacia (1911)
Alpha Chi Rho (1905)
Alpha Epsilon Pi (1947)
Alpha Sigma Phi (1925)
Alpha Tau Omega (1950)
Beta Epsilon (1957)
Beta Sigma Rho (1950)
Beta Theta Pi (1889)
Delta Chi (1967)
Delta Kappa Epsilon (1871; SU's first fraternity)
Delta Tau Delta (1910)
Delta Upsilon (1873)
Kappa Sigma (1906)
Lambda Chi Alpha (1928)
Omega Pi Alpha (1949)
Omega Psi Phi (1922; reactivated in 1968)
Phi Alpha (1963)
Phi Delta Theta (1887)
Phi Epsilon Pi (1917)
Phi Gamma Delta (1901)
Phi Kappa Psi (1884)
Phi Kappa Tau (1922)
Phi Sigma Delta (1949)
Pi Alpha Chi of Theta Alpha (the two houses merged in 1947; would become Tau Kappa Epsilon in 1962)

Pi Kappa Alpha (1913)
Pi Lambda Phi (1949)
Psi Upsilon (1875)
Sigma Alpha Epsilon (1907)
Sigma Alpha Mu (1913) ("Sammies")
Sigma Beta (1911)
Sigma Chi (1904)
Sigma Chi Psi (1959)
Sigma Delta Phi (1968; previously Sigma Alpha Epsilon)
Sigma Nu (1906)
Sigma Pi (1949)
Sigma Phi Epsilon (1906)
Tau Delta Phi (1948)
Tau Epsilon Phi (1922)
Tau Kappa Epsilon (1962)
Theta Alpha (1909)
Theta Chi (1928)
Zeta Beta Tau (1911)
Zeta Psi (1875)

SERVICE FRATERNITY

Alpha Phi Omega (1931)

SOCIAL SORORITIES

Alpha Chi Omega (1906)
Alpha Delta Pi (1924)
Alpha Epsilon Phi (1919)
Alpha Gamma Delta (1904)
Alpha Lambda Phi (1961)
Alpha Omicron Pi (1914)
Alpha Phi (1872; SU's first sorority)
Alpha Sigma Tau
Alpha Xi Delta (1904)
Beta Chi Alpha
Chi Omega (1911)
Delta Delta Delta (1896)
Delta Gamma (1901)
Delta Phi Epsilon (1949)
Delta Zeta (1941)

Gamma Phi Beta (1874; the first women's fraternity to be called
  a sorority)
Iota Alpha Pi (1939)
Kappa Alpha Theta (1889)
Kappa Delta (1923)
Kappa Kappa Gamma (1883)
Mu Phi Epsilon (1905)
Phi Kappa Epsilon
Phi Mu (1920)
Phi Sigma Sigma (1927)
Pi Beta Phi (1896)
Sigma Delta Tau
Sigma Kappa (1905)
Sigma Tau Upsilon (1961)
Theta Phi Alpha (1923)
Zeta Tau Alpha (1923)

SERVICE SORORITY

Delta Sigma Theta

PROFESSIONAL FRATERNITIES AND SORORITIES

Alpha Chi Sigma, chemical (1914)
Alpha Delta Sigma, advertising
Alpha Epsilon Delta, pre-medical
Alpha Kappa Kappa, medical (1899)
Alpha Kappa Psi, business administration
Beta Alpha Psi, accounting fraternity and professional honor society
Beta Phi Mu, library science
Delta Chi, law (1898)
Delta Nu Alpha, transportation
Gamma Eta Gamma, law (1908)
Kappa Phi Delta, forestry (1953)
Nu Sigma Nu, medical (1896)
Phi Alpha Delta, law
Phi Delta Kappa, education fraternity and professional honor society
Phi Delta Phi, law (1899)
Phi Epsilon Kappa, physical and health education
Pi Alpha Mu, professional publishing, advertising, public relations,
  and management

Pi Lambda Sigma, library (1903)
Sigma Alpha Iota, professional music sorority
Sigma Delta Chi, journalism
Tau Delta Sigma, engineering (1905)
Theta Tau, engineering
Zeta Phi Eta, professional speech arts and sciences (1914)

ACADEMIC HONORARIES

Alpha Delta Iota, advertising design
Alpha Delta Rho, oratory
Alpha Lambda Delta, freshmen women's scholarship honor society
Alpha Pi Mu, industrial engineering
Alpha Tau, architecture
Alpha Xi Sigma, senior forestry
Beta Gamma Sigma, business administration
Delta Sigma Rho, forensics
Eta Pi Upsilon, senior women's honor society
Janus, literature and oratory
Justinian, law
Omicron Nu, home economics
Order of the Coif, law honor society and fraternity
Phi Alpha Theta, history
Phi Beta Kappa, liberal arts
Phi Kappa Alpha, senior men's honorary society
Phi Sigma Iota, romance language
Pi Kappa Lambda, music
Pi Landa Theta, professional education
Pi Mu Epsilon, mathematics honor society and fraternity
Pi Sigma Alpha, political science
Pi Tau Sigma, mechanical engineering
Psi Chi, psychology
Sigma Theta Tau, nursing
Sigma Xi, natural sciences
Tau Beta Pi, engineering
Tau Kappa Alpha, forensics
Tau Theta Upsilon, senior men's honorary society

PHASE I: BASIC NEEDS

Central University Library	8,000,000
Internal Grad School of Communications	15,000,000
Physical Sciences Complex:	
Physics, #2 Engineering Completion, Life Sciences,	
Research Computation Center Buildings,	
Chemistry Addition	9,000,000
Endowment	5,000,000
TOTAL	37,000,000

PHASE II: CONTINUING NEEDS

Continuing Education Building	2,000,000
School of Social Work Building	1,000,000
Behavioral Sciences Building	1,000,000
University Theatre	1,150,000
Chancellor's Campus Fund	2,000,000
TOTAL	7,150,000

PHASE III: STUDENTS AND FACULTY

University Community Center	5,000,000
Center for Overseas Operation and Research	2,000,000
Administration Building	3,000,000
Endowment:	
Grad Fellowships—Humanities	5,000,000
Faculty Salaries—Science and Engineering	5,000,000

Presented by Chancellor Tolley to the board of trustees on Mar. 25, 1961.

Infirmary and Health Center		700,000
Buildings and Grounds Building		1,000,000
Grad School of Business Building		1,000,000
	TOTAL	22,700,000

PHASE IV: FACILITIES EXTENSION

School of Art: Architecture Addition		2,500,000
Hall of Languages Remodeling		1,000,000
College of Law Auditorium		500,000
Chapel		1,000,000
Heating Plant Addition		1,800,000
Chancellor's Campus Fund		1,500,000
	TOTAL	8,300,000

GRAND TOTAL   76,150,000

A Note on Sources

ABBREVIATIONS

AVC Archives-Vault Collection, SUA (AVC entries are followed by the call number)

CF Clipping File, SUA

MOS Michael O. Sawyer, Files and Notes, RG 43, SUA

WTR William P. Tolley. Records of the Chancellors Office, RG 1, SUA

RG Record Group (classification of SUA)

SUA Syracuse University Archives

SP Syracuse University Press

In lieu of a tedious amount of footnotes, a short discussion of the most important sources used in the preparation of this book follows. An annotated copy of this manuscript has been placed on reserve at the Syracuse University Archives (SUA).

THE SYRACUSE UNIVERSITY ARCHIVES (SUA)

Syracuse University is fortunate to have an archival facility that rivals the Presidential Library system in its organization, archival care, and inclusiveness. The Clipping File (CF), indexed and organized both by subject and person, is the place to begin any serious research project on Syracuse University. The Archives-Vault Collection (AVC), also beautifully indexed, includes printed and published material—not only books, but catalogues, course descriptions and syllabi, handouts and flyers, programs, and schedules. The Photo File covers every aspect of the institution's history — all photographs in this volume were chosen from the SUA's Photo File.

ARCHIVAL AND MANUSCRIPT MATERIAL

Four archival collections form the basis of the primary source research for this volume. The fundamental source for this study was the files of William Pearson Tolley, Records of the Chancellor's Office (WTR), RG 1, SUA. This particularly well-organized collection consists of 152 archival boxes and twelve oversize packages. The WTR offers very little coverage on the World War II years, but the period 1945–69 is represented in detail. Of equal importance are the files and notes of Michael O. Sawyer (MOS), RG 43, SUA. The original researcher for this volume, Sawyer compiled six boxes of notes, taken on primary and secondary material. There are also transcripts of research interviews with Tolley and several other top administrators (see below, "Oral Histories and Interviews"), and a singular collection of Tolley's original scrapbooks. A third collection of invaluable research material is the notes of Alexandra Mitchell Eyle as research assistant for William P. Tolley, *At the Fountain of Youth: Memoirs of a College President*. RG 1, SUA. These three boxes of material, which also includes research interviews (see below, "Oral Histories and Interviews"), represent at least two years of systematic note-taking as well as some correspondence and chapter drafts. The records and files of Melvin A. Eggers while serving as vice president and vice chancellor (RG 30, SUA) are the best manuscript records of the student crises of the late sixties. The actions of both Eggers and Frank Piskor in the 1968 administration building lock-in and the 1969 black student protest both can be traced through these files.

Other manuscript collections utilized for this volume include: American Association of University Professors (AAUP), Syracuse Chapter. General Records: 1926–1958, RG 63, SUA; Paul Appleby, Papers, RG 4, SUA; Norman Balabanian, General Records, RG 13, SUA; Martin Barzelay, Files, RG 14, SUA; Lyndon B. Johnson Presidential Papers, White House Central Files, Lyndon B. Johnson Presidential Library; Ivan Mestrovic, Papers, RG 13, SUA; Lorimer Rich, Papers, RG 3, SUA; Ben Schwartzwalder, Papers, RG 13, SUA; and Women's Athletics, Records, RG 12, SUA.

NEWSPAPER AND MAGAZINE SOURCES

The *Daily Orange,* Syracuse University's student daily, is the newspaper of record. However, it must be read cautiously; as with any student publication, there are errors. For the most part during the Tolley years, the *DO,* as it is referred to at the university, reflected the beliefs of the administration and agreed with its policies with virtually no dissent. There are, of course, exceptions over a twenty-three year period, but they are few (one noted in this text are the 1944 fight for coed student government). The *DO* during the Tolley years, then, was a mainstream conservative publication, much like its sister metropolitan dailies, the *Syracuse Post-Standard* (morning), and the *Syracuse Herald-Journal* (evening), both Newhouse papers. These papers dutifully followed the success of Tolley's Building Bulge, and they were often the best window for a student of university sports (consult the *Herald* for the better sports reporting). But the editorial stance of these papers, particularly during the sixties, dripped vitriol at any movement they considered to be in any way "liberal." The university, probably through the influence of Director of Public Relations Kenneth Bartlett, was also surprisingly successful at finding its way into the *New York Times,* even before the success of the Building Bulge. The *Binghamton Sun* was particularly helpful for establishing Tolley's early career.

The *Syracuse University Alumni News* (complete set at SUA) is a good example of the genre. Throughout this period it was printed in magazine format, with feature stories that accompanied the usual litany of classmate accomplishments. The *Alumni News* is the best place from which to follow Syracuse sports, with Lew Andreas's monthly report. However, as with any public relations piece, one must watch for hyperbole. The most obvious example: the *Alumni News* consistently exaggerated the university's financial figures. An excellent window for an overview of student life is the university yearbook, *The Onondagan* (complete set at SUA).

ORAL HISTORIES AND INTERVIEWS

The author and his assistants conducted over eighty interviews for this work. Those that were taped and transcribed have been deposited at the SUA. When appropriate, interviewees are cited below by specific chapter topic.

These interviews were augmented by the research interviews of Sawyer and Eyle. Sawyer did an excellent series of twenty-five interviews with Tolley, aided by Sawyer's research assistant, Bruce Thompson. The rest of the interviews, in both tape and transcript form, are with Tolley's top administrators and deans. Eyle also interviewed Tolley at great length as she prepared drafts of *At the Fountain of Youth.* Several of these interviews are transcribed; others are the basis of chapters in the book. One, on the search for Corbally, did not make it into Tolley's book. Other interviews include William P. Tolley interview with Bruce H. Yenawine, WTR, box 114—an often thoughtful interview on Tolley's relationship with his board of trustees.

GENERAL STUDIES: SYRACUSE UNIVERSITY IN THE TOLLEY YEARS

One must consult the first three volumes of this series in order to get a full view of the growth of Piety Hill. W. Freeman Galpin authored the first two volumes. The first, *The Pioneer Days* (SP, 1952) is a well-written survey of the first twenty years of the institution's history. The second, *The Growing Years*

(SP, 1960), deals primarily with the tenure of Chancellor Day. It is not as gracefully written, but it is all-inclusive, with quite useful appendixes, which were not included in volume one. The third volume, *The Critical Years* (SP, 1984) is a poor volume, most likely because it became a patchwork project finished after Galpin's death in 1963. His notes were given to history professor Oscar T. Barck, Jr., who also did not complete the work. It was up to public relations specialist Richard Wilson to piece the text together. The result is stylistically disappointing, although not one that features any glaring errors.

The researcher must turn next to Tolley's memoirs, *At the Fountain of Youth: Memoirs of a College President* (SP, 1989). Tolley is at his best in this brief book when describing his early, pre-chancellor days. His stories of his chancellorship are interesting and useful, but all too often interrupted by long lists of people to whom he feels that the university owes a debt. Tolley completely omits any discussion of his retirement or the search for his successor. However, this is not a tome that should be ignored. In most places, it is engagingly written, and the tone of the writing is true to the writer's beliefs—rather than writing a dry, encyclopedic narrative, Tolley allows his beliefs to come through. For a complete list of Tolley's books, articles, and speeches, consult this volume's appendix A.

A useful overview of the period, although replete with overstatement, can be found in the *Syracuse University Alumni News,* May 1968 issue—an entire issue dedicated to a retrospective of the Tolley years. Several errors of fact mar an otherwise useful Patricia A. Orsino, ed., *A Century on Piety Hill: Syracuse University Centennial History* (vol. 2 of 1970 *Onondagan*). A useful student paper, Dora Lee Dauma, "A Brief Study of the Stresses and Presses at Syracuse University in the Post–World War II Period" (Dec. 1964, SUA, AVC 1.2) gives a comprehensive listing, with little analysis, of the headline stories of the *Daily Orange* from 1945 to 1963. Students wishing to get a unique perspective of Syracuse in the postwar period will want to consult the script given to those students who conducted campus tours (ca. 1949–54), found in CF, Traditions, General, SUA. The best single piece written on residence life during the Tolley period is Doris M. Seward, "A Historical Study of the Women's Residence Program at Syracuse University" (Ph.D. diss., Syracuse Univ., 1953), which delves into the official records to paint a full picture of residence life—for both men *and* women—during the period.

The best single volume history of American higher education is Christopher J. Lucas, *American Higher Education: A History* (New York: St. Martin's, 1994). It has been used with profit to contextualize each chapter. See also Paul Westmeyer, *A History of American Higher Education* (Springfield, Ill: Charles C. Thomas, 1985).

1. NEW LEADERSHIP[1]

For Tolley's early life, *At the Fountain of Youth* is the source of record. See also *Alumni Record of Drew Theological Seminary, Madison, New Jersey: 1867–1925* (1926), and Tolley's interview with Michael O. Sawyer, Jan. 27, and Jan. 29, 1981, MOS, SUA. For information on the Graham chancellorship, see Richard Wilson, W. Freeman Galpin, and Oscar T. Barck, Jr., *Syracuse University: The Critical Years* (SP, 1984). For the city of Syracuse in the fall of 1942, see Henry W. Schramm and William F. Roseboom, *Syracuse, from Salt to Satellite: A Pictorial History* (Woodland Hills, Calif.: Windsor Publications, 1979). See also the reminiscences of Frank Woolever in Zoe Cornwall, *Human Rights in Syracuse: Two Memorable Decades* (Syracuse: Human Rights Commission of Syracuse and Onondaga County, 1989) and John C. Greene, interview with author, July 9, 1995.

2. THE CHALLENGE OF WORLD WAR II

An excellent primer on American society during World War II is John Morton Blum, *V Was for Victory: Politics and American Culture During World War II* (New York: Harcourt, Brace, Jovanovich, 1976). See also Richard R. Lingemann, *Don't You Know There Is a War On?* (New York: G. P. Putnam's Sons, 1970), and William L. O'Neill, *A Democracy at War: Americans Fight at Home and Abroad in World War II* (New York: Free Press, 1993). For the effect of the war on higher education, the best source is Willis Rudy, *Total War and Twentieth Century Higher Learning: Universities of the Western World in the First and Second World Wars* (New Jersey: Fairleigh Dickenson Univ. Press, 1991). For the sacrifices of the faculty during the period, see paper by George B. Cressy, *Geography at Syracuse* (Apr. 1962, AVC 6l69, SUA) and Jesse Burkhead, interview with Sawyer and Thompson, Sept. 30, 1981, MOS. The story of the attempt to gain a single student government is told in the *Daily Orange*, Jan. 6, Apr. 10–29, 1943. See also Grafton F. Willey III, interview with author, June 3, 1995. The story of the founding of the school of nursing was well told by Dean Emeritus Edith Smith at a September 1963 luncheon of the Syracuse University Nurses Alumnae Association (copy of speech in Tolley Papers, box 93, Nursing folder 2). See also Virginia Mulroy, interview with author, July 5, 1995, and Charlotte Clair Brown and Mary Lou Raedler Lamphear, interview with author, June 2, 1995. For a discussion

---

1. The specific chapter entries that follow do not include articles from routine secondary material such as the *Daily Orange, Alumni News,* and the two Syracuse newspapers. When directly quoted in the text, the source is so noted.

of the medical school during the war, see Raymond Stoddard, interview with Karrie A. Baron, Oct. 8, 1994.

For the plight of the Japanese Americans during the war, begin with Edward H. Spicer, Asael T. Hansen, Katherine Lumala, and Marvin K. Opler, *Impounded People: Japanese Americans in the Relocation Centers* (Tucson: Univ. of Arizona Press, 1969). For their story at Syracuse University, see Jim Naughton, "Forty Years Ago: SU A Haven for Japanese Americans," *Syracuse Post-Standard,* Dec. 7, 1983.

3. TOLLEY AND HIS ADMINISTRATORS

Tolley's interviews with Sawyer and Thompson are particularly revealing on his managerial style. See interviews dated Jan. 27, Feb. 11, and Mar. 13, 1981. For Tolley's view towards the board of trustees, see Tolley interview with Bruce Yenawine, Apr. 15, 1992, in WTR, box 114. Tolley's correspondence with Ahlberg is found in WTR, box 4. See also Clark and Rowena Ahlberg, interview with Sawyer and Thompson, Oct. 13, 1985, MOS; Guthrie Burkhead, interview with author, Aug. 16, 1994; Richard Crawford, interview with author, June 8, 1995; Melvin Eggers, interview with author, June 13, 21, 1994; and John Prucha, interview with author, Oct. 11, 1994.

4. THE "GI BULGE"

The place to begin any study of the "GI Bulge" is with Alexandra Eyle, "Once the War Was Over," *Syracuse University Magazine,* Feb., 1987, 14–24, a superb survey of the period 1944–50, which covers all aspects of university development. Also helpful: "Remember When the GI's Came to SU?" *Syracuse Post-Standard,* May 30, 1977, 13. The federal report cited at the beginning of the chapter is *Higher Education for American Democracy: The Report of the President's Commission on Higher Education* (New York: Harper and Bros., 1947). Also on this report, see William P. Tolley, "Some Observations on the Report of the President's Commission on Higher Education," *Educational Record* (Oct. 1948), 371–80. The details of the Servicemen's Readjustment Act of 1944 can be found in *Digest of Public General Bills and Resolutions.* 78th Cong., 2d sess., 1944. Senate Bill 1767. Also helpful to an understanding of the GI Bill is J. M. Stephens, "A B.A. for the GI . . . Why?" *History of Education Quarterly* 24 (1984), 513–17. Specific information on the registration figures for veterans can be found in WTR, box 101, Registrar: Kennedy folder. For details on the curriculum at Syracuse for returning vets, see pamphlet, "A Personal Word to Returned War Veterans," AVC 5.2, Veterans in Training Under GI Bill. On life at Syracuse as a returning veteran, see Randy

Christensen, interview with author, June 2, 1995; Luke LaPorta, interview with author, Aug. 9, 1994.

On Triple Cities, see Report, "Transfer of Triple Cities College from Syracuse University to State University of New York," Undated, WTR, box 58, Triple Cities folder 2, and Stephen McIntire, *Harpur College in the Bartle Era.* (New York: SUNY Press). On the benefactor, see William Rodgers, *Think: A Biography of the Watsons and IBM* (New York: Stein and Day, 1969). See also "Triple Cities Extension Center, 1942–1943," and "1949–1950 Bulletin of TCC," AVC 6t, SUA. For Utica College, consult Joan Wishbod Reardon, "History of Utica College," Eyle Papers, SUA, and "Utica College of Syracuse University. College Bulletin: 1948–1949," AVC. For thoughts on the changes in the student body, see Jesse Burkhead, interview with Sawyer and Thompson, n.d., MOS; Dick Clark, interview with author, June 30, 1995; and James Powell, interview with author, July 7, 1994.

5. THE BUILDING BULGE, PART ONE: THE BUILDING AND DEVELOPMENT FUND

The report cited at the beginning of this chapter is *The Report of the Syracuse-Onondaga Post-War Planning Council* (Dec. 15, 1945). Tolley's correspondence with Gamble is found in WTR, box 53, Gamble folder. For information on the Building and Development Fund, see Tolley's correspondence with Rossman in WTR, box 39. An excellent summary of the building fund is "Policy and Procedure Statement of the Syracuse University Fund Council," Apr. 14, 1954, WTR, box 39, Rossman folder 1. For the Design Board, see "The University Design Committee," Nov. 9, 1953, WTR, box 38, Design Board folder. Tolley's correspondence with both Lorimer Rich and Harry King is in WTR, box 11. For views on Pinebrook, see WTR, box 4, Pine Brook folder, and Francine Harbach Lausin, interview with author, June 2, 1995.

Eyle's interviews with Tolley, Ann Lubin Goldstein, and Barbara Lubin Goldsmith Perry contribute to our knowledge of the relationship with Lubin. See also H. Bruce Horel, *A Man Named Lubin* (Pace College Publication, 1971). Tolley's correspondence with Arents is in WTR, box 13. One of the best sources for the description of the new buildings are the various releases from the Syracuse University News Bureau, given to the press at the time of a building's dedication (found in SUA, Clipping File, "Buildings and Grounds"). See also Frank and Anne Piskor, Interview with Sawyer and Thompson, Feb. 16, 1982; Clark and Rowena Ahlberg, Interview with Sawyer and Thompson, Oct. 13, 1985, MOS; Newell Rossman, Interview with Sawyer and Thompson, Sept. 30, 1981.

6. THE RESEARCH INSTITUTION

An excellent overview can be found in Alexandra Eyle, "1950–1970: The Golden Age of Research," *Syracuse University Magazine*, Aug., 1987, 26–29. Tolley's memoranda to Galbraith, found in WTR, box 44, Galbraith folders, form the core of the material for this chapter. The Tolley Records also hold invaluable information on the IRR (Box 103), and SURC (Box 103). Of inestimable help for this topic was Ralph Galbraith, interview with Sawyer and Thompson, Oct. 8, 1981, MOS. The Annual Report, College of Engineering, 1968–1969 (WTR, box 44, College of Engineering folder 5) is very helpful for an overview of the history of the College of Applied Science/College of Engineering during the period. See also "History of the Research Institute," Eggers Records, SUA, RG30, box 10, Research Institute folder. For student reactions to the "T-Road" experience, see John F. Jureller, interview with author, June 2, 1995. For the building of Hinds Hall, consult Tolley's correspondence with Hinds in WTR, box 50; for the establishment of SURC, consult Tolley's correspondence with Baker, WTR, box 21.

7. THE PROFESSIONAL SCHOOLS, ADULT EDUCATION, AND THE LIBERAL ARTS

An excellent summary of the development of the school of art during the period is Laurence Schmeckebier, "Random Notes on the W. P. Tolley Years at Syracuse University, as seen from the Art School," MOS, box 6, Schmeckebier's Notes folder. Tolley's correspondence with Dillenback, Rice, and Schmeckebier is in WTR, box 14. On Mestrovic, see Lawrence Schmeckebier, *Ivan Mestrovic: Sculptor and Patriot* (SP, 1959). Tolley's correspondence with Mestrovic is in WTR, box 83. See also David S. Tomkinson, interview with author, Oct. 8, 1994; Dr. Dian Fetter, interview with Karrie A. Baron, June 3, 1995; Prof. Domenic Iacona, interview with author, Aug. 14, 1995. On Tolley's art acquisitions, see Newell Rossman, interview with Sawyer and Thompson, Sept. 30, 1981, MOS. The story of the battle over the Everson estate begins with the files in the WTR, box 46. Falk's correspondence with Tolley is in WTR, box 42. Also helpful were Jerry Stiller's remarks at the Syracuse University 125th Anniversary Dinner, June 2, 1995. For the school of journalism, see Roland E. Wolseley, *Still in Print: Journey of a Writer, Teacher, Journalist* (Elgin, Ill.: David C. Cook Foundation, 1985). See also Dick Clark, interview with author, June 30, 1995.

A useful starting point for Maxwell is "The Citizenship Program at Syracuse University: A Thirty-Fifth Year Report." AVC 6m46, SUA, box 11. Tolley's correspondence with Appleby and Cleveland, as well as his files on the development of the Doctor of Social Science program are in WTR, box 82. The D.S.S is explained in "The Doctor of Social Science Program at Syracuse University: A New Program for the Training of College Teachers" (SUA, AVC 6m46), and "The Doctor of Social Science Program at Syracuse University: A Thirteen-Year Evaluation" (SUA, AVC 6m46). See also Guthrie Burkhead, interview with author, Aug. 16, 1994, and Melvin Eggers, interview with author, June 21, 1994.

A useful beginning for the history of University College is the *Syracuse University Continuing Education Diamond Anniversary Yearbook*. For more detail, consult Roy Ingham, "University College, Syracuse University: A Period of Transformation, 1958–1965." in WTR, box 31, Charters folder 1. Tolley's correspondence with Charters is in WTR, box 117. See also Alexander Charters, interview with author, Aug. 30, 1994, and John Mulroy, interview with author, July 5, 1995. For Syracuse University Press, see "The University Press," *Focus* (1948), 7, and "A Brief History of Syracuse University Press," in WTR, box 119, University Press folder 3.

8. THE CHALLENGE OF SUNY

Oliver Cromwell Carmichael, Jr., *New York Establishes a State University: A Case Study in the Processes of Policy Formation* (Nashville: Vanderbilt Univ. Press, 1955), a readable history of the Young Commission, is the place to begin any study of SUNY. *Sixty-Four Campuses: The State University of New York to 1985* (Albany: Office of University Affairs and Development, 1985) is a collection of vignettes of each campus. A copy of the Young Commission Report, "The State Commission to Examine Into the Need for a State University: Statement by the Association of Colleges and Universities of the State of New York," can be found in WTR, box 89, Committee on State University folder. Tolley's correspondence regarding SUNY can be found in WTR, boxes 91–92, and his records on the College of Forestry in WTR, box 51. George Armstrong, ed., *Forestry College: Essays on the Growth and Development of the New York State College of Forestry, 1911–1961* (Buffalo: William J. Keller, 1961) offers little depth on the Syracuse/SUNY fight over Forestry. See instead *A Statement on the Relationship Between Syracuse University and the New York State College of Forestry at Syracuse University, with Reference to Future Student Status and Services* (Syracuse Univ., 1956), in SUA, AVC 6.F71. Tolley's correspondence on Triple Cities is in WTR, box 58—see the important "Transfer of Triple Cities College from Syracuse University to State University of New York," n.d., WTR, box 58, Triple Cities folder 2.

Correspondence relating to the sale of the medical school is found in the above mentioned WTR folders on SUNY. Kenneth W. Wright, *Foundations Well and Truly Laid: A History Leading to the Formation of the State University of New York Health Service Center at Syracuse* (Syracuse: Alumni Association, SUNY Health Science Center, 1994) is the only monograph on the subject. But it is disjointed—more of a list than a narrative—replete with aggravating typesetting errors. Better sources are H. G. Weiskotten, "A History of Syracuse University College of Medicine" (Syracuse: Onondaga Co. Medical Society, 1957), and "Statement of Future Relationships Between Syracuse University and the State University Medical Center at Syracuse," July 30, 1954, CF, College of Medicine. On the issue of the endowments, see WTR, box 79, George L. Manley folder 1.

9. THE CHALLENGE TO ACADEMIC FREEDOM

David Bennett, *The Party of Fear: From Nativist Movements to the New Right in American History* (Chapel Hill: Univ. of North Carolina Press, 1988) sets the scene with a graceful narrative. The above-mentioned Lucas, *American Higher Education,* and Westmeyer, *History of Higher Education,* are particularly strong on the challenges of the postwar period. John S. Brubacher, *Higher Education in Transition: An American History, 1636–1956* (New York: Harper and Row, 1958) is without the historical depth of either of these volumes. Still, its chapter on academic freedom is a useful primer to the subject. For Tolley's role regarding faculty salaries, see WTR, box 38, Deans and Directors folder, and box 48, Faculty Salaries folder. See also Clark and Rowena Ahlberg, interview with Sawyer and Thompson, Oct. 13, 1985, MOS, and Melvin Eggers, interview with author, June 13, 1994. For good background on Maxwell during this period, see Jesse Burkhead, interview with Sawyer and Thompson, n.d., MOS; and Melvin Eggers, interview with author, June 13, 1994. Anti-Communist works written by Syracuse University faculty include Edward E. Palmer, ed., *The Communist Problem in America* (New York: Thomas Y. Cromwell, 1951), and Warren Walsh, *Readings in Russian History* (SP, 1948). The Paul Appleby Papers, SUA, box 3, contain a great deal of helpful correspondence for this topic. See also Appleby's *Big Democracy* (New York: Knopf, 1945), referred to in this chapter. Gelbart's testimony before HUAC is in House of Representatives, Committee on Un-American Activities. *Communist Methods of Infiltration—Education* (1953), 1565–82. Tolley's response to Gelbart's testimony, "Academic Freedom and Tenure," Statement to the Board of Trustees, May 29, 1953, is in SUA, AVC 9.2.

10. SPORTS, PART ONE

Several books have been written about Syracuse University sports. Malcolm R. Alama, *Mark of the Oarsmen: A Narrative History of Rowing at Syracuse University* (Syracuse: Estabrook Printing, 1963) is to date the most gracefully written, and the most interesting, book on sports at Syracuse University. Alama does not—as do several of the extant books on football and basket-ball—sacrifice readability and narrative for records and scores; *both* are there. For football, the best source is Michael A. Mullins, *Syracuse University Football: A Centennial Celebration* (Norfolk: Downing Company, 1989). All the key statistics are there, and Mullins does employ a game-by-game approach to the text. But he has a balanced writing style, outstanding pictures, excellent captioning, and a fuller, more inclusive look at the growth of the sport at Syracuse. Much weaker is Ken Rappoport, *The Syracuse Football Story* (Huntsville, Alabama: Strode Publishers, 1975). Utilizing a writing style that drips hyperbole (particularly its unvarnished glorification of Schwartzwalder), the book is a disappointment, particularly on the 1940s and early 1950s. The years 1941–45 are covered in two sentences—the decision to fire Ossie Solem is never adequately explained. The entirety of the terms of Munn and Baysinger is discussed in less than a page, and excused with the comment that the programs "went no place at all" under them. It is at its most useful for its interviews with the best-known athletes. See also Robert C. Gallagher, *Ernie Davis: The Elmira Express* (Silver Spring, Md.: Bartleby, 1983). For basketball, the standard source is Roderick Macdonald, *Syracuse University Basketball, 1900–1975* (Syracuse: Syracuse Univ. Printing Services, 1976). Privately printed, the book's typestyle makes it a difficult read. It offers a game-by-game discussion that is helpful as a reference.

Much of Tolley's correspondence on athletics is in WTR, box 18. For football, see Tolley Interview 1 and 12, MOS; Lew Andreas, interview with Michael O. Sawyer, n.d., MOS; Bernie Custis, telephone interview with author, Aug. 15, 1994; Luke LaPorta, interview with author, Aug. 9, 1994; and John Mackey, interview with author, June 3, 1995.

11. THE CAMPUS

For views of the Greek system at Syracuse, see Randy Christensen, interview with author, June 2, 1995; Dick Clark, interview with author, June 30, 1995; Richard Crawford, interview with author, June 8, 1995; Glory Katz, interview with author, Oct. 8, 1994; and David S. Tomkinson, interview with author, Oct. 8, 1994. There is a useful chapter on Syracuse University in B. G. Rudolph, *From a Minyan to a Community: A History of the Jews of Syracuse* (SP,

1970), which suffers only from its errant conclusion that there were never any quotas placed on the acceptance of Jewish students at Syracuse University. A more scholarly study is Harvey Strum, "Discrimination at Syracuse University," *History of Higher Education Annual* 4 (1984), 101–22. Tolley's correspondence with Dean Noble, including the fight with Father Gannon Ryan, is in WTR, box 59. See also Jesse Burkhead, interview with Sawyer and Thompson, n.d., MOS, and James Powell, interview with author, July 7, 1994.

12. THE BUILDING BULGE, PART TWO:
THE SYRACUSE PLAN

For background on Newhouse, see "Publisher With A Cure," *New York Times,* Jan. 26, 1960. Tolley's correspondence on the journalism school is in WTR, box 67; his correspondence with Newhouse is in box 88. See also Melvin Eggers, interview with author, June 21, 1994. Material on the building of Newhouse can be found in WTR, box 11, King folder. See also "The 1965 AIA Honor Awards," *AIA Journal,* July 1965, 23–30. For the planning and the controversies surrounding the dedication, see Lyndon B. Johnson Presidential Papers, White House Central File, Lyndon B. Johnson Presidential Library, Name File: Syracuse University folder, and General: TR20, Trip to Syracuse University folder. A copy of Johnson's speech can be found in *Papers of the Presidents of the United States: Lyndon B. Johnson, 1963–1964,* vol. 2 (Washington, D.C.: Government Printing Office, 1965), 928–30. Tolley's correspondence with Arnold Grant is in WTR, box 56. David Stam, "Peaks of Joy; Valleys of Despair: An Illustrated Epitome of the History of the Syracuse University Library, 1871–1942," *Syracuse University Library Associates Courier,* 30, 1995, is a good primer on the subject. Tolley's correspondence dealing with the library is in box 75; correspondence with and about Ernest S. Bird is in box 22. See also Melvin Eggers, interview with author, June 21, 1994, and Horace Landry, interview with Karrie A. Baron, June 29, 1995.

13. SPORTS, PART TWO

See comments on Mullins, *Syracuse University Football,* Rappoport, *Syracuse Football Story,* and Macdonald, *Syracuse University Basketball,* above. Tolley's correspondence with George Manley is in WTR, box 79. On the building of Manley Fieldhouse, see *General Construction Specifications for the George Leroy Manley Fieldhouse* (King and King Architects, 1960). See also Lew Andreas, interview with Michael O. Sawyer, n.d., MOS. On the 1965 Sugar Bowl against LSU, see Marty Mule, *Sugar Bowl: The First Fifty Years* (Birmingham:

Oxmoor House, 1983). An excellent short history of baseball at Syracuse is a two-part series by Rick Jacobsen in the *Daily Orange,* Apr. 5 and 6, 1978. There has been no synthesis yet written on lacrosse. The best short history is offered in Franz Lidz, who profiles Roy Simmons, Jr., in "My Teams are Collages," *Sports Illustrated,* Mar. 23, 1984, 43–49. For the Women's Athletics Association (WAA), see Women's Athletics Records, RG 12, SUA. On the fight over athletic contests with segregated schools, see WTR, box 18, Athletics, Men's, folder 3, and box 9, AAUP folder 3. See also Bernie Custis, interview with author, Aug. 15, 1994; and John and Sylvia Mackey, interview with author, June 3, 1995.

14. THE CHALLENGE OF CIVIL RIGHTS

Tolley's correspondence on the whole of the CORE protests is found in WTR, box 35. It should also be noted that the *Daily Orange* did a particularly good job of covering these protests—certainly better than either of the two Syracuse dailies—probably because several *DO* reporters were allowed to get closer to the protests than any establishment reporter. Ronald David Corwin, "School Desegregation in Syracuse: A Study in Community Decision-Making" (Ph.D. diss., Syracuse Univ., 1968), offers useful material on the 1962 clash between CORE and the school board. It is also useful for background information on Syracuse itself. Philip G. Altbach, *Student Politics in America: A Historical Analysis* (New York: McGraw-Hill, 1974) offers an excellent introduction to the whole of student politics. George Wiley has received a sympathetic yet balanced biography in Nick Kotz and Mary Lynn Kotz, *A Passion for Equality: George A. Wiley and the Movement* (New York: W. W. Norton, 1977). Zoe Cornwall, *Human Rights in Syracuse: Two Memorable Decades* (Syracuse: Human Rights Commission of Syracuse and Onondaga County, 1989) sets the stage for the civil rights movement in Syracuse. See also Faith Seidenberg, interview with author, July 13, 1994. For his reminiscences on the day that Kennedy was assassinated, see David S. Tomkinson, interview with author, Oct. 8, 1994.

15. CHALLENGED CURRICULA

On the development of the Citizenship requirement, see *The Maxwell School of Citizenship and Public Affairs: Twenty-Fifth Anniversary* (Syracuse Univ., 1949). Tolley's correspondence with Brown on the matter is in WTR, box 81. See also David H. Bennett, interview with author, Aug. 29, 1995; and Guthrie Burkhead, interview with author, Aug. 16, 1994. For Haagstrom and the CATC, see again Cornwall, *Human Rights in Syracuse.* Tolley's correspondence on the CATC matter is in WTR, box 118. See also Walter M. Beattie, interview with author, Aug. 29, 1995.

16. VIETNAM

The most thoughtful survey of America in the 1960s is Allan J. Matusow, *The Unravelling of America* (New York: Harper and Row, 1984). The full text of "The Hershey Letter" can be found in *AAUP Bulletin,* winter, 1967, 412–13. Tolley's correspondence on the lock-in at the administration building can be found in Tolley Files, box 5, Administration Building Disturbance folder. See also David H. Bennett, interview with author, Aug. 29, 1995.

17. NEW LEADERSHIP, REDUX

For the choice of Corbally, see Melvin Eggers, interview with author, June 13 and June 17, 1994; John Prucha interview with author, Oct. 11, 1994, and Tolley interview with Alexandra Eyle, n.d., "The Selection of My Successor." For the protest of African-American Students, see Melvin Eggers Records: Vice Chancellor, RG 30, box 1, Black Students folder.

18. SOME CONCLUSIONS

Tolley's view of higher education can be found in his *Adventure of Learning* (SP, 1967).

Index

Page numbers in italics denote illustrations.

283

Book design by Christopher Kuntze
Printed and bound by Thomson-Shore